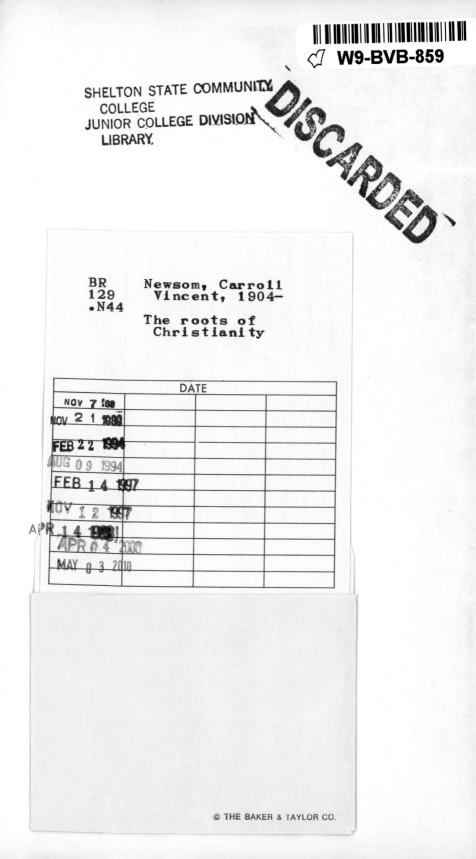

THE ROOTS OF CHRISTIANITY

Also by Carrol V. Newsom:
A University President Speaks Out
A Television Policy for Education

Contributor to:
An American Philosophy of Education
Mathematics, Our Great Heritage

Carroll V. Newsom

THE ROOTS OF CHRISTIANITY

PRENTICE-HALL, INC., Englewood Cliffs, New Jersey

Book Designer, Linda Huber
Art Director, Hal Siegel

The Roots of Christianity
by Carroll V. Newsom
Copyright © 1979 by Carroll V. Newsom
Printed in the United States of America
Prentice-Hall International, Inc., London
Prentice-Hall of Australia, Pty. Ltd., Sydney
Prentice-Hall of Canada, Ltd., Toronto
Prentice-Hall of India Private Ltd., New Delhi
Prentice-Hall of Japan, Inc., Tokyo
Prentice-Hall of Southeast Asia Pte. Ltd., Singapore
Whitehall Books Limited, Wellington, New Zealand
10 9 8 7 6 5 4 3 2 1

Library of Congress Cataloging in Publication Data

Newsom, Carroll Vincent,
The roots of Christianity.
Includes index.
1.   Christianity—Origin.   I.   Title.
BR129.N44   209   79–9246
ISBN 0-13-783050-5

CONTENTS

FOREWORD

The present work, concerned with a significant part of the story of the evoluton of the Christian tradition, represents the culmination of a lifetime of study in particular areas of history and cultural anthropology. As a young adult I began to realize, although I had been a serious student of the Christian Bible, that my knowledge of the development of the Christian tradition was extremely incomplete in many significant respects. Shortly thereafter I embarked upon a systematic program of studies to fill in the gaps in my knowledge. But I soon discovered that the historical materials easily available to Christian readers were singularly dissatisfying; they seemed to ignore many factors of obvious significance for one who seeks to develop a true understanding of the origins of his faith. So, for more than forty years, I have traveled extensively for the purpose of visiting geographical locations important in the history of the Judeo-Christian tradition and of having access to important resource materials, including the Dead Sea Scrolls and many important early Christian and Judaic manuscripts. Moreover, I have made it a practice to supplement my studies by discussing various aspects of my interest in the field of religion with a variety of knowledgeable scholars, both Christian and Judaic; my involvement in such discussions has assisted me in making decisions on some controversial subjects and has enabled me to refine many of my ideas, especially in difficult problem areas.

My writing of the present volume was motivated in part by my growing realization, which for me has been the cause of increasing concern, that, like myself as a young man, a large number of professing Christians know very little about the historical aspects of the foundation upon which their faith is built. I readily admit that my thinking on religious subjects, which differs significantly from that of many other students of religion, has been influenced strongly by my many years of research and study in the fields of mathematics and science and especially by my active involvement in the field of cultural anthropology. The present volume, in fact, might very well be regarded as a specialized work in cultural anthropology. Thus in the treatment of its content, the term "man" is employed in the anthropological sense.

It is not possible to express my appreciation individually to the many Christian scholars both in this country and abroad, including representative members of both the Eastern and Western Christian sects, who have encouraged me in my endeavors and have provided constructive commentary upon some of my ideas and my writings. However, I must make note of the fact that probably the earliest stimulus to my studies that ultimately led me to the writing of the present work came from a series of discussions that I had about thirty years ago with the late Dr. Clarence T. Craig, a colleague of mine Dr. Craig was then involved in working with others on a revision of the Christian New Testament, so we talked at length about some of the historical uncertainties that have been responsible for endless debate in the field of Christian doctrine. Moreover, I acknowledge the great amount of encouragement along with the constructive comments that I have received in recent months from Dr. Donald Harrington, minister of the Community Church in New York City, and from Dr. R. L. Wilder, mathematical scientist and student of anthropology, who is a member of the National Academy of Sciences. To Reverend Frederick Poorbaugh, who read my manuscript with great care, I express my appreciation of his wise judgment. In addition, I am indebted to Dr. K. M. Simon, specialist in Near Eastern Christianity, for some distinctive kinds of assistance.

Early in my studies I became troubled as I realized that some of the common works by Christian authors on Biblical exegesis appear not to be properly objective in certain aspects of their treatment; this, in general, seems to stem from the fact that the authors are restrained in their points of view by their rigid adherence to particular sets of tenets within the broad framework of Christianity. Possibly of even greater importance, I became much disturbed as I realized that most of the reference works on Christian history that are commonly employed by Christians seem to possess a critical weakness in the fact that they fail to recognize in an adequate manner that Christianity derived many of its forms and much of its substance from its Judaic ancestry. Thus while developing the present work, I consulted frequently with Dr. Gerson Cohen, historian and chancellor of the Jewish Theological Seminary of America, with the late Dr. Solomon Zeitlin, Horace Stern Professor of Rabbinic Law and History, the Dropsie University, Philadelphia, with President Emeritus Abraham I. Katsh of the Dropsie University, and with Dr. Norman Lamm, philosopher-historian and president of Yeshiva University, New York, upon subjects having to do with Judaic philosophy and history; to these scholars I express my sincere appreciation. But I accept complete responsibility for any errors of fact and for any fallacious judgments that I may have introduced into my writing.

I would be remiss if, in conclusion, I did not acknowledge my great indebtedness to the late Clyde Kluckhohn, distinguished cultural anthropologist at Harvard University, who at one time was my close friend and colleague and with whom I spent a vast number of hours in discussion of basic cultural problems. And once again, I express my gratitude to my wife, Frances, who throughout our married life has accepted the arduous responsibility of preparing my writings for publication.

The Biblical citations in the text of the present work, in the case of the Christian New Testament, refer to the *Revised Standard Version of the Bible*, completed in 1952 and published by the A. J. Holman Company, Philadelphia. I thank the Division of Christian Education of the National Council of the Churches of Christ in the United States of America, which holds the copyrights on the Revised Standard Version of the Holy Bible, for permission to quote from that publication. When making reference to the Judaic Torah, I have relied upon the comparatively recent translation of the Masoretic Text of the Torah, copyrighted in 1962 and published by the Jewish Publication Society of America, Philadelphia.

C.V.N.

Chapter One
INTRODUCTION

SOME FOUNDATION IDEAS FROM THE PHILOSOPHY OF SCIENCE AND FROM ANTHROPOLOGY

It is believed by most anthropologists that very early man, long before the dawn of history, was merely one component of the complex natural ecology of his time. He hunted and was hunted. He killed and was killed. He ate what nature provided and starved when no food could be found. He fled with the other animals before flood and fire. His apparent mental reactions differed remarkably little from those of other members of the animal kingdom. But, like the other animals, according to evolutionary theory, man slowly, slowly, slowly, chiefly as a result of selective processes, underwent a series of physiological modifications. It is accepted generally as a part of evolutionary theory, however, that man's physiological development in certain significant respects, especially those which provide the physiological basis for intellectual endeavor, ultimately moved ahead of the other animals and, consequently, man was able to achieve a superior position in the animal kingdom.

In fact, in the earliest days of history that we have been able to document, man, the human animal, although he still reacted much like the other animals to many elements of his natural environment, possessed a brain that had attained such a remarkable state of development that he could cope with many very difficult factors in his environment; he could make decisions that made it possible for him to have shelter and a variety of conveniences; he could create objects and develop ideas that had great value for him in improving his way of life; he was able to communicate with others of his kind. It is likely, in fact, that earliest man of whom we have historical knowledge already possessed a brain with intellectual potentials considerably greater than those to which his attainments would seem to testify. But, in comparatively recent years, chiefly because of man's virtually unbelievable achievements in the field of science, there has been a rapidly increasing appreciation of the fact that man is endowed with an "instrument of thought" of fantastic capacity for creativity and accomplishment; there has been growing appreciation of the apparent fact that the human brain possesses potential powers that transcend man's comprehension. In truth, it has become common among scholars to assert that the study of the brain must now be recognized as the most important subject upon the frontiers of scientific

1

investigation. The reasons for this comparatively new recognition of the fundamental importance of the human brain are not hard to find.

Most members of the public have become accustomed to the idea that the virtually unbelievable behavior of a satellite in space as it finds its way to the moon or to a distant planet is a consequence of the fact that it is under computer control. Likewise, it no longer seems strange to most people when it is reported that the complex operation of some entire industry is under computer control. Usually the same members of the public, however, find that they must struggle to comprehend even partially the fact, if and when they consider it, that mere man has been able to create the computers which possess such capabilities; a technological accomplishment of that order of difficulty taxes the credulity of most people. And the wonderment of interested individuals is increased when they realize that, because of new understandings of the properties of matter, it has become possible in comparatively recent years to decrease the size of computers that possess such vast capabilities from their original several tons to a very few pounds. The significance of this accomplishment becomes even greater when there is comprehension of the fact that each man and woman goes through life under the control of his or her own personal three-pound computer, the human brain. Each individual's physical and mental behavior, including the mental processes of the scientist who creates and perfects the computer that controls a satellite, is determined by his or her brain. It is now known that the human brain and the man-made computers with which we are becoming familiar have many elements of similarity; in fact, much is being learned about the functioning of the brain from studies of the functioning of man-made computers. But, simultaneously, scientists have developed an increasing appreciation of the fact that the human brain and any man-made computer also possess pronounced differences—so much so that possibly they hardly deserve comparison. A man-made computer can do and will do only that which it has been told to do by some person's brain; there is no similar restriction upon man's instrument of thought. Studies of the findings of scientists who indulge in research on artificial intelligence reveal that the early hope of some of them of being able to develop computers that can think in the same way that man thinks are fading rapidly. It is becoming common belief that man cannot re-create his brain.

The serious scholar who attempts to indulge in studies of the functioning of the brain soon realizes that in his work he must accept the existence of inherent limitations; he can go only so far before reaching an epistemological impasse: A person can go only so far in asking his brain to explain how it functions. Nevertheless, certain very important observations in regard to the structure of the brain and its functioning have been made, especially in recent years, by neuroscientists supported by mathematicians, but much more remains to be done. When studying the functioning of the brain, it is recalled that for many years psychologists have been impressed with the tremendous capacity of the memory unit of the brain. Some slight indication of the magnitude of that capacity is revealed by the fact that a complete record of the intricate instructions to the muscles of the fingers, the arms, and other parts of the body, necessary for the performance of a difficult composition on the piano without reference to a musical score, is often stored in the memory unit of a performer's brain so that he or she, actually without conscious effort, can carry out the performance in flawless fashion; having a brain with a memory unit of such capacity, most persons would agree, borders on the miraculous.

But it is when man attempts to grasp the full significance of the statement that it is his brain which controls his creative endeavors that his powers of comprehension seem to be overwhelmed. By employing the cultivated inherent creative powers of his brain, man has developed rules, laws, principles, even institutions, that make it possible for him to overcome at least partially the threat of social and physical chaos to which he is constantly subjected; in truth, by employing his creative powers, man has been able to make his life livable.

Some indication of the fantastic creative powers of the human brain is revealed by an examination of the methods employed by the scientist in his development of principles to assist him in his efforts to understand and control nature. Mature natural scientists know that nature is fundamentally inscrutable; we can talk about many aspects of nature, but actually we do not know that of which we speak. At the present time we talk glibly about energy but what, really, is energy? No one knows. Only through its effects and through the various ways in which it is experienced is man aware of something in nature which he designates by the term "energy." In the technical writings of the scientist, the term "energy," a mere abstraction, is characterized as an undefined term. And amazing as it may seem to some individuals, the man of science does not need to associate meaning with the term to indulge in discussions of natural phenomena in which energy is involved. Only a very few other

3

terms which are employed in discourses upon natural phenomena are regarded as undefined; the rest of the terms that appear to be necessary are given definition through the contexts in which they are used with the undefined terms.

Critical analyses of the methodology employed by scientists have revealed that in many notable instances a man of science has displayed the truly remarkable capability of being able to create a mechanism that serves to relate the terms, undefined and defined, associated with a particular phenomenon in such a way that the mechanism becomes invaluable in helping man obtain answers to many important questions that arise in studies of the phenomenon. Such a mechanism may be in the form of a formula, a diagram, or a verbal statement (often cast into the language of mathematics). In view of the necessary close relationship that must exist between the mechanism and the phenomenon with which it is associated, often the mechanism is described as a model of the phenomenon. The model of a phenomenon must be similar to the phenomenon in many of its fundamental structural aspects, much as the model of a house possesses fundamental elements of similarity to the house it represents.

One cannot doubt that the development of a model which has such properties requires tremendous exploitation of man's creative powers. To initiate the process leading to the development of the desired model of some natural phenomenon, the creative scientist attempts to extract from his imagination, often a seemingly impossible task, a general concept of a mechanism that hopefully will prove to be of appropriate type; that is, the mechanism is supposed to be of such a nature that it will yield acceptable answers to important questions that may be raised pertaining to the phenomenon. To provide an explanation of the procedure followed by the creative scientist in extracting from his imagination a rudimentary concept of the desired mechanism transcends man's capabilities; there is little doubt, however, if success is to be achieved, that the creative scientist must exercise tremendous ingenuity and must utilize in an important way his powers of intuition. After the general concept of the desired mechanism has been enunciated, usually it will be necessary to subject it to much refinement as the scientist repeatedly checks the answers to questions about the phenomenon as given by the proposed mechanism against the answers to the same questions as given by direct reference to the phenomenon itself. Often the creative scientist must

4

display much patience and skill while, as just explained, he attempts to refine the proposed mechanism. It is likely that he will never succeed.

If, ultimately, however, the creative scientist achieves success in the development of a scientific model, a mechanism created by man, that has the capability of being able to answer questions about a natural phenomenon without the necessity of going directly to the phenomenon, many of the values associated with the accomplishment become obvious. Much scientific investigation can be carried out through the use of pencil and paper and without the creation or acquisition of possibly elaborate and expensive equipment. And, actually, in virtually every kind of scientific endeavor, there are frequent occasions when the obtaining of information by direct reference to nature is impossible. The fact that so much of the study of science has been reduced to working with models has provided a tremendous stimulus to the development of scientific theory and understanding. In addition, there have been many incidental results of tremendous importance. For instance, modern scholars have been fascinated by the fact—of vast philosophical, religious, and scientific significance—that it appears to be possible to characterize the behavior of the forces that seem to underlie all natural physical phenomena by means of not more than four super mechanisms; Albert Einstein before his death was studying the possibility of reducing the number to one.

Careful consideration of the method of "thinking by means of models" that is employed by modern scientists, as just briefly described, and that has enabled them to achieve their remarkable successes, reveals the indisputable fact that the so-called laws of nature treated in textbooks and in scientific reference books are, in reality, merely models created and employed by men in their study of nature. Actually, probably it is inappropriate even to employ the phrase "laws of nature." Man does not know and possibly cannot know the laws of nature. Each one of the scientific mechanisms employed by the scientist is a product of man's imagination; it is a demonstration of the remarkable creative capabilities of the human brain. Most nonscientists seem to believe that the scientist collects data in connection with his studies of a particular natural phenomenon and then, from his examination of the data, he is able in some manner to employ logical procedures to derive a law or theory. Such a point of view is false. Instead, as already implied, before even attempting to study in a systematic manner collections of data that have been derived from observations of a particular natural phenomenon, the scientist accepts as necessary strategy that he must have a preconceived notion of the rudiments of a formulation, some kind of mechanism, to which he suspects that any one of the collections of data will conform. As one scholar has said, "Even though a scientist in his study of a particular natural phenomenon ultimately may become involved in elaborate logical procedures as he indulges in the development of theory, he must start his systematic endeavors with a mere hunch." C. S. Peirce, early American philosopher-mathematician, asserted that it is the business of science and mathematics to guess. Thus, contrary to the expositions in many textbooks in the field of science wherein it is implied that a science is characterized by its rational approach to knowledge, there are basic ingredients in the methodology of the scientist that cannot be described as rational. Now it is accepted generally by scientists that the foundation of an organized natural science, such as astronomy, physics, or geology, is provided by a carefully synthesized collection of the models created by man to assist him in answering questions that arise in his studies of phenomena that occur in a particular, possibly an arbitrarily designated, section of nature.

Some happenings in the history of atomic theory may provide some clarification of previous comments. Ernest Rutherford, early in the twentieth century, developed what was commonly described at that time as a simple geometric model of the atom. The device that Lord Rutherford created involved the portrayal of a small mass, described as the nucleus, at the center of a series of concentric circles; upon these circles he located a collection of small entities which he designated as electrons. The term "electron" was regarded as undefined. By reference to such an unlikely symbolic representation, including its possible variations, physical scientists who were contemporaries of Rutherford were surprised and delighted to learn that they could answer many basic questions about atomic behavior; previously some of the most important questions had been unanswered. In their enthusiasm, some scientists of that time endorsed the idea that the "Rutherford Atom" must provide a conventionalized sketch of a real atom. But now, three quarters of a century later, scientists operate on the assumption that the symbolic device developed by Rutherford was merely an artificial mechanism—the product, obviously, of a high order of imagination—created by Rutherford and others to facilitate their efforts to try to understand and explain fundamental concepts of atomic behavior. John von Neumann, greatest of the mathematical scientists of the twentieth century, warned repeatedly, "identifying the real physical or biological world with models constructed to explain it is indeed dangerous." Most modern scientists agree with Neumann.

As scientists proceeded in their study of atomic behavior after the time of Rutherford, more and more questions arose that could not be answered by means of the Rutherford device. It has been a frequent experience in the history of scientific endeavor to find that some commonly accepted scientific model must be modified or refined, or even completely reconstructed, the better to serve the purposes for which it was supposed to have been designed. That proved to be true of the model created by Rutherford; the Rutherford device was virtually discarded as it underwent many modifications. The net result of the contributions of many scientists was virtually a new model that has assisted man to answer most of the major critical questions that have arisen since the time when Rutherford created his original device. By answering such questions, ultimately it became possible to tap the vast amount of energy that is inherent in the nucleus of the atom, an accomplishment that has been described as the miracle of miracles. Much of the rest of that particular story in science, as we know it up to the present time, is common knowledge.

What is this brain that has been given to man and which in the case of his early studies of atomic theory guided him in writing down in preliminary form a diagram that proved to have tremendous value in assisting him in the development of his atomic studies? What is this brain that has been given to man and which guided him in enunciating formulations that proved to be so important in assisting him in the design of the computer? What is this brain that has been responsible for the fact that man has been able to create models that have enabled him to achieve tremendous successes in many of his studies of nature? There is no disagreement with the idea that the brain is composed of the same basic chemical materials that are common to the rest of nature. Moreover, one cannot doubt that the chemical and physical behavior of those materials is like that of the same materials in other parts of the universe. Yet, when they are brought together as they have been to form the brain, the result is awesome and not what the present status of our knowledge of scientific principle would permit us to predict. It is conceivable that some day our knowledge will be sufficiently great that it will be possible to explain all the various aspects of the functioning of the brain. Many scientists, however, doubt that such a prospect should be anticipated. Perhaps there are reasons why explanations of the powers of the brain cannot be found within the realm of man's present or future knowledge; in fact, some religions teach that each person possesses capabilities that can be explained only on the assumption that each man has within himself "something of the spirit of God." And one recalls with interest the Biblical assertion that "God created man in his own image."

The fact that the scientist has been so successful through the use of his models in explaining many important aspects of the behavior of nature has served intuitively to increase confidence within the scientific community in the validity of the fundamental assumption of science that there is a "natural order" behind the behavior of nature. One is reminded of Einstein's remark that "God does not play dice with the world." Undoubtedly the confidence of scientists in the validity of the idea that the behavior of nature is subject to law has been increased with the realization that four principles, possibly even a smaller number, are sufficient to explain the forces involved in all natural phenomena. As a consequence of man's amazing successes associated with his use of models, products of the brains of men, in explaining the workings of nature, some men have indulged in speculation upon the possibility that the brains of men are not isolated from the inner workings of nature. Of even greater importance, some scientists, usually after much reflection upon the question of their relationship with nature, admit that they possess a predisposition toward the acceptance of some kind of religious belief. Many cultural anthropologists have long insisted that the same statement may be made of mankind in general.

A science and a religion differ in most respects. Yet, it is a notable fact that an organized science and an organized religion possess some elements of similarity that cannot be ignored in the present exposition. There is little doubt that religion had its origin in early man's concern with his own relationships with the Powers, the God or Gods, whom he believed to be in control of the phenomena of nature. Primitive man believed that he was satisfying most of the demands that such relationships made upon him, as discussed later, when he indulged in certain patterns of behavior. As man matured intellectually, however, he developed an understanding and appreciation of the behavior of nature which transcended that of very early man. As a consequence of that fact, man's questions about his relationships with nature became increasingly sophisticated, and the development of answers to those questions demanded greater and greater ingenuity. At the same time, man was inclined to extend his presumption of the inherent orderliness of the physical universe to include the presumption that orderliness is supposed to be a characteristic of the universe of men. Thus the realm of religion became enlarged.

One may assume that the later "more advanced" religions, such as Christianity, Judaism, and Islam, that evolved as a result of man's greater intellectual maturity, were stimulated in their development by the need of man to answer questions about issues that became inevitable as the realm of religion was expanded. Typical of such questions were and are those that pertain to the ultimate control of events in a person's life, to man's destiny after death, to man's purposes in life, and to the values that man should seek from his indulgence in the various activities of life. Probably it is impossible to write down a generally acceptable definition of the word "religion." However, the content of the four questions just enunciated may be regarded as providing some insight into the realm of man's thought that properly may be associated with the word "religion."

To provide himself and others assistance in answering questions such as the four just phrased, man has developed the tactic of drawing upon his tremendous intellectual powers of imagination and creativity to create a collection of carefully conceived verbal statements or principles, designated upon occasion as doctrines, that will provide a basis for the determination of acceptable answers. The net result of such a tactic, especially since it has proved to be very helpful to man when he tries to answer questions pertaining to issues in the realm of religion, is the fact that a collection of principles as thus developed and used has become accepted as actually defining a particular organized religion. Since many collections of principles that provide guidance to man in dealing with questions arising from a consideration of religious issues are possible, many organized religions are possible, and, in fact, a great variety of organized religions have been and are now in existence. Consequently, unique answers to questions in the broad field of religion are not to be expected.

It is of primary importance to note that, in general, the individual principles of a collection that defines a particular organized religion as well as the total collection are the result of a long evolutionary process, and any contributions made to one of the individual principles or to the collection as a whole must be recognized as a product of the cultivated inherent intellectual powers of the men who were the contributors.

By contrast with what is true of the organizational structure of a mathematical science, for example, the tradition exists within the field of religion that the collection of principles, or doctrines, that defines an organized religion is not displayed as such. Thus one or more of the principles that are regarded generally as basic to Christianity may be found in various places in Christian literature. However, it may be observed that the letters of Paul in the Christian New Testament are an important source of information on the basic principles of classical Christianity. Paul was Christianity's first great organizer; his life and work are the subject of a later chapter. The lack of attention by Christian theologians to the development and the display of a carefully organized and useful collection of the basic principles of Christianity may be due in part to the fact that adherents to the Christian faith, as is true of adherents to other religions, do not employ logical deduction to derive from Christianity's basic tenets their own personal principles to provide them guidance in the "fulfillment of a Christian way of life." Man's intellectual life in the field of religion is based on faith, not on the use of logic.

The following sentence from the Christian New Testament is regarded by many Christians as a statement of the most important principle of the Christian faith: "God shows his love for us in that while we were yet sinners Christ died for us." (Romans 5:8.) Many similar statements occur in the New Testament. The principle, that through the crucifixion of Jesus man received redemption, has given Christianity some distinctive characteristics. Another principle of Christianity that is regarded generally by Christians as basic to their faith is implied in the many sentences in the Christian New Testament which describe Jesus as the Son of God.

An organized religion, as is true of an organized science, must be strongly involved with abstractions. In writings pertaining to religion, as is true of treatises in science, a particular abstract concept is denoted by an undefined term. For several reasons, the concept of a defined term, as used in an organized science, is devoid of significance in an organized religion.

It is agreed by men of religion that the most important undefined term in an organized religion is the word "Deity," a term employed to denote an abstraction that generally is regarded as the most fundamental concept in any religious structure. Upon occasion, the term "God" or "Supreme Being" or possibly "Supreme Authority" may be used in a religious discourse as a synonym for the term "Deity."

When a man of religion tries to assist a prospective recruit to his particular religion in the development of an understanding of the values

10

of his religion, it is common for him to suggest for each of the religion's undefined terms some descriptive terminology expressed in the recruit's vernacular in the hope that such a tactic will assist the recruit in using the term in appropriate contexts. For instance, the Christian missionary in his attempt to assist a recruit in developing some facets of a useful meaning to be associated with the undefined Christian concept of the Deity, also known as God, may quote from the letter to the Hebrews that appears in the Christian Bible (Hebrews 4:11–13): "The word of God is living and active, sharper than any two-edged sword, piercing to the division of soul and spirit, of joints and marrow, and discerning the thoughts and intentions of the heart. And before him no creature is hidden, but all are open and laid bare in the eyes of him with whom we have to do." In Christian literature, the Deity, also referred to as the Lord, is described as a shepherd, as a father, as merciful and gracious, and as master. Christian advocates hope that the tactic of using such descriptive terms will assist the prospective adherent to Christianity to gain some understanding and appreciation of the desired Christian meaning, admittedly very complex, to be associated with the term "Deity." The term "heaven," another undefined term, is referred to in the Christian Bible as God's dwelling place, as God's throne, as the location of precious things, and as a place of happiness. Thus the attempt is made through the use of man's common language to explain why life in heaven is to be regarded as a desirable award for living a righteous life on earth.

By associating carefully chosen descriptive terminology with each of the undefined terms, as just explained, that occur in the principles that provide the basis of a particular organized religion, it becomes possible to provide for many people a kind of extension to and clarification of the formal structure of a religion in ways that considerably increase its significance and usefulness. Then it becomes possible through the use of understandable language to develop rules and regulations that are regarded as appropriate for the particular religion. Moreover, traditions are inaugurated, and a variety of activities, regarded as religious activities, are an inevitable result. In general, each particular religion, as characterized by its own collection of principles and its own special version of meanings to be assigned to the undefined terms, takes on a distinctive set of characteristics, all of which are subject to interpretation; as a result of differing interpretations, many sects of the same religion have become common. So, theoretically speaking, a person who is not pledged to a particular religion can choose for himself, from among the vast array of religions and their various interpretations that are in existence, a religion or a special sect of a religion that appears to be most compatible with his needs and interests. Many men seek a religion that will provide them assistance in making decisions when, as often may be true, the men making the decisions must contend with problems that involve issues which are regarded generally as within the realm of religion; other men are content to become affiliated with a religion that seems to have special value for them in their desire to lead a life of satisfaction and happiness and, in addition, will provide them comfort and guidance when and if they are involved in personal difficulties, possibly with emotional elements. As a result of the fact that during the time span of human history a tremendous number of religions and sects have been created and continue to be created, the diverse needs of a vast number of men have been served.

Even this very brief discussion of an organized religion may serve partially to explain the fact, as is true of a systematic organized science, that a true understanding of an organized religion cannot be separated from an understanding of the contributions of man to its origins and to its development. Moreover, hopefully, the discussion will provide a basis for understanding the present trend among scholars to categorize within the broad field of cultural anthropology the systematic study of the evolution and the characteristics of religions. This trend is in keeping with the fact that cultural anthropology is concerned with products of the brains of men. The culture of a society, as it is broadly defined in the field of cultural anthropology, refers to the elements, all of which are a product of the brains of men, that may be regarded as characterizing the way of life of that society. It follows that the culture of a people, as thus broadly defined, comprises, at least in part, their language, their arts, the sets of principles adopted by them to define their sciences and their other highly systematic disciplines along with the collection of principles accepted by them to define, for example, their political system, their moral code, and their system of religion.

The importance of having a science created for the purposes of examining the characteristics of individual cultures and of comparing differing cultures, tasks which are accepted by cultural anthropologists, becomes clear when it is realized that members of populations found anywhere on earth must face essentially similar problems. All men must have food; they must clothe themselves; they must develop shelter against the weather; they must propagate their kind; they must have emotional outlets; and they must take steps to give proper recognition to the political, sociological, and economic needs of their particular society while simultaneously recognizing the fact that individuals seek and need security, happiness, and comfort. Such social and individual needs are satisfied in many ways within the great variety of environmental frameworks found upon our little planet.

Again, it must be emphasized that most modern students of cultural anthropology accept as basic to their professional activities the principle that a culture is man-made; each of its components is a product of the brains of men. A fundamental consequence of such a statement is that man can and does introduce new elements into his culture, and he can modify and does modify existing elements of his culture. A few, a very few, elements of a culture, especially the sciences, are introduced into that culture by individuals whose thought processes have been disciplined in a rigorous manner. But most elements of a culture—the common institutions, for example—are usually a consequence of long and elaborate evolutionary processes that have provided much of the essence of history. A study of such evolutionary processes reveals that often the origin of an important present-day institution was characterized by utter simplicity but from such a start it progressed to great complexity —the result of man borrowing from other cultures, the introduction of modifications virtually forced upon man by pressures from within his society, and the introduction of artificial changes in the hope that they would assist man in adapting to new needs. To understand this historical process is fundamental for the person who, for example, may desire to comprehend the development of the religion to which he adheres. That is also true of the individual who desires more than a cursory understanding of the legal code, the moral code, the political system, the sciences, and all other systems of ideas, as well as all the institutions that are a part of the culture of his particular society; in general, each of these cultural elements represents the cumulative contributions of the brains of many men, often over a time span of a vast number of years.

Yet, it seems to be a natural characteristic of man that he wants to believe that the particular culture and its elements with which he has familiarity are to be preferred; he may even regard them as inherently desirable and right; in fact, often he regards them as uniquely right. Individuals who belong to other cultures, he may believe, are living in sin; what they do and think is wrong. It is even very difficult to persuade some people to indulge in serious thought about the merits or demerits of some of the institutions of their particular culture; it has been said that most of such people, if they finally decide to engage in such serious thought, believe sincerely that they are doing so when they are merely rearranging their prejudices. Wars have been fought over religious and political differences; often members of each side fervently believed that they were defending that which was uniquely right. The field of international relations is complicated by the fact that too few people, including diplomats, understand the importance of cultural differences as a factor that usually must be recognized when an attempt is being made to arrive at an understanding upon some difficult issue. The world is being faced with new and increasingly difficult problems because too many people are serving as crusading missionaries for their respective cultures or subcultures. As the world becomes smaller, cultural clashes become increasingly common and their consequences become increasingly serious, even critical.

A system of religion is a very important element of virtually every culture; in fact, during human history there have been many instances of a society in which the system of religion espoused by its members has been the controlling factor within its culture. Often this has been due to an interesting aspect of the evolution of most religious traditions. Virtually every religion, in its basic principles and in the descriptive terminology assigned to the undefined term "Deity," convey the impression that the idea of very great wisdom and tremendous power must be associated with the Deity. Since many men, especially primitive men, as a result of their experiences, only associate very great wisdom and tremendous power with rulers or with others of great authority, it is not surprising that many men through the ages have adopted an anthropomorphic point of view when they attempt to portray the Deity, or, as in the case of primitive man, many Deities. Thus the Deity in some cultures has been assigned characteristics, even mental characteristics, that might be assumed to be associated with a superman. Frequently it is then assumed, as such a portrayal of the Deity continues to evolve, that the man-God becomes actively involved in the affairs of man, and, consequently, has a strong influence upon man's way of life. Having accepted such a portrayal of the Deity, it is virtually inevitable that some men, assuming the validity of their own mental processes for the task, would attempt to describe the will of the Deity and would then enunciate hypotheses pertaining to that will. Moreover, usually because of some

14

unusual personal experiences, some men will assert and possibly will believe that they can communicate with the Deity.

Cultural anthropologists have given much attention to primitive religion. Such attention is essential, for religion was and is a dominant factor in the life of primitive man. In fact, it always has been a prime characteristic of a primitive society that its very culture is based strongly on the idea that the supernatural and the real world of man's experience are closely interwoven. Thus it is necessary to understand the ideas of the members of a primitive society in regard to the supernatural world and to the nature of their Deity or Deities before it is possible to understand the motivation of that society for some of its common activities. And, of great importance for the purposes of the present work, the primitive religions provided a foundation upon which later "more advanced" religions were built. In particular, the primitive religions and associated cultures of the early peoples of the Near East contributed heavily to the foundation of Judaism, of Islam, and of Christianity. In fact, much of Christian principle can be traced back to the efforts of very early man to create concepts and principles that would provide him guidance and even a sense of well-being in what often must have seemed to be a hostile world. So some attention to primitive religion, especially to the primitive religions of the Near East, becomes desirable.

THE EARLY CULTURES OF THE NEAR EAST:
A NECESSARY PRELUDE TO JUDEO-CHRISTIAN CULTURE

The primitive religions, it would appear, originated to great extent as an early by-product of man's efforts to try to comprehend and interpret nature's behavior. Although, as already noted, religion and science are fundamentally different in many respects, they both had their origin in man's yearning for explanation, for understanding, and for an interpretation of many of his experiences. Very early in the history of man's intellectual development, certain elementary kinds of regularity in nature were being noted. Man became aware, for example, of the recurrence of many celestial events, the periodicity of the seasons, and the fact that thunder follows lightning. In the course of time, then, but still before the dawn of history, he began to develop reasons for some of the natural phenomena that featured regularity of occurrence. The fact that the sun appears in the eastern sky each morning, moves across the heavens, and

15

then disappears each evening beneath the western horizon was undoubtedly one of the first natural phenomena to awaken the intense curiosity of man as he began to indulge in the most elementary kinds of analysis. Since there seemed to be no apparent cause for such a sequence of events, primitive man usually explained the phenomenon by creating the concept of a Supernatural Power in the form of a manlike creature, known as a God, who had the daily task of moving the very bright object across the celestial dome. What better solution to his puzzling problem could be expected from a primitive man? Some of the earliest religions were built upon the concept, created by man, of a Sun God.

In general, the Gods of early man were created by him in essentially his own image. Although there were many differences in the Deity concepts as they were developed by members of the various societies about the world, it was a common tactic to create concepts of special Gods to be responsible for virtually all of the otherwise unexplained happenings of man's day-to-day experiences, including his own triumphs or defeats, life and death, the success or failure of his crops, and the appearance of pestilence and disease. The wind, felt and heard but unseen, was explained as an expression of the activity of a particular God; the same kind of explanation was offered in the case of the ripple of water in a stream and the mystifying fire that devoured a tree or a forest. Primitive man, by contrast with most modern men, saw Divinity in nature, and that fact caused him to hold nature in tremendous reverence.

There is some tendency by modern man, when discoursing upon the reasons for various natural events, to speak disparagingly of the approach employed by primitive peoples as he tried to answer their questions about natural phenomena. The truth would seem to be, however, that early man had already attained a rational state of considerable sophistication when he was able to develop abstract concepts of the causes of various natural events, which he designated as Gods, and then was able to carry his ideas further by assigning characteristics to those Gods which would assist him in explaining many of the complex phenomena of nature. Obviously it would be foolish for anyone to try to minimize the importance of the remarkable intellectual accomplishments, including the elaborate systems of principles, that characterize the modern sciences. Nevertheless, perhaps the scientist of the twentieth century has not gone quite as far in refining some aspects of primitive man's approach to understanding his environment as some persons might believe. How does the modern physicist explain the fall of an apple from a tree? The occurrence, he asserts, is one of the observable consequences of the pull of gravity. What is gravity? It is, according to treatises on the phenomenon, that particular force in nature, as experienced on the earth, which pulls objects toward the center of the earth. Mathematical formulas explaining the magnitude of the effects of gravity have been perfected, and, in general, the properties of the "force" have been described. The modern scientist, in fact, deals with the abstraction "gravity" as if it were as real as the object that can be seen and felt. But, in actuality, gravity is merely an undefined term, denoting an abstract concept, invented by physicists; it is described only in terms of its effects and is postulated as the cause of certain natural phenomena. Perhaps the physical scientist, venerated by midtwentieth society for his intellectual conquests, has, at the very foundation of his endeavors, merely replaced the abstract Gods of antiquity by such abstract hypothetical scientific entities as gravitational force, magnetic force, and energy.

It was inevitable that early man, having accepted the idea that the Gods, actually a product of his imagination, were strongly in control of his destiny, ultimately would speculate upon his own relationships to those Gods; thus, rudimentary principles and practices pertaining to such relationships, which became the elements of a primitive religion, began to emerge as an essential part of man's culture. The performance of acts to propitiate the Gods, usually doing what man would do under similar circumstances in dealing with another person of superior rank, became a fundamental aspect of man's purpose in life. Moreover, the time would come when the various hypothetical Deities, as conceived by virtually all men in the early stages of their cultural evolution, would be endowed by their human creators with many of the psychological and sociological characteristics possessed by men. In fact, man would assume that his own social and political inclinations must provide a way of life for the Deities. Consequently, elaborate systems and societies of Gods became a significant aspect of accepted religious beliefs. Some of the ancient peoples even accepted the idea that attractive Goddesses might be wooed—or even raped—by male Gods, and frequently they had offspring. One God might indulge in intrigue against another God or Gods, and struggles for supremacy were regarded as common among those who comprised the Godly kingdom. And it was not unusual for some early societies to accept as fact that certain mortal men had close relationships with the Gods and frequently became involved in their political or social chicanery. It was even accepted in some societies that a

God might have offspring by a mortal woman, and a mortal man might be the father of a child of a Goddess.

The composite picture of the many primitive religions of antiquity reveals an amazing diversity of Deities. There were lesser Gods and major Gods; there were demons and there were spirits; there were evil Gods and good Gods. Some early societies had several hundred assorted Deities. Almost any activity in which a person might participate could easily intrude on the domain administered by some God; it was common, therefore, for an individual to attempt an appeasement of the appropriate controlling Powers before embarking upon an important project. Misfortune, it was generally assumed, would invariably overtake the person who incurred the wrath of an ever-watching God.

It was often true that a particular Deity became associated with an animal. In societies where this was the case, the next step in the evolutionary process involved the actual identification of the God or spirit with the animal; consequently, the animal became the recipient of special attention and respect. Often the Sacred Bulls of Egypt were accorded the respect and honor, even at death, that usually were reserved for royalty. The ultimate identification of an animal with some Deity may well be regarded as a very human kind of development, for man finds it very difficult to work with abstract notions. The modern theoretician must symbolize his abstract concepts to facilitate his development of theory that has relevance to his efforts to understand some segment of nature; without the use of notations, often complex notations, made on paper or on blackboard, the theoretician's mental processes fail him. The scientist developing a theory may struggle a long time even before he is successful in developing a symbolic representation of an abstract idea in such a way that creative discussions of the idea become possible.

The same need to symbolize some hypothetical Deity was satisfied frequently by ancient men through their creation of a material image to represent the God. As generations of men indulged in displays of deference before such an object, a gradual change in man's attitude toward it often took place. Ultimately the image was no longer regarded as a mere symbol employed to represent some Deity; rather, it became the Deity and was venerated as such. Idol worship, in fact, was common among early peoples; it was not unusual for a particular community to worship two or three hundred different idols.

The many, diverse activities that man developed as a result of his assumed relationships with his Gods became basic, as already noted, to much of his culture. There is little doubt that many of his rituals came into existence as a result of his evolving notion of what he should do to propitiate certain Gods and thereby win their goodwill. But after many years of man's indulgence in commonly approved practices designed to accomplish such a purpose, the ritualistic ceremonies often lost most if not all of their original meaning; they became accepted as inherently significant as procedures to be followed when certain objectives were desired. Thus, in essence, man ultimately reached a stage in his cultural evolution when he implicitly accepted the principle that through specific kinds of formalized behavior he could release particular forces in nature that would make possible the accomplishment of ends which he desired. Many dances and dance forms, for instance, had their origin in man's attempts to symbolize certain aspects of his attitudes and actions toward his Gods. Much early art in all its various forms had such a religious motivation.

An important part of the religious tradition of antiquity was provided by men who professed to know the will of the Gods, and, could, if desirable, communicate with them; some persons even claimed that they had been designated as representatives on earth of a God or Gods. Among such individuals were the diviners and the soothsayers, and even some of the prophets of later eras of history seemed to imply in their sayings that they possessed such a distinction; some of the early magicians must also be included in the category. Often such persons were consulted before the making of crucial decisions; their opinions, in general, were amazingly influential.

As ancient man attempted to develop patterns of behavior that he assumed to be consistent with the desires of the Gods, some of the practices which he adopted, as judged on the basis of criteria commonly accepted by our own culture, would be regarded by many people of today as detestable; among such practices were human sacrifice and various kinds of behavior that featured sexual displays and even compulsory sexual intercourse. Slowly, as man's moral sense evolved, many such practices were discarded. But, it must be emphasized, many of the primitive religions included much that today we would regard as good and desirable in addition to that which we would now condemn. In particular, the ancient religions of Mesopotamia, Canaan, and Egypt in the Near East, the cradle of the three great religions, Judaism, Christianity, and Islam, possessed some especially praiseworthy characteristics that contributed greatly to the betterment of the lives of their adherents;

some of the Mesopotamian, Canaanite, and Egyptian Gods were venerated, in spite of their supposed occasional instances of capricious behavior, as the patrons and advocates of cultures that, as we would judge them, possessed many fine attributes. In fact, various types of religious expression, including some that involved the common art forms, reached an unusually high level of development in many societies of the Near East during the era that preceded the days of Biblical history. Some of the early Gods of the Near East were respected for their supposed insistence upon elementary types of justice and morality, and many customs for which the Gods were regarded as advocates provided a focus for various kinds of desirable community action. In antiquity, acceptance of the idea of life after death was common in the Near East, and for some of the early peoples of that part of the world, notably many generations of Egyptians, the anticipated nature of life after death was a dominant factor in the thoughts and in the determination of the activities of the living.

Each of the great present-day religions, Judaism, Hinduism, Buddhism, Taoism, Confucianism, Islam, and Christianity, which are so influential in the lives of vast populations of people, has drawn heavily in some major ways and in a vast number of minor ways upon earlier religions; a little reflection upon the principles and practices that define present-day Judaism and Christianity reveals the validity of such a comment for those two religions. In general, however, by contrast with what was true of the early religions, it is a notable characteristic of the great religions of the present day that a significant part of the orthodox doctrine of each particular religion is based strongly upon the purported ideologies of a specific individual who was regarded by early adherents to that religion as a major contributor to its tenets.

Christianity, in its multiple versions, which for many years has been the favored religion of more persons in the world than has been true of any of the other great present-day religions and which has been an extremely important factor in the development of Western civilization, regards Jesus of Nazareth, a Judaic reformer of the first century A.D., as its nominal founder. Much Christian doctrine is built around ideas associated with the message and mission of Jesus as they were understood and interpreted by his early followers. In addition, orthodox Christianity involves doctrines, introduced by some of the first followers of Jesus, that were designed to testify to the Divine nature of Jesus.

Of very great importance, Christianity, by contrast with virtually all the early religions, accepts monotheism as a fundamental tenet; that is, persons who accept the religious philosophy of Christianity adhere to the belief that there is one and only one Deity, or God. In general, advocacy of the monotheistic idea represented a major break with the philosophy of the ancient religions, but instances may be cited in the history of the early religions when the monotheistic doctrine was supported. For example, the Egyptian ruler, Amenhotep IV, 1379–1362 B.C., issued a proclamation to the effect that Aten, who was the Sun God at that time in Egyptian history, must be worshipped as the only Egyptian Deity; then Amenhotep embarked upon a campaign to erase the names of other Gods from Egyptian temples and monuments.

As men became more sophisticated in their approach to the solution of problems encountered during their attempts to refine the religious principles and concepts which they accepted, especially during the two millennia preceding the Christian era, probably it was inevitable that the time would come when many of them would prefer monotheism to polytheism. With polytheism, man's religious interests are dispersed; with monotheism, those interests are concentrated and unified. Also, when compared with the polytheistic idea, the monotheistic concept seems to be more consistent with the assumption implied in the ideas and activities of virtually all peoples that there is unity and coherence in the universe. Although for many centuries monotheism has been accepted as fundamental doctrine by such religions as Christianity, Judaism, and Islam, it remains and probably always will remain a subject for debate and critical discussion by theologians and philosophers. Through the years, in fact, some theologians with a philosophical turn of mind have carried out laborious logical exercises purporting to demonstrate propositions pertaining to the existence of a unique God and also pertaining to certain characteristics of the relationship with men of such a God, but it appears that in general the resulting discourses, although they may bear the superficial marks of great skill and learning, do not display the logical rigor that the mathematical scientist demands of his proofs. What has been offered by many Christian philosophers, notably Thomas Aquinas, as a logical demonstration of the existence of a God, and a unique God, usually has violated accepted principles of logical deduction. Moreover, it has been common in such fallacious logical demonstrations to base the argument on premises, both those which are explicitly stated and those which are merely implied, that have been drawn from interpretations of some kinds of information provided by the sense organs of man, which probably modern trial lawyers would question, or from sources that depend on little more than opinion. Similar statements may be made in regard to purported logical demonstrations of the nonexistence of God, such as have been advanced by some atheists. In truth, a position adopted by a religious society or by an individual in regard to the existence of God, the nature of God, and the role of God in the physical world and in the world of man cannot originate as a consequence of a logical exercise. Any particular religious "belief" or doctrine accepted by an individual or by a society is a product of man's undefined creative powers; its acceptance by an individual may be a consequence in part of the possibility that it will provide an hypothesis upon which certain, usually desired, processes of thought may be built, or by the possibility that it appears to be a necessary consequence of already accepted tradition, especially a religious tradition, or by the possibility that it receives the support of individuals for whose wisdom there is great respect. But a person's ultimate acceptance in a meaningful way of any intellectual position in regard to a God, to the characteristics of God, and to the relationship of God to the natural universe, which includes man, must depend upon the happiness and satisfaction that the accepted position provides; that is the ultimate test, a test that depends strongly upon a person's educational and psychological background. Because of the many ways in which individuals may have arrived at their decision about a God or Gods, it is now realized that there can be no unanimity of opinion upon characterization of the God concept. The spectrum of opinions in regard to the God concept is indicated by the following extremes: For some persons, their God concept is that of an all-wise Being out there somewhere; for other persons, their God concept is that of a universal principle which provides explanation for all or virtually all happenings in the universe.

It is an interesting fact that in many instances the objections expressed by an individual to the acceptance of any God concept have not really constituted a rejection of the idea of the concept but a rejection of some common anthropomorphic characterization of that concept. That seems to be true of many persons living in nations that accept the philosophy of Marxism. Too often, unfortunately, even in modern times, the God concept of many people seems to have been cast into the image of a man, possibly a white man with whiskers, who pulls the strings that control the universe, probably in a capricious manner, while he sits on a throne in heaven surrounded by attractive angels; such is the image of God inherent in many popular expositions of religious subjects.

The first positive enunciation of the monotheistic doctrine that represented a *lasting* break with the polytheistic doctrine of most early men was not made by adherents to Christianity; it was made by the Hebrew religious who were among the founders of Judaism. The great importance of that action by some of the Hebrew wise men becomes clear, at least in part, when it is realized that Judaism, a predecessor of Christianity, provided the foundation and much of the substance of both Christianity and Islam. In truth, even a brief study of the evolutionary development of the religious institution called Christianity, which is an essential ingredient of the present work, must give significant attention to the fact that Judaism provided much of Christianity's ancestry. The phenomenon of Jesus, previously described as the nominal founder of the Christian faith, must be regarded by the true student of the development of Christianity as merely one of the factors, although an important factor, in a very long and complex evolutionary process, with an extensive history before the time of Jesus, that produced the Christian tradition as we know it today. It is important to realize, in fact, even in this introductory statement, that in the early part of the so-called Christian era, until well into the second century A.D. (Jesus died before the middle of the first century A.D.), Christianity, as then conceived, was properly regarded as a special form of the Judaic faith accepted by the members of a particular cult of Judaism, already a well-established religion at that time. In general, during the very early years of the Christian era, the name "Christian" was not even associated with the particular Judaic cult that accepted many of the new religious ideas associated with the name of Jesus. As time progressed, however, the cult, with respect to the body of beliefs and practices which it advocated, moved farther and farther away from its Judaic heritage, and ultimately it became known as the advocate of a new religion, described as Christianity. Bearing such a designation, the new faith born of Judaism then underwent its own distinctive evolutionary development.

But before giving attention to the particular phase of the evolution of the Christian tradition that has occurred since the time of Jesus, proper recognition must be given to the already implied fact that Judaism, the distinctive religion of the Hebrew people and the religion which provided much of the substance of Christianity, was itself the product of a long evolutionary process which borrowed heavily from the primitive religions. The early Hebrew people usually identified with the beginnings of that evolutionary process lived midst Near Eastern peoples now described as pagan.

The adjective "pagan," properly employed to designate those people who do not accept the monotheistic doctrine, is used frequently in a derogatory sense; that is unfortunate, for the ancient pagan peoples of the Near East, who possessed cultures based to great extent upon their distinctive religions, were responsible for the development of the magnificent early civilizations of that part of the world. The evidence is clear that the culture of the early Hebrew people, including their religion, benefited greatly from the fact that it evolved in close contact with those civilizations. In truth, the early wise men of Hebrew history who contributed so much to the tenets of Judaism reveal in their words and works that they were the product of civilizations that were remarkably advanced in many areas of human accomplishment. Thus it is desirable to give attention, at least briefly, to some of the important early civilizations that occurred at the eastern end of the Mediterranean Sea. The specific geographic area of interest may be described roughly as that which encompasses—employing modern geographical and political terminology—Greece, Turkey, Iraq, Syria, Lebanon, Israel, Saudi Arabia, Jordan, Sudan, Egypt, and Ethiopia. Virtually all of these countries continue to provide fertile opportunities for research by modern archaeologists and historians upon the remarkable civilizations, some of the earliest that historians have been able to document, that existed within their borders. Possibly it is not too surprising that studies of civilizations in antiquity have found a focus in the Near East, for man has had an extremely long history in that part of the world; moreover, physical conditions existed there during the latter millennia B.C. that were favorable to human life. And the cultures of societies of men in the area under consideration, as the dawn of history approached, profited greatly from the extensive migrations of peoples of diverse background between Africa and Asia, probably even including China.

In the fourth millennium B.C., Sumerian civilization had already attained a remarkable state of development in Mesopotamia. The white, non-Semitic Sumerians had created a civilization in Sumer on the fertile soil between the Tigris and Euphrates Rivers that featured distinctive and advanced styles of architecture, elaborate irrigation systems, copper tools and utensils, cuneiform writing, the extensive use of tables as a basis for a well-developed mathematical system, a practical knowledge of astronomical events, and a system of religion built around a priesthood.

Also in the fourth millennium B.C., Egyptian civilization was beginning to display some of the characteristics that within a few centuries would make Egypt a tremendous political and cultural factor in the history of the Near East; such a role for Egypt persisted until Greek and Roman conquerors, just before and just after the start of the Christian era, created drastic changes in the political situation in the region. It appears from archaeological findings that the ancient civilization of Egypt developed slowly as peoples from Africa and immigrants from Asia fused their cultures and learned to cultivate the rich but often swampy land of the Nile valley and delta. Even in the fourth millennium B.C., the Egyptians were displaying an unusual mastery of techniques pertaining to the use of stone in architecture and the utilization of both metal and stone in creating works of art as well as useful household and agricultural implements. The high state of artistry and technical skill to which the early Egyptians attained astounds present-day artists and archaeologists as they recover more and more works of art and useful artifacts in gold, copper, and ivory of even the second and third millennia B.C. Today the accomplishments of the Egyptians of antiquity are becoming familiar to vast numbers of people because of the publicity given to the remarkable array of objects removed from the tomb of Tutankhamen (constructed in approximately 1400 B.C., and discovered in 1922), and other similarly important discoveries made as a result of recent excavations of other commemorative monuments and old habitations. The great ability of the early Egyptians as architects and builders is attested to by the remarkable perfection of measurement that still exists, for example, in the great Pyramids, mostly constructed during the Egyptian Third Dynasty, 2686–2613 B.C. Ancient Egyptian hieroglyphics also reveal that the early Egyptians possessed advanced knowledge of the commercial and mathematical arts. As a military power, Egypt was long a feared adversary.

The very nature of Sumerian and Egyptian cultures was such that raw materials had to be obtained from geographic areas other than those over which they had direct control. So the Sumerians roamed far and wide seeking stone and metal for their needs, and Egyptian caravans, which at that time employed the donkey since the domesticated camel was not yet available to them, conveyed raw materials to Egypt from distant points and then transported finished goods to communities throughout a large area, especially to the east of Egypt. Many of the same peoples who used the caravan trails also operated by sea; heavily loaded boats plied the Mediterranean, the Red Sea, and the Indian Ocean as well as the larger rivers.

Although the Sumerians and Egyptians, sometimes at war but more often at peace, dominated much of the earliest known history of the Near East, there was frequent intrusion into the area by tribal and family groups of people of other ethnic backgrounds. These communities of intruders settled or moved about at the sufferance of the controlling nations, sometimes fighting with each other and sometimes fighting with the people whom they were trying to displace; some of the tribal groups and clans stayed in particular areas for long periods of time, whereas other groups were essentially nomadic. The Bible tells of many such tribes and family groups. A few of the intruders from outside the region ultimately became political powers in the area; some left significant cultural marks upon the peoples of the region and of the world; most merely moved in and out of history.

Starting in about 2000 B.C., tribal groups of people who spoke languages of Oriental origin as well as a few people who employed dialects that were definitely European began to move into the eastern Mediterranean area. Presumably the comparatively advanced state of civilization that prevailed in parts of the Near East was proving attractive to the "have nots." Among the new people coming into the region were the powerful Hittites, apparently of Oriental extraction, who founded a great empire centered on the Anatolian plateau in what is now Turkey. The Hittites ultimately extended their influence several hundred miles north into a part of the modern Soviet Union, and they were involved in military activities deep into Egypt. Of considerable importance for students of Judaism and Christianity is the fact that the Hittites became a major force at one point in history, as recorded in the Bible, in much of Palestine. The aggressive Hittites possessed a culture that was advanced in many respects. Recent archaeological discoveries in Turkey have revealed that the Hittites had achieved considerable competence in the creation of ceramic utensils, and they possessed a remarkable knowledge, especially for that time in history, of the metallurgical sciences. The Hittites demonstrated unusual military and political sagacity, and they maintained a highly disciplined kind of society. Other tribal groups from outside the Eastern Mediterranean area became the forerunners of such aggressive peoples as the Chaldeans and the Assyrians.

As early as 6000 B.C., some Semitic tribesmen were migrating into parts of the Near East; they were merely the forerunners of an extensive movement of Semitic peoples into that region some two or three thousand years later. The origin of the Semitic intruders remains a mystery; there is considerable acceptance of the idea that originally they were desert people. The descriptive term "Semitic," originally "Shemitic," is applied to a tribe or society if the language of its members is Semitic. The term "Semitic language" was introduced by August von Schlözer in 1781 because he argued that those who employed such a tongue were descendants of Shem. (Note Genesis 10 and 11.) All the Semitic languages, of which Hebrew is the best known example, are closely related in structure and in vocabulary but there are interesting and often important differences between the various Semitic tongues.

Much can be written about the contributions of the Semitic immigrants, especially during the latter two millennia of the B.C. period, to the developing cultures of the Near East. The Moabites, the Ammonites, and the Edomites, all of whom were involved in events noted in the Bible, were Semitic. Ancient Canaan, a congeries of city-states and many people outside the city-states, which during Biblical times occupied a significant part of the land bridge between Africa and Asia, including modern Israel, was extremely important during Biblical times, for, as already noted, there was much movement of people and goods along the caravan routes within the land occupied by the culturally advanced Semitic Canaanites. The Phoenicians, who are known in history for their extensive programs of trade throughout the Mediterranean area that reached a peak in approximately the eleventh century B.C. and from whose script the Greek and Roman and all western alphabets were derived, had Canaanite ancestry. The Aramaeans, also great merchants of antiquity, were descendants of Semitic people who became dominant in Syria. At some point in the late history of Sumer, Semitic people began to dominate its political and economic life; then, it appears, they became a significant factor in the development of the great Babylonian civilization which had its seeds in Sumerian culture. There is little doubt that Hammurabi, wise Babylonian ruler and statesman, was Semitic. The contributions of Babylon toward an improved way of life for man are well known; its magnificent architecture, its great literature, its science, and its remarkable legal and related social codes had profound influence upon the culture of later societies, including that of the Hebrews.

Much doubt exists in regard to the origin and the very early history of the particular Semitic people described by historians as Hebrews. The idea has become widely accepted, however, that certain tribes of the Semitic people of Biblical history had their origin in Mesopotamia, of which Sumer was a part. It is the opinion of some knowledgeable historians that a large number of those Semitic people from Mesopotamia, who may have been seeking peace and economic opportunities, migrated into Egypt whereas others moved into areas to the east of Egypt, including Canaan, during the troubled times that accompanied and followed the fall of the Sumero-Akkadian Empire of the third Dynasty of Ur, 2170–2062 B.C. A different view of the origin of the Hebrews in Egypt, which is especially common among some Egyptian historians, seems to have originated with the early Egyptian scribe Manetho. Manetho wrote that in the early part of the second millennium B.C., an "ignoble race" from farther east, apparently Mesopotamia, known as Hyksos, came into Egypt as conquerors and easily subdued the Egyptians. The great historian Josephus of the first century A.D. expressed agreement with Manetho that the Hyksos were the early ancestors of the Hebrew people of Biblical history, but only a few later historians have accepted the judgment of Josephus upon the subject. Irrespective of the story that one accepts in regard to the circumstances surrounding the emigration into Egypt from Mesopotamia of a large number of the early Semitic people, it is important to note that they were the possessors of the legends, customs, and other traditions of the part of Mesopotamia from which they came; ultimately considerable blending must have taken place between their culture and Egyptian culture.

According to Biblical testimony, with which most historians seem to agree, there came a time in the history of the Semitic people who were the descendants of those who settled in Egypt, when many of them were very unhappy with their life in Egypt and decided to leave; consequently they became involved in a very difficult migration to Palestine, an event known in Jewish history as the Exodus. Although it is possible, even quite probable, that the Semitic people who ultimately journeyed from Egypt to Palestine adopted native languages when they lived in Egypt, there came a time, after going to Palestine, when Hebrew became their written and spoken language, so it has become common to designate the people of the Exodus, their descendants, and even their forebears as Hebrew.* Originally, Hebrew may have been a Canaanite dialect. It was the

---

*According to custom, the Hebrews of Biblical history were not known as Jews until after the time of the Babylonian Exile, 586 B.C.

particular Semitic people to whom reference has just been made who were chiefly responsible for the development and nurture of Judaism, so special attention is given to them in this work. (Their story as it pertains to the development of the present exposition is told in the next few chapters.)

By 2000 B.C., Semitic peoples had so infiltrated the Near East and had assumed so much control of the commercial and cultural activities of the area that they had become a dominant factor in the life of the region. Some of the Semitic people roamed the countryside with their flocks; some were traders, and their caravans moved from community to community along the caravan routes; and some were merchants and artisans in the city-states, the common political units of the day. Simultaneously, Semitic traders sailed the Mediterranean with their raw materials as well as finished merchandise, moving from port to port in—using modern geographical terminology—Greece, Turkey, Lebanon, Syria, Israel, and Egypt. Some of the seafaring Semitic traders also made voyages into the Persian Gulf in their quest for markets, sailing from ports that now appear on the maps of modern Iraq and Iran.

The cultural diffusion that was supported by such extensive travel and trade by the Semites and others was magnified by the fact that people were also regarded as a commodity. Although many expert craftsmen moved by choice from one locality to another, often they were bought and sold. And the conquered in war usually became slaves. The very extensive slave traffic which existed at that time was accepted generally by the peoples of the region as something inevitable in human society. Moreover, men of one tribal group bought, wooed, or stole women of other tribes; promiscuity, as presently defined, was common. So the Near East during the pre-Christian era was the locale of tremendous biological as well as cultural cross-fertilization; a great variety of individual human traits was represented in the intermixing. It is the belief of some historians and anthropologists that, over a time span of many generations, the intellectual and social development of the Hebrew people, later to be known as Jews, who provided the human foundation for the development of the unique and tremendously significant Judaic tradition, was greatly stimulated by such intermixing of genes and cultures.

Much of the Near East in Biblical times was, as is true today, a desert country; some was utter desolation. Yet, as a result of the ingenuity of the people, a substantial agricultural program, necessary to sustain the progressive civilizations of the day, was maintained. More of the countryside, except for that in modern Israel, was cultivated in those days than is true at the present time; remains of ancient water collection basins are still easily detected and many now barren hillsides reveal traces of ancient terracing, sometimes elaborate, that was developed to facilitate agricultural pursuits. Forests were undoubtedly much more extensive than today; many boats transported timber from the forests of Lebanon, the "cedars of Lebanon," and from other forested areas to buyers in ports along the Mediterranean. Irrigation, even more common than today in most regions, was widely practiced in the then fertile valleys; many of those rich valleys, one notes with regret, are now essentially sterile because of the impregnation of the soil with salt, the usual end point of the process of irrigation unless necessary controls are introduced. The Nile valley and delta were extremely fertile and supported a large population; the soil was renewed periodically by the river floods. Extensive irrigation systems provided water to the rich soil of the Tigris and Euphrates River valleys, an area which was truly a wonderful garden spot; it is not surprising that traditions exist which place the Garden of Eden in that particular locality. The mouth of the Euphrates River in the early part of the Biblical era was a fine harbor where many ships, outbound for or inbound from ports as far away as India, could always be found loading and unloading finished merchandise and raw materials. Now much of the ancient harbor and the riverbed just above it are filled with silt; in fact, although extensive efforts at restoration of the land are now under way, a large amount of the old valley still remains barren and deserted, its soil no longer fertile because of its high salt content. The land area of ancient Canaan, on which modern Israel occupies a central position, was described by Sinuhe, a famous Egyptian traveler, in approximately 2000 B.C., as "an excellent land." He said further that the soil produced abundant crops of figs, grapes, and grain; wine, he reported, was more plentiful than water. Continuing, he noted that honey was in great supply and the olive trees of Canaan, some of which from later Biblical days still survive, were highly productive.

So the Near East, which in so much of its area is now plagued with extreme human misery and often reveals itself to the visitor as a land of despair, was for many centuries, long before the era of the important accomplishments of the ancient Greeks and Romans, the dynamic focus of man's cultural development; it was the locale, along with China, of man's first great civilizations. From such civilizations of the Near East came advanced principles and practices in art, in mathematics, in architecture, in literature, in science, in commerce, in law, in philosophy, and in religion, that provided foundational elements for many of the traditions that became the nucleus of Western culture. Among those traditions was the Judaic religious tradition which, along with its offspring Christianity, was probably the most influential of all the recognizable elements contributing to the development of what we now commonly characterize as Western civilization.

The next few chapters treat what appear to have been some of the most important factors in the evolution of the Judaic tradition as it was based on and grew out of the ancient highly developed Near Eastern cultures. Later chapters reveal how the evolutionary process that was responsible for Judaism underwent a distinctive branching at one point in its history; one branch, which soon began to feature its own evolutionary process, ultimately was responsible for introducing to mankind a new religion, now universally known as Christianity, which for nearly two millennia has been a major factor in the way of life chosen by many nations and by a vast number of people.

Chapter Two

THE HEBREW PATRIARCHS

Great arbitrariness exists in connection with the selection of events and persons to be designated as primary in the history of the evolution of Judaism, the distinctive religious and cultural tradition of the Hebrew people. Any particular tradition actually is the product of the creative efforts of an uncountable number of persons and of an uncountable number of events for which no beginning in time can be specified. The early Hebrew wise men who were responsible for the development of the Judaic Bible,* the Holy Book of Judaism, seemed to accept Abraham as the individual who should be designated as the original patriarch of the Hebrew people. Nevertheless, the same wise men developed a genealogical record, obviously mythical, that appears in Genesis, the first book of the Judaic Bible, which represented their attempt to relate Abraham to the first people who inhabited the earth. Much of the Judaic Bible possesses considerable historical and geographical validity, but, as noted later, a substantial part of its first five books, generally known as the Pentateuch by Christians and as the Torah by followers of Judaism, obviously was constructed essentially from legends. Moreover, the development of the Torah has a history that severely limits its factual trustworthiness. Thus a skeptical attitude is appropriate when reading the Biblical accounts of Abraham and his deeds. In view of the attention, however, that was given to Abraham by the authors of the Judaic Bible, he and his supposed involvement in the early history of the Hebrew people cannot be ignored when trying to isolate and analyze some of the most significant factors that were responsible for determining the nature of the Judaic tradition.

Abraham is introduced in the Biblical record (Genesis 11) as the son of Terah, who, according to the Biblical presentation, was a native of Ur of the Chaldees; Ur was the capital city of Sumer, already mentioned as the locale of the first highly developed civilization of which we have any trustworthy knowledge. The fact that the Bible specifies that Abraham came from Mesopotamia seems to provide some confirmation of modern theories pertaining to the origins of the Hebrew people. The

*The term "Judaic Bible," the Christian version of which is "Old Testament," is used in this treatment in preference to the usual term "Hebrew Bible."

story of Abraham, as narrated in Genesis, is inaugurated with an account of a lengthy expedition undertaken by Terah and his family to relocate in Canaan, the "land of milk and honey"; the journey originated in Ur. Associated with Terah at the start of the trip, along with his flocks and a large retinue of aides, were his son Abraham, his grandson Lot, and Abraham's wife Sarah. Originally Abraham and Sarah were named, respectively, Abram and Sarai, but later, reputably at God's direction, they were renamed. To provide a break in the long journey to Canaan, the party decided to stop in Haran, now a town in present-day Turkey, where, according to the Biblical account, Terah died. Later (Genesis 12:7), after Abraham and other surviving members of the expedition had left Haran and had finally reached Canaan after a difficult journey, the Biblical narrative records the occurrence of an episode that is obviously legendary but which has been acknowledged generally by the Jewish people to have been an event, fictitious or not, that has had great influence upon the development of their attitudes and thoughts toward their future role in human history. Myths, stories created by man although they may have had some factual basis, as well as actual sayings and events, often have had a pronounced influence on human belief, on his traditions and institutions, and on his behavior. The legendary episode to which reference has just been made involved an appearance of the Lord before Abraham. During the dialogue that followed, as narrated in the Bible, the Lord is reported to have asserted, "I will give this land (Canaan) to your offspring." Much of the land thus designated by the Lord is now part of modern Israel. Upon other occasions, according to the Biblical text, the Lord also promised Abraham that he would be "the father of a multitude of nations" and his offspring would be as numerous as "the dust of the earth." Those promises, the Book of Genesis reports, were confirmed in an emphatic manner at a later date (note Genesis 17), upon the occasion of the creation of an important covenant between the Lord and Abraham. Over a time span of many centuries, that covenant, which seemed to imply that a mutual spirit of understanding and cooperation between the Lord and Abraham and his descendants must exist and will exist in perpetuity, has provided the reason for much courage and hope on the part of the Jewish people; moreover, the covenant, which has become very important as a significant part of the Jewish and Judaic traditions, has been responsible for some elements of Jewish political policy. So that future generations of Hebrew people would give proper recognition to the existence and to the importance of the covenant, the Lord, according to the Biblical account, specified that every male in Abraham's household, including slaves, must be circumcised at the age of eight days. Thereafter, circumcision was to be accepted by all male descendants of Abraham as a "mark in their flesh" of the "everlasting pact" between Abraham and the Lord. Thus, as a consequence of the tradition which, according to the Biblical account, originated in the time of Abraham, the minor surgical operation of circumcision has retained through the ages its deep significance for the Hebrew (the Jewish) people; today, each male Jewish child, as mandated by the covenant, is circumcised when he is eight days old.

Any idea however that the circumcision of males originated with the covenant between the Lord and Abraham cannot be sustained, for the circumcision of young males is a very old practice with an unknown origin; it took place long before any date ascribed to Abraham. In fact archaeologists have found evidence of the early existence of the practice of circumcision in many parts of the world; pictorial representations appearing on ancient Egyptian ruins reveal that the operation was carried out on young boys as early as 4000 B.C. Moreover, some historians believe that circumcision did not become an important element in the Judaic tradition until approximately the fifth century B.C.

The sex organs were the focus of much interest on the part of early man, undoubtedly because of their apparent relationship to the most irresistible biological drive to which men and women are subjected. Thus, it is not surprising that in the evolution of some religious traditions practices involving the sex organs, such as circumcision, would ultimately become endowed with religious significance, irrespective of the origin of the practices.

It is an interesting fact that no Christian sect, although Christianity drew much of its substance from Judaism, authorizes the practice of circumcision, but the operation has become increasingly common among some classes of Christians, notably Anglo-Saxon Christians, because of its sanction, for reasons of health, by many medical authorities. Some Christians have expressed the belief that Chapter 15 of the Book of Acts, as they interpret the chapter, exempts them from the instruction pertaining to circumcision as supposedly given by the Lord to Abraham. But, as revealed later, Christians do not adhere to the practice of circumcision because the first Christian advocates, who still regarded themselves as followers of Judaism, found it undesirable to attempt to enforce the custom as they began to recruit non-Jews to accept their religious ideas.

There are elements in the story of Abraham that seem to have historical contexts which traditionally have led most historians to place the time of his life near the start of the second millennium B.C.; recent discoveries in Syria, however, have been interpreted by some scholars as meaning that Abraham lived at a much earlier date. But such observations do not mean that a man named Abraham, as he and his life are portrayed in the Bible, actually lived. Abraham may have been and possibly was a fictitious character created by the much later Biblical authors, actually poets and singers, to provide a vehicle for the introduction of several significant ideas and to satisfy certain needs of the carefully conceived plot of the story told in Genesis. In fact, no historical evidence presently exists that confirms the Biblical account of Abraham's life and activities. It is likely, however, that his extensive nomadic wanderings, as described, were typical of those of many families and tribal groups during early Biblical times. There is little doubt, if a man Abraham did live, that much of the religious philosophy and many of the religious practices attributed to him actually became a part of the Judaic tradition long after his death. Nevertheless, fictitious or real, Abraham may be regarded as typical of some of the dominant personalities among the very early predecessors of the Jewish people; they lived amidst civilizations based strongly on pagan religious ideas and, it is to be presumed, they accepted polytheism and indulged in pagan practices.

Early Christians found in the character of Abraham, since he is portrayed as a man of great spiritual strength, many of the ideals which they advocated; moreover, Christians of later periods believed that they saw in some of Abraham's recorded experiences a prefigurement of events of special significance for Christianity. For instance, Chapter 18 of Genesis tells of a visit to Abraham by three angels; the fact that there were three angels has been interpreted by some Christians, especially medieval Christians, as providing an introduction, many centuries before the time of Jesus, to the Christian concept of the Holy Trinity. Since the three angels, when talking to Abraham, prophesied the birth of a son to his wife Sarah, previously barren, the event was also interpreted by some early and especially medieval Christians as prefiguring the much later visit of an angel to Joseph, reported in the Christian New Testament, to foretell the birth of a son Jesus to his wife Mary; Mary is described in the Christian New Testament as a virgin at the time when the conception of Jesus took place.

During the five centuries or more between the time of Abraham and that of Moses, most venerated of those who generally are regarded as major contributors to the development of the Judaic tradition, there occurred, according to the Biblical text, a series of interesting and complex events, familiar to all readers of the Bible, in which Abraham's son Isaac, Isaac's son Jacob, and Jacob's son Joseph, and some members of their families were participants. Among the stories that are told in the Bible is the fascinating tale of the adventures of Joseph; it will be recalled that Joseph was sold by his older brothers to a caravan of Ishmaelites on their way to Egypt, and some time later he was able to ascend to a position of such great influence in Egypt that he could save his father and brothers during a time of severe famine and then give them a new opportunity for livelihood in Egypt. The stories of the experiences of Isaac, Jacob, and their families and the intricate plots woven about the characters in those stories undoubtedly were based on legends that were part of the folklore of the Hebrew people. It is possible that the legends had their origin in real events that occurred during the long period of time, for which there is virtually no historical record, between the days of Abraham and those of Moses.

Some Judaic Biblical analysts have given much thought to the meanings and the significance that should be associated with the stories that are told in the Book of Genesis about Abraham and about some of the early generations of his descendants. Increasingly, it would appear, the historical value of the stories is being questioned. Many rabbis now suggest that the stories should be regarded as allegories, folklore cast into stories that are designed to teach lessons. The stories take on special meaning for followers of Judaism when read from that point of view. For instance, the stories serve to give emphasis to the idea that in the early days of the Hebrew people God was truly their guardian, and the implication exists that such a relationship will continue as long as the Hebrew people accept God's mandates. When judged against the demand for continuity in the narrative that tells of the early history of the Hebrew people, as related in the Book of Genesis, it may be observed that by means of such stories the ingenious early poets and singers who were responsible for much of the content of the Book of Genesis succeeded in locating in Egypt a large number of Hebrews, predecessors of the Jews, at about the time in history, approximately the middle of the second millennium B.C. when, in conformity with both legend and historical evidence, Hebrew people were living in Egypt. Among those people was

Moses, who, according to the Biblical text, was born in Egypt. The validity of the Biblical assertion that Moses was of Egyptian background is supported by legends, by some of the cultural elements in his reported ideas and actions, and by the significant fact that the name "Moses" as well as the names of some of his associates are easily recognized as having Egyptian origin.

It appears that the Hebrew segment of the populace in Egypt continually grew in size so that ultimately it constituted a large fraction of the population. In fact, according to the Biblical narrative, the Egyptians "came to dread the Israelites." It is likely that this dread was based in part on the possibility that the Israelites, whom the Bible asserts were held in "bondage," might indulge in violent tactics as they sought to attain a higher status in Egyptian society.

As reported in the Bible, it was during a time when life for the Hebrew people in Egypt had reached a very low state that Moses, one of the truly great leaders and teachers of history and also a person universally revered by the Jewish people, became the most significant character in the important story that was unfolding. Because of the tremendous significance of Moses in Jewish and in Judaic history, the singers and poets who contributed so much to the content of the Torah must have felt impelled to dramatize significant events in his life; that seems to be apparent as one reads pertinent sections of the Torah. In fact, some rabbis believe that much of the Biblical account of Moses and his career must be regarded, along with the stories about Abraham, as belonging in the realm of allegory. Shortly after Moses was born, according to the Biblical narrative, a new and insecure Pharaoh, not identified by historians, decided that curbs had to be introduced upon the growth in population of the Hebrews. Supposedly for such a purpose, an order was given by the Pharaoh to oppress the "Israelite people with forced labor." In spite of the edict, the number of Hebrew people continued to increase. Finally, in desperation, the Egyptian king decided to take a more direct step for introducing population control among the Hebrews by ordering every newborn Hebrew boy to be thrown into the Nile. Moses, of Hebrew parentage, survived the Pharaoh's order, according to the Biblical account, because of his mother's astuteness in hiding her very young son in a basket among the papyrus reeds of the Nile. The Biblical report continues by noting that the Pharaoh's daughter found the infant and then, unknowingly, employed the child's mother as his nursemaid when he was removed to the chambers of the palace. So, if the Biblical story is essentially true, Moses, throughout his youth, enjoyed many uncommon opportunities. The unknown Hebrew lad, along with the other children then living in the palace, studied under scholarly teachers, and he was given the opportunity to develop the abilities and obtain the knowledge then regarded as a prerequisite for a future leadership role in Egypt or in one of its colonies. At that time many aspects of Egyptian culture were remarkably advanced. The Biblical report of the educational opportunities made available to Moses is provided support by the fact that Egyptian historians have found that it was not unusual for the Egyptian Pharaohs of approximately the Moses period of Egyptian history, notably King Thutmose, 1504–1450 B.C., to give special attention to the education of a few apparently competent non-Egyptian children; the Pharaohs wanted to be certain that they would have the necessary administrative personnel for any lands which they might conquer.

After Moses had grown up, according to the Biblical text, he observed an Egyptian in the act of assaulting "one of his kinsmen." In some manner he had learned of his Hebrew ancestry. So Moses in his anger slew the Egyptian and then fled from the wrath of Pharaoh to "the land of Midian," then an extensive area in what is now Jordan and Saudi Arabia. So the adult Moses is introduced in the Biblical text as a man of physical strength and as a vengeful man, greatly disturbed by the tribulations to which the Hebrew people were being subjected. Possibly it was during the years of his reported stay in Midian that Moses decided that the Hebrew people must be freed from their bondage, and that this could only be accomplished by making it possible for them to have their own nation. Moreover, during the same period of time he may have found himself virtually forced to accept the idea that a new code of social principles must be developed and accepted by his people to bring order and justice into their chaotic way of life, an apparent consequence of the fact that their many years of subjection to the control of their Egyptian masters had led to a critical deterioration in their own social standards and in their appreciation of values. Only a person who had been raised outside the degrading cultural framework in which apparently the Hebrew people in Egypt were living could fully appreciate the necessity for the development and adoption of such a code. Possibly revealing, at least in part, the influence of some aspects of his religious education in the Pharaoh's household, Moses, at some point in his career, also decided that he could no longer accept pagan concepts common in his day pertaining to the ultimate wisdom and the ultimate powers of control within the universe.

Controversy in regard to Moses, his life, and the contributions to Judaism that are attributed to him is inescapable because of the fact that no acceptable historical evidence exists that Moses ever lived. Possibly he and his career were the creation of later generations of imaginative and ingenious singers and poets. But it would be difficult to accept such a suggestion without modification. In fact, modern students of Judaic history generally accept the point of view that the Moses of the Bible was not a fictitious character; they believe that there was a real Moses who proved to be a true genius in his chosen role of leader and teacher of the Hebrew people. Undoubtedly it is true, however, that a great amount of legend was incorporated into the Biblical story of Moses. Even the well-known moral and ethical code and its ramifications that are associated with the name of Moses in the Torah were undoubtedly adaptations of principles that were a part of the cultural tradition of the Babylonians, the Canaanites, the Egyptians, and others; moreover, the record of the original contributions of Moses to Judaic principle was probably modified, extended, and perfected by later priestly editors before it was incorporated into the Biblical text.

One must not believe that Moses ever demanded a discontinuation of the major religious customs that were basic to the pagan way of life in which he had been educated. He himself, according to Biblical accounts, practiced and apparently advocated animal sacrifice. Although a person with a perspective provided by present-day moral principles is inclined to condemn animal sacrifice, the practice was consistent with the mores of virtually all the peoples of the Near East at that time in history.

Many years after Moses had gone to live with the Midianites, the troublesome Pharaoh died. But the Israelites continued to suffer severely under the oppression that remained in effect. Since, according to the Biblical narrative, "God heard their moaning," He sent a message to Moses by way of an angel who appeared before Moses in a blazing fire in a bush which "was not consumed"; the angel informed Moses that he was the choice of the Lord to intercede with the Egyptian ruler in behalf of the Hebrew people, his kinsmen. Moreover, as related in the Biblical text, the angel informed Moses that he had been designated as the person who ultimately would lead the great mass of Hebrew people out of Egypt into the land that the Lord had promised to Abraham as the ultimate home of his offspring.

The Biblical story of the circumstances under which Moses is supposed to have been enlisted by God to accept the responsibilities associated with the leadership of his people undoubtedly reveals much about the dramatic and imaginative capabilities of the early poets and singers who contributed so much to parts of the Torah. Probably, however, it would be a mistake to regard the story as mere fiction devoid of significance. Rather, the story seems to involve the implication, of special interest to psychologists as well as to students of Judaism and Christianity, that Moses underwent an experience essentially similar to those described in the biographies of many persons who have believed that they were "called by God" to undertake an important service in behalf of mankind. After an individual has indulged in a prolonged mental struggle while debating his personal obligation in connection with a particular cause, some unusual emotional experience, even a dream, often serves to trigger the making of a firm decision to pursue a preferred course of action. Also it may be noted that the part of the Bible text that pertains to the assignment of Moses to the role of liberator of his people is of interest to the sociologist and historian in view of the fact that it is a common phenomenon in history that a person who becomes a liberator is prepared for his role by those who are the oppressors.

The Biblical account of the initial as well as later instructions from God to Moses, newly designated by God to be the leader of the Hebrew people, later to be known as Israelites, includes reference to some very impressive signs that Moses was authorized to employ to prove to his people that he was truly a representative of God. The same signs would also be useful to Moses in providing a demonstration of his powers, which he could assert were derived from God, during his negotiations with Pharaoh. The signs included the changing of his rod into a snake, the changing of water from the Nile into blood, the production of extensive destructive plagues of frogs, of lice, and of insects, and the invoking of damaging hailstorms and pestilences.

During much of antiquity, magic and magicians were very important in Egyptian culture, including the Egyptian religion; it was not unusual for a person to employ magic when attempting to display his God-given powers or when trying to win a point in a debate. Thus the original authors of the story of the negotiations of Moses with Pharaoh had good reason to believe that probably Moses employed magic. In this connection it may be observed that accounts of rods being turned into snakes and of water being turned into blood are often found in the annals of

Egyptian magic; some Biblical commentators believe that the Biblical reports of such activities by Moses serve to give the story of his negotiations with the Pharaoh an authentic Egyptian coloration. Some of the signs, such as the predictions of plagues and natural catastrophes, purportedly employed by Moses, cannot be explained as demonstrations of the use of magic; other explanations are necessary. But severe plagues of insects (locusts), which in a very short time can turn a green countryside into wasteland, have been common in the history of Egypt and of neighboring areas; the devastating hordes of locusts as well as other plagues and pestilences, and even severe storms, were and still are regarded by many people of the region as having been instigated by God, actually as God's way of punishing men for their misdeeds.

In spite of the reported demonstrations by Moses of his powers supposedly bestowed upon him by the Lord and which were to prove that he was acting at the Lord's behest, the Biblical text observes that his insistent demand that the Hebrew people be released from their bondage was consistently rebuffed by the Pharaoh. Consequently, as the story is narrated in the Bible, the Lord informed Moses (note Exodus 11) that yet one more plague would be visited upon Pharaoh and upon Egypt. After that, the Lord asserted, Pharaoh would capitulate, and Moses and his people would be free to leave the country. Exodus 12 records directives said to have been issued by the Lord pertaining to necessary preparations to be made by Moses and his people in anticipation of the forthcoming plague. Each family of the "whole assembly of Israel," it was specified, was to select a lamb "without blemish" to be slaughtered at twilight of the fourteenth day of the month. Specific directions were given for roasting and eating the flesh of the lamb on the very night of the slaughter. Previously, however, the two doorposts and the lintel of the house in which the feast was to take place were to be marked with the lamb's blood. That same night, the Lord promised, He would strike down every firstborn in Egypt, both man and beast, except for those who occupied the houses marked with blood.

According to the Biblical record, these elaborate instructions were given to Moses on the tenth day of the month; that particular month, the Lord is said to have mandated, was henceforth to be designated as the first month of the year. It was further directed by the Lord (again refer to Exodus 12) that the momentous event, the Passover, should be celebrated "throughout the generations" as a festival to the Lord. The festival was to last from the evening of the fourteenth day of the month to the evening of the twenty-first day; a sacred convocation, during which no work should be done, was to be held on the first day of the festival and again on the seventh day, and only unleavened bread should be eaten during the festival period.

The Biblical narrative reports that events occurred as predicted, and the distraught Pharaoh ordered Moses and his people along with their flocks and herds to "depart"; they were free to leave the country. The "miracle of the Passover," as it has often been described in Judaic literature, had been effective; the Exodus of the Hebrew people from Egypt under the leadership of Moses had become possible. If the story of the dealings of Moses with the Pharaoh and their consequences is regarded as allegory, obviously part of the lesson that it teaches is that one does not defy the will of God.

The festival of Passover had its origin as a religious event to celebrate the triumph of Moses in winning freedom for the Hebrew people, thereby making possible the Exodus; without doubt, the series of events associated with the Passover and the Exodus are the most spectacular and the most crucial of any series of events described in the Judaic Bible. Thus, the festival of Passover has always possessed tremendous significance for those who are followers of Judaism. The undoubted importance of Passover for adherents to the Judaic faith is emphasized in rabbinical teachings, and many references to the Exodus occur in the Siddur, the Judaic Book of Daily Prayer. It may be noted, however, that some scholars, who have been impressed with the common tendency of men to associate religious significance with important traditions, already existing, have suggested that the actual origin of the Passover celebration may be found in one or another of three possible sources: ancient ceremonies that gave recognition to the spring equinox; a spring festival of the pre-Moses era that provided its participants atonement for past misdeeds; or an ancient ceremony designed to give emphasis to old beliefs in the sacrosanctity of the firstborn. Moreover, some Judaic scholars are quite certain that several of the Judaic festivals, if not most, are adaptations of festivals celebrated by the pagan Canaanites; virtually all of the festivals in Canaan seem to have originated as celebrations pertaining to the significance of the seasons and to the planting, growing, and harvesting of crops. It is conceivable that many years after the conquest of Canaan, the festival of the Passover had such an origin. Even if it is ascertained that the Passover celebration had such an origin, there would be no implication in the finding that the Exodus, as an historical event, did not occur.

The Jewish calendar, actually two overlapping calendars pertaining respectively to the *chronological* or *agricultural* year and the *ecclesiastical* year, has a long history of development although it was not given a fixed form until Hillel II did so in the fourth century A.D.; the calendar is based essentially upon the motions of the moon but with large periodic corrections (the leap year effect) to keep it in a proper relationship with the solar cycle; each of the two kinds of years comprises twelve months. The names of the twelve months of the Jewish year, given in the order in which they appear in the chronological or agricultural calendar, are Tishri, Heshvan, Kislev, Tebet, Shebat, Adar, Nisan, Iyar, Sivan, Tammuz, Ab, and Elul; Tishri, the first month of the chronological year, usually has its first day in September. But to be consistent with the purported instruction from the Lord to Moses upon the occasion of the original Passover, the Judaic ecclesiastical year starts with Nisan, the month of the festival of Passover; Nisan occurs in the spring.

The Jewish calendar provides an interesting illustration of the strong influence of Babylonian customs upon the development of Jewish traditions. The names of the months of the Jewish calendar come directly from the Babylonian; moreover, the basic design of the calendar to conform to the cyclical appearances of the moon was derived from Babylonian practice. In the Jewish chronological calendar, the term Rosh Hodesh denotes the first day of a month; consequently, according to the very manner in which the calendar was conceived, Rosh Hodesh must designate the date when the new moon first appears. Tishri 1 of each Jewish chronological year is designated as Rosh Hashanah, which also denotes the beginning of the Ten Days of Penitence; the ten days end with Yom Kippur, which for the Judaic faithful is the most solemn day of the year.

The celebration by the Jews of the festival of Passover, with its long history and the grand tradition behind it, has become highly stylized. On the night of Passover, the faithful indulge in a ceremonial meal, the Seder, at which bitter herbs and unleavened bread in the form of crackers are eaten to symbolize remembrance of the Passover events. Also, in connection with the ceremonial part of the meal, the participants indulge in the Haggada, (Haggada means "recitation"), which is a stylized interpretation of or midrash on the Exodus and the meaning of Passover.

During each year, as a part of the Judaic tradition, there are numerous religious holidays and festivals in addition to the festival of Passover; they have varying degrees of significance for those who are adherents to Judaism. Rosh Hashanah, the Jewish New Year, and Yom

Kippur, the Day of Atonement, have already been mentioned. The Sabbath must be observed, according to Exodus 20:8–11 and Deuteronomy 5:12–15, as a particular day of each week to be devoted to rest and religious observance; Judaic tradition specifies that the Sabbath is on Saturday. The celebration of the Sabbath, with special prayers prescribed by Judaic liturgy, begins at sundown on Friday. (All Jewish holidays are from sundown to sundown.) Christians, when adopting much of the Judaic tradition, accepted the concept of the Sabbath, but only a few Christian sects celebrate that particular holiday—i.e., holy day—on Saturday; most Christians observe the Sabbath on Sunday.

Followers of Judaism accept the principle that the religious holidays and festivals are ordained by God and are essential and fundamental to the maintenance of an acceptable religious life. (Note the instructions given in the latter part of Leviticus, starting with Leviticus 23.) Certainly the conscientious celebration of the religious festivals and holidays has had a remarkable unifying effect upon the worldwide Jewish community. In addition, the celebrations have served as a constant reminder for the Jewish people of those important events and circumstances that have provided meaning and value to the Judaic tradition; the religious celebrations and holidays have also been responsible in part for the unusual knowledge of their historical background that most Jews possess. Christianity has attempted to imitate Judaism in its advocacy of the regular celebration of certain events of great significance for their faith, notably the birth of Jesus and his "resurrection."

When Moses undertook the task of leading his kinfolk on their Exodus from Egypt, he accepted a horrendous task, for the people under his command were an undisciplined rabble. Since apparently the Hebrew people who were following him had been living in an abject state of bondage for many generations, they were ignorant and superstitious and were generally incapable of accepting responsibility. Even the thought of freedom, although strongly desired, often aroused deep fear. Moreover, the large body of Hebrews under the command of Moses, apparently recruited from much of Egypt, was actually composed of distinct communities of individuals of somewhat diverse cultural background.

Interesting statistical information on the refugees from Egypt is provided in Chapter I of the Book of Numbers, which reports that early in the second year after the Exodus took place a census that Moses authorized revealed that he was the leader of 603,550 men, aged twenty years and over. Each man was a member of one of the twelve clans of the ancestral houses of the whole Israelite community; each clan possessed distinctive cultural characteristics. The clan with the largest number of individuals, 74,600, was composed, according to the tradition accepted by Biblical authors, of descendants of Judah, son of Jacob. The statistical data provided by the Book of Numbers are regarded by some scholars as greatly exaggerated, possibly because of a faulty translation at some point in the development of the particular version of the Book of Numbers that presently is the accepted version. It appears, as the later history of the Israelites developed, that the members of the tribe of Judah provided unusual stability in the political entity that ultimately was created in the Promised Land, and they maintained a special loyalty to the ideals promulgated by Moses.

The Biblical story reports that the huge company of Hebrew people fleeing Egypt was subjected to a frightening experience in the early part of the flight when it was realized that the army of Pharaoh was in pursuit. Many attempts have been made to provide a scientific explanation of the episodes, described in dramatic fashion by Biblical writers, during which Moses and his followers succeeded in evading the pursuing Egyptian forces when an opening miraculously occurred in a body of water that had impeded their progress, but the opening ceased to exist when the members of Pharaoh's army arrived at the scene; thus the members of Pharaoh's pursuing army were drowned. A universally accepted identification of the body of water in which the event is supposed to have occurred has not been made, but there were treacherous swampy sections in the part of Egypt where the reported event may have taken place; a portion of the modern Suez Canal is located in that general region. Some traditional readings of the Book of Exodus which specify that the Red Sea was the locale of the episode are not accepted by most modern Judaic scholars. The entire route followed by Moses in going from Egypt into the Sinai peninsula has been the subject of much conjecture by Biblical scholars; the limited information provided by the Biblical account of the expedition has provided little assistance to geographers.

It appears from the story of the Exodus, as told in the Book of Exodus, that for a period of some three months after their escape from the pursuing Egyptians the wanderers underwent a variety of severe hardships that caused much grumbling and dissension; Moses, however, maintained the stern discipline within the total community that always characterized his leadership. Finally the fugitives created a temporary abode at a great camp at the base of a mountain, designated in the Biblical

45

narrative as Mount Sinai. There is much uncertainty in regard to the precise mountain in the Sinai that was described as Mount Sinai. Several tall hills have been suggested; evidence can be mustered to support each suggestion. It is unlikely that the mountain in the lower extremity of the Sinai peninsula that presently is named Mount Sinai, at the base of which is the famous fourteen-hundred-year-old monastery of St. Catherine, is the mountain associated with the exploits of Moses.

At times, especially during the rainy season, the clouds hang low over the high hills of the rough Sinai country, and during the fierce storms that often occur in that area heavy lightning plays between the clouds and hill tops and thunder echoes through the valleys; such meteorological displays must have been extremely frightening and mystifying to the naive and superstitious people who had lived nowhere except in Egypt. The terrifying phenomena associated with a severe electrical storm probably signified to the Hebrews that they were in the presence of God. One may conjecture that it was upon the occasion of such a storm or storms, when "the people witnessed the thunder and lightning . . . and the mountains smoking," that, according to the Biblical account, Moses went up into the mountain, and the Lord appeared before him. As a part of the purported dialogue that ensued, the Lord is said to have delivered to Moses the basic principles of an elaborate code of behavior that provided the basis, after much editing, for the well-known Ten Commandments, also known as the Decalogue. The Decalogue would come to be regarded as fundamental to the Judaic tradition.

The authors and editors of the Judaic Bible, it seems clear from the very nature of the Biblical story that tells of the manner in which Moses obtained the Ten Commandments and other directives, accepted the point of view, which was not unique with them, that regulations pertaining to human behavior possess a special kind of authenticity for many people if it can be asserted that the regulations were issued by God or by His designated representative. Through all known history such a stratagem has often been adopted by religious leaders, especially by originators of religious doctrine, to provide an authoritative basis for the principles they desired to promulgate.

Starting with Chapter 19 of the Book of Exodus, much attention is devoted to the experiences of Moses and his followers at Mount Sinai and to an elaboration of the comprehensive instructions, which had the Ten Commandments as their basic theme, that Moses is said to have received from the Lord. In addition, it is reported in the Biblical text that directions were given to Moses in regard to the conduct of acts of worship, and specifications were provided for the construction of a tabernacle that would become a sanctuary for the Lord. The tabernacle would contain the Holy Ark of the Covenant, which ultimately became an object of very deep religious meaning for the faithful; the Ark of the Covenant as originally conceived was a special kind of cabinet that housed stone tablets upon which were inscribed the Ten Commandments. Directives pertaining to several aspects of man's conduct, attributed to Moses, appear at various places in the Torah, but all the treatments appear to represent interpretations of or variations upon a basic theme of principles that has the Ten Commandments, with which all followers of Judaism and most Christians are familiar, at its heart.

Central to the utterances attributed to Moses in the Bible, as a result of his reported experiences on Mount Sinai, was the concept of a unique God. In fact, the idea of one and only one God, a powerful God, and a "jealous God," ultimately became basic to the Judaic tradition. At a later date, as already noted, the same concept became fundamental to the bodies of doctrine espoused by both Christianity and Islam, both of which derived much of their substance from Judaism. It is doubtful, it must be noted, that Moses made as complete a break with the pagan polytheistic tradition as the Biblical record implies, but there is essential agreement on the part of Judaic scholars that his utterances formed the basis for the ultimate acceptance by Judaism of the monotheistic doctrine.

From the perspective of the present, so different in its cultural characteristics from what it was several millennia ago, one can only speculate upon the motivation and justification of Moses when, according to Judaic history, he insisted that there is one and only one God, Yahweh or Jahveh in Hebrew terminology.* One must assume, however, that Moses, when he is supposed to have enunciated the monotheistic doctrine, did not operate in an intellectual vacuum. As already noted, for a person who accepts the position, possibly implicitly, that the universe possesses unity and coherence, the monotheistic position is more intellectually satisfying than the polytheistic. Moreover, one cannot ignore the probability that the boy Moses received the kind of education in Pharaoh's household

---

*In the King James version of the Christian Bible, Jahveh was translated as Jehovah. It appears that the scholars working on the King James version were familiar with the Hebrew tradition that the exact pronunciation of the name of the Lord is unknown. Their own term for the Lord was developed as a result of their attempt to vocalize the consonants in the term employed by the Hebrews.

that provided the elements for the religious philosophy which he later founded.

Irrespective of the intellectual route that Moses followed in arriving at his conclusions pertaining to a Deity, one may well believe that in addition to other justifications which he may have had, he hoped, by insisting upon a common devotion to a great and powerful God, to create a kind of unifying purpose, so necessary at that time, within the community of his followers. Moreover, in a forceful manner Moses advanced the principle that the basis for the kind of society which he believed to be desirable was to be found in the will of that God, as expressed in an approved code of morality, a code of principles that defines man's proper relationship to man. Such a code of morality, it is clear from the teachings of Moses, must be consistent with and supplemental to a God-approved code of ethics, a code of principles that defines man's proper relationship to his God. Undoubtedly, as a result of the strong emphasis on morality in the enunciations of Moses, Judaism as it evolved under the impact of a great variety of sociological and political factors gave ever increasing attention to the notion that an ethical society is a moral society. Morality became accepted as a basic religious value; in fact, to characterize God properly, in the Judaic view, demands attention to the moral attributes which should be associated with the behavior of man but which actually should be regarded as having their origin with God. Followers of Judaism accept as an often-stated axiom of life, "Be like Him: as He is gracious and merciful . . ." Christianity, it may be noted, continued as a fundamental tenet of its faith the Judaic idea that the promulgation and maintenance of a system of principles of morality, regarded as consistent with the will of God, should be a significant part of its doctrinal basis.

The ultimate net effect of the ideas that had their origin with the philosophy of Moses was the development of a truly ethical society, a truly ethical nation, a God-centered nation of people who would be the forebears of the Jews. That fact must be understood and appreciated before one can comprehend many attributes and actions of the Jews as well as the role of Judaism in their philosophy of life; it must be understood and appreciated to comprehend many aspects of Jewish history, even some facets of the history of modern Israel; it must be understood before one can comprehend the tremendous sense of pride that the Jewish people have in their distinctive cultural heritage—a sense of pride that ultimately was reflected in the fact that the Jews became strong advocates of personal independence of thought and action.

The foundation for the dominant ethical aspect of traditional Judaic society is centered in the very first commandment of the Decalogue. That commandment, while emphasizing that there is only one God, is very explicit in its assertion that any God other than Yahweh must be a false God, and, consequently, there can be no worship of any other God. As a result, the thought and actions of the Israelites, the followers of Moses and their descendants, were focused in a most unusual way on a single basic concept. But the fact that the monotheistic idea survived, even in a preliminary form, especially in the early centuries after Moses, must be regarded as truly remarkable, for the concept had to face a variety of critical challenges; that the concept as suitably interpreted and elaborated did survive was due essentially to the traditional prestige of Moses and to the tremendous support given to the idea by a comparatively few prophets and other strong religious leaders.

The commandments which follow the first commandment of the Decalogue reveal something of the importance that Moses attached to moral principle. In addition, they may be interpreted as providing for the Israelites the rudiments of a practical sociology. It may be assumed, in fact, that the second to tenth commandments were promulgated by Moses, at least in some preliminary form, in an attempt to introduce needed order and desirable notions of justice and responsibility into the chaotic Israelite society. The essentiality of the advocacy of such commandments becomes clear when it is realized that among the Israelites, after their many tragic years in Egypt, human life had become cheap; little significance was attached to family life; and women, irrespective of their marital status, had virtually no rights and no purposes in society other than carrying heavy burdens of menial chores and providing sexual pleasures for demanding males.

Certainly the ethical and moral ideas advanced by Moses, even after giving due recognition to the undoubted fact that as they are known today they are the result of much elaboration and interpretation as Judaism and Christianity evolved, have had a profound effect upon the nature of life within the framework of Western culture. Legal codes that evolved in societies which accepted the Judaic tradition have been responsible for improved notions of order and justice, and the philosophies of life accepted by both scholars and nonscholars in the Western world reveal, possibly in a subtle way, the influence of the events that are purported to have taken place at Mount Sinai. Even the origin of dominant elements in the concept of American democracy can be traced to ideas found in the Torah (the first five books of the Judaic Bible which often are described as the Five Books of Moses) or in interpretations of the Torah, as such interpretations evolved through the centuries in both Judaism and Christianity. Indirect influences of the Judaic tradition are found in the literature and even in the music and art of many Western societies. And, more than we may realize, the scientists responsible for the tremendous scientific accomplishments of the West received encouragement from the fact that they were members of a society such as the one for which Judaism provided a foundation. Many scientists, as noted earlier, accept as basic to their scholarly endeavors the principle that a strong faith in the values of the natural order, a faith which is sustained by a compelling belief in the existence of a superior wisdom within the universe, is required if men are to dedicate themselves to an elucidation of that order.

Through the ages the actions and attitudes of the Jewish people often have been influenced by the fact that inherent in Judaic doctrine, as it originated with Moses and then was expanded and interpreted by later thoughtful teachers of Judaism, is the principle that the spiritual and the nonspiritual must be fused. Thus, it appears to be part of the message in Deuteronomy and Chronicles that it is the will of God that man be judged and rewarded on earth for the excellence and integrity of his accomplishments. Ideas pertaining to life after death, including concepts that resemble Christian notions of heaven and hell, have been basic to many pagan religions and have always been central to the Judaic faith. But it has been the Christians, the product of a religious movement strongly influenced in its early days by then existing forces in Judaism, not the followers of traditional Judaism, who have given very great emphasis to the notion of an award after death for those persons who have lived a life on earth that has been pleasing to God. By contrast, the Judaic faithful believe sincerely that they have received a reward on earth, expressed in the statement that "God has smiled upon them," in addition to any posthumous award to which they may be entitled, if they can succeed in life in such a way that their accomplishments are recognized as good by their fellowmen. Thus the Jewish people have been dominated by a strong desire to learn and to achieve. The consequences of such strong personal motivation are revealed in the indisputable historical fact that, in general, the people of no other cultural group have equaled the Jewish people in the significance of their contributions to the betterment of life for mankind. Many of the true geniuses of human history, in the arts, in business and industry, in science, in philosophy, and in religion, have been Jews; among the very large number of such geniuses in the field of religion, one must recognize Moses, Jesus, and Paul. "We pass this way but once" is an axiom of life that dominates the thoughts and actions of most of those who subscribe to the Judaic faith.

The philosophy of Judaism, as simply but broadly portrayed in previous paragraphs, was the major factor in determining the nature of Jewish thought and conduct and the nature of Jewish society during the time of Jesus. So the attempt to provide some understanding of the philosophy of Judaism has been essential for the purposes of the present work if one would truly understand Jesus, his motivations and his interests.

The material goal of the Israelites and their leader Moses that was dominant in their thought and planning during their stay in the Sinai wilderness was, in fulfillment of their understanding of the Lord's wishes as first expressed to Abraham, the winning and occupation of the land of Canaan, the Promised Land. But the people were ill-prepared for such a task; they did not have the necessary military training or materiel to challenge the well-equipped and well-disciplined Canaanites. In fact, the Israelites, whose behavior often taxed the patience of Moses, possessed little sense of discipline. Early probing actions undertaken by the Israelites against the military might assembled against them by the city-states of Canaan invariably ended in defeat. So the decision was made by Moses not to hasten any major military actions; rather, the Israelites would continue to maintain a camp in the desert, with headquarters in the Negev. Apparently the delay was planned deliberately by Moses so that more military preparation could be made and, probably of greater importance, so that a number of disturbing sociological and psychological problems that interfered with any attempt at unified endeavor could be resolved. Some historical analysts believe that no significant military actions were attempted by the Israelites for at least a decade, and probably much longer, after their arrival in the Negev. It was during the stay in the Negev that Moses died, in approximately 1200 B.C., and the competent Joshua, who had been groomed for the task, took over the leadership of the people of destiny.

The Book of Joshua in the Judaic Bible provides a record of the conquest of the Promised Land under Joshua's generalship. There is growing belief, however, that the record is biased, for Joshua seems to have been a favorite of later priestly writers and editors; he is portrayed in the Book of Joshua as such an accomplished military strategist and disciplinarian—a point of view still common among many Jews—that with a little assistance from the Lord he was able to engineer a series of remarkable victories and, consequently, succeeded in routing the Canaanites. It is likely that the true record of the conquest would yield quite a different story. In fact, the Book of Judges, which may be older than the Book of Joshua and probably was subjected to less reworking by later Biblical editors than may have been true of the Book of Joshua, provides information pertaining to the conquest of the Promised Land that is regarded by some Judaic scholars as more authentic than the account given in the Book of Joshua. It is likely that the process of conquest was laborious and painful and lasted for several generations. In truth, most of the military operations were probably small and guerrilla in nature, and, in keeping with the times, the victor was extremely ruthless in dealing with the loser. One may assume that, during the long period of military activity before Canaan was finally conquered, there was continuous infiltration of the Promised Land by the Israelites. It also seems likely that other Semitic peoples, including some who probably were distant relatives of the Israelites but who had no background in Egypt, moved to take advantage of the pressures being exerted on the Canaanites by the Israelites so that they might gain a foothold for themselves on the comparatively rich terrain of Canaan.

As has been true many times in history, there was substantial cultural transfusion from the conquered to the conqueror. It has been noted previously that there is much in the Judaic tradition, including the law and the religious festivals, that had its origin in or was strongly influenced by Canaanite precepts and practices. And many of the Israelite conquerors, tending to imitate those who were already resident in the land, ceased being nomadic wanderers and became merchants, tillers of the soil, and village craftsmen. But some of the Canaanite influence, as judged by present-day standards, was not good. For instance, many of the Hebrew people found much that was alluring in the religious beliefs and practices of the Canaanites. Possibly a major factor in the readiness with which so many Hebrews accepted the pagan Canaanite religion was the apparent fact that the concept of Yahweh was too abstract for ready acceptance by many of the Hebrew people at that stage in their intellectual and religious history; the Canaanites worshipped idols and they deified various animals. The Baalim worshipped by the Canaanites were essentially Gods of nature and often possessed special significance for workers in the field; they could assume a variety of inanimate and animate forms. Rituals involving sacrifices and a diversity of ceremonial practices were associated with Baal worship. Certain of the rites featured extreme sexual displays by Baal priests as well as mandatory prostitution for selected women. In such a religious environment, with its appeal to a variety of human passions and interests, a large number of the descendants of the people who had followed Moses out of Egypt made the decision to desert Yahweh and to adopt the pagan practices and ideas of the people whom they had conquered. Only very strong leadership, one must believe, made possible the survival during this critical period of the religious principles promulgated by Moses.

For our knowledge of the development of the first Hebrew nation in Palestine, following the conquest of the Promised Land, we must rely heavily upon the Biblical text. Many of the key elements in that narrative, however, have been confirmed by other ancient documents of accepted historical authenticity. The evidence indicates that even as the Hebrew tribes that composed the conquering mass of people began to be a dominant force in Palestine, after finally overcoming most of the opposition which they had encountered in Canaan, they were beset by new conquerors from the outside. During the twelfth century, B.C., the militant and aggressive Philistines, probably a non-Semitic people from island areas of the Mediterranean, moved into northern Egypt; there, however, they met violent opposition, so they moved on into the coastal area of Palestine. Soon they encountered the Hebrew tribe of Dan whose strong man Samson and his exaggerated strength are featured in certain Biblical legends, obviously derived from Hebrew folklore; in spite of the reported exploits of Samson and his associates, the military power of the Philistines soon prevailed. After the people of Dan had fled, the victorious Philistines pushed on, conquering and slaughtering, into the new homeland of other Hebrew tribes, descendants of peoples who had followed Moses out of Egypt. The Philistine armies were not stopped until Saul, apparently a couragous lad, displayed extraordinary skill as a leader and tactician in reversing the enemy's progress. As a consequence of his accomplishments, Saul won great acclaim which finally led to a demand by a coalition of several Hebrew tribes that he become their ruler. In the year 1020 B.C., Saul acceded to the demand and thus became head of a small kingdom that was the political entity which immediately preceded David's Israel.

The Biblical account of the accession of Saul to the throne of the small, newly formed Hebrew kingdom reports that he was anointed by Samuel, thus introducing to Biblical readers the first of the great Biblical prophets to whom, according to tradition and Biblical testimony, followers of Judaism owe so much. The Books of the Prophets, comprising a section of the Judaic Bible that was canonized at a later date than the part known as the Torah, are devoted to the works and sayings and sometimes to brief biographies of particular prophets who had pronounced influence upon the thought and attitudes of the Hebrew people, and who were highly regarded by the Biblical compilers as transmitters of the word of God; probably much more than is commonly realized, Judaism in many of its aspects reflects the ideas of some of the prophets. Undoubtedly many of the prophets occupied distinctive positions of prestige within the society of which they were a part. Often displaying great moral courage, they provided strong judgments on men and on events of their times and, upon occasion, they projected their judgments into the future; it was common for them to condemn in the name of God the sins of the Hebrew people. A national crisis seemed to stimulate prophetic activity; during a time of crisis a prophet had an excellent platform from which to deliver his message that the troubles of the people and those of the nation were the result of moral decay and a denial of God's precepts, as revealed in the laws of Moses. The dire predictions by some of the prophets of terrible things to come unless there was a return to principles acceptable to God often were mollified by a prophecy of the ultimate redemption and salvation of the people, possibly through the arrival of a great king who would provide the necessary leadership.

Samuel, who anointed Saul, must have played a many-faceted role among the Hebrew people while, in spite of their harassment by the Philistines and others, they were developing a strong sense of identity and a feeling of unity that provided a necessary basis for the political consolidations later achieved by David. Apparently Samuel was significantly involved in several episodes that led to the ascendancy of David to the throne of the kingdom after the death of Saul. Most important, the recorded utterances of Samuel reveal that he tried to serve as the conscience of the Hebrew people at that critical time in their history. Frequently, revealing his talent as a great teacher, he attempted to help the Hebrews understand the practical inferences for them of the Mosaic code as well as the responsibilities that they must accept as a result of their unique heritage. And he often emphasized the idea, accepted by the faithful among the Israelites, that, in spite of any temporary reverses, God was always on their side in their struggles with their adversaries.

The great significance of Samuel and the other Judaic prophets in both the religious and political history of Israel is irrefutable. Moreover, they occupy distinctive positions of honor in the history of religion because of the manner in which they served their society by being astute analysts of the human condition. But history tells of other sages of an even earlier date who served their particular societies in much the same way. For instance, just before and just after the start of the second millennium B.C., Egyptian society featured some unusually wise social philosophers and prophets who, especially through their writings, exercised tremendous influence upon the ideologies of the people. Some of their writings were read, studied, and even memorized by Egyptian schoolchildren for more than five hundred years. *The Admonitions of a Prophet,* written early in the second millennium B.C., by a sage named Ipuwer, describes in vivid terms the misery that prevailed among the people of the nation during his time; to solve the tremendous social problems that existed, Ipuwer urged upon his readers the continuing necessity of fighting against evil and of maintaining their faith in the wisdom of the Gods. It is possible, and even probable, that the Judaic prophets derived inspiration from some of the sages of the pagan peoples with whom they may have had some acquaintance.

Saul, when he became ruler of the little Hebrew kingdom, continued to be harassed by the Philistines and other enemies, and, in addition, soon he had to contend with the popularity of David, a personable youngster whose physical exploits in military combat had attracted much public attention. Ultimately, David was forced to flee because of Saul's enmity. In the course of time, however, the influence of Saul declined, and he actually became a pathetic character; his rule was terminated when he was killed in battle. Then David, one of the most revered characters in Jewish and Judaic history and literature, rejoined his countrymen and was proclaimed king, the choice of Yahweh, according to the Biblical text.

Chapter Three

THE FOUR CENTURIES OF THE DAVIDIC MONARCHY

In spite of his tremendous popularity with many Hebrew people, David had to overcome initial opposition from ten of the tribes of Israel before he could consolidate his rule. Then he embarked upon a major campaign of conquest that brought about the creation of the original nation designated as Israel, the first significant Hebrew political entity. The great and powerful empire which David finally controlled extended from modern Lebanon to the Red Sea.

An important feature of David's military success was his conquest, in approximately 1000 B.C., of Jerusalem, which at that time was a small community of no obvious importance. During the Bronze Age, however, Jerusalem had been a Jebusite stronghold. Jerusalem provided David an excellent base for the conduct of his military operations because he was able to locate major defensive positions high up in the Judean hills. So under David's guidance Jerusalem became a mighty military bastion. In addition, the city soon became a center for trade and commerce, and, of very great importance, it would become the religious center of the Hebrew people, the home of the Holy Ark of Yahweh. So, Jerusalem, often described in Hebraic and Judaic literature as the City of David, was to become a permanent symbol for the Hebrew people of their proud heritage and of their hopes and aspirations. Jerusalem remained the capital city of the Davidic monarchy for slightly more than four centuries, until it was destroyed by the Babylonians in 587/586 B.C.; even before the Babylonian conquest, however, the kingdom created by David had already become much smaller than it was originally. After the destruction of Jerusalem by the Babylonians, the city slowly regained much of its previous importance, as noted later, chiefly because of its deep significance for the Jewish people, and it actually underwent somewhat of a renaissance under later Persian, Greek, and Roman rulers. But in A.D. 70, an infamous date in history for all the Jewish people, the noble city was ravished by Roman legions under the command of Titus. The Old City walls, a landmark in modern Jerusalem, follow the approximate boundaries of the city as it existed before its destruction by the Romans, but the actual walls as they are seen at the present time are the result of efforts at reconstruction undertaken by the Muslim leader Sultan Suleiman and completed in A.D. 1541.

David, as he is characterized in legend, in history, and in the Biblical narrative, was a man of many talents. As a military leader and as a statesman and political organizer he must be acclaimed as an individual of great stature among the personages of history; it appears to be true, however, that often he was amazingly ruthless and brutal when attempting to achieve his ends. As an indication of his versatility and of the contrasts that characterized his intellectual life, David was also a poet and a pious religious leader. Although he seemed to possess some weaknesses of character that became increasingly apparent during the latter years of his career, his reputation in history is secure; testimony to his greatness is provided by the fact that he was the person who succeeded in bringing about significant political unity for the forebears of the Jewish people, and in the city of Jerusalem he created a material focus for the important religious tradition that developed from the enunciations of Moses.

Partly through intrigue, Solomon, one of David's sons, became successor to his father. Possibly as a result of inheritance and certainly as a result of his experiences as a youth in the ruling household, Solomon possessed many of his father's strengths. His reputation among the Jewish people as a man of great wisdom is supported by legends that supplement well-known Biblical stories. It is likely, however, that the legends preceded the organization and writing of the Biblical text; if so, they undoubtedly were an influential factor in persuading the later Biblical writers to attribute sayings and actions to Solomon that enhanced his stature as a man of tremendous intellectual capability.

Although much legend undoubtedly provides the basis for our knowledge of Solomon's life and accomplishments, his reputation as an astute statesman and as a great builder has not been questioned. He expanded the boundaries of the young nation; he made treaties with troublesome neighbors; and although his reign was characterized by religious tolerance, he took specific steps to make Jerusalem the religious center for the growing numbers of people who were subscribing to Judaism. A major part of the plan which Solomon developed to increase the significance of Jerusalem for Judaic worshipers involved the construction of the great Temple that had been envisaged since the days of Moses. The large and ornate building which ultimately resulted, with its special facilities for housing the Holy Ark of Yahweh, was the original

Judaic Temple of Biblical history. Vast quantities of materials needed for the construction of the magnificent religious structure were imported from neighboring countries, and tremendous numbers of slaves were involved in its construction.

Unfortunately, Solomon suffered from critical weaknesses of character. His great accomplishments as a statesman, conqueror, builder, and religious leader have been partially negated in the minds of some students of history by the heartless manner in which he disposed of his enemies and by the fact that he subjected the peoples whom he conquered to often intolerable conditions of slavery. Solomon's reputation also has suffered from stories of his excessive indulgence in sexual pleasures. But criticisms of Solomon based on the latter observation must be tempered, for it was consistent with the mores of his time in history that the people generally expected their rulers and the great among them to acquire many concubines and to enjoy the pleasures of the harem.

Solomon, there is reason to believe, was not a strong administrator. Partly because of some of his administrative weaknesses, which became increasingly noticeable in the later days of his reign, Israel began to show signs of demoralization and disintegration even before Solomon's death in 933 B.C. Shortly after his death the Jewish state as created by David was separated into two parts. And, unfortunately, each of the two new nations into which the kingdom was divided was politically and militarily weak. In keeping with the political disintegration of the kingdom that occurred after the time of Solomon, there was also deterioration in the religious faith of the people. Many of the inhabitants returned to paganism, especially Baal worship; only a few tribal communities, notably Judah, remained steadfast in their worship of Yahweh. Jerusalem lost much of its religious significance for many of the Hebrew people, and competing centers of worship were created. From that time on, except for short interludes, the Hebrew people, descendants of those who had fled Egypt and who with great hope had finally been able to settle in the Land of Promise, were to lead a very unhappy and even tragic kind of life.

But during the reign of David and for much of the time during the rule of Solomon, life for the Israelite people was good. They had great pride in their heritage and in their accomplishments; their enemies had been conquered; and they were established in the land of their dreams. Within the environment of tranquility and happiness that prevailed, singers and poets entertained audiences on the streets, and fathers repeated for their children some of the legends and historical tales that had special meaning within the Israelite tradition.

It was during that time, a number of Biblical scholars believe, that a popular religious epic now known as the Yahwist Epic, an epic with Yahweh as its hero, began to take form in the works of several poets and singers in the southern part of the kingdom. It would appear that the prime purpose of the epic was to memorialize some notable aspects of the supposed relationship of the Israelite people with the major events of previous history, including the creation of the world, as that history had taken form for them through the medium of several popular legends and commonly accepted traditions. Some of the legendary tales brought together in the Yahwist Epic probably had a very early origin with singers and poets of non-Hebrew tribes; in fact, there is little doubt that the stories were part of the folklore of many people, non-Hebrew as well as Hebrew, in a large geographic area at the eastern end of the Mediterranean. The development of the Yahwist Epic must be regarded as an event of considerable importance in any study of the evolution of Judaism, as well as Christianity, for the epic, it appears, became an early part of the oral tradition of the Hebrew people. Approximately four centuries later, that tradition provided a substantial part of the content of the material that was assembled and edited to become the earliest version of the Torah. A person who understands the manner in which the Torah was constructed and who indulges in close reading of that great work can easily detect the thread of the Yahwist Epic in its content.

The story of Noah and the great flood, as it appears in the Book of Genesis, came from the Yahwist Epic. But without doubt an old Sumerian/Babylonian legend provided a prototype for the story. Although several versions of the ancient legend have been discovered by archaeologists as a result of their excavations in Mesopotamia, the oldest known version is that which appears as a part of the famous Gilgamesh Epic, the best known and certainly one of the most important literary works of the ancient Babylonians. The Gilgamesh Epic is an elaborate epic poem that is concerned with the quest of King Gilgamesh for eternal life. The story of the flood is only a small portion of the larger work, and it is recorded by the authors of the epic as it was supposed to have been told by Ut-Napishtim, the hero of the saga (who corresponds to the Noah of the Biblical story), to King Gilgamesh. The plot, the structure, and even the details of the Biblical story of the flood are remarkably similar to those same aspects of the Gilgamesh story of the flood, but it must be observed that the story of the flood in the Bible possesses a moral-monotheistic quality not found in the Gilgamesh Epic. In both stories the flood was ordered by the God, or the Gods, and one man was designated to build a large boat and in other respects prepare for the great disaster. As the time neared for the rains to start, the designated individual loaded his family as well as sufficient animals for breeding purposes into the boat. Then, for many days, the day turned to night as the rains drenched the earth. After a considerable delay following the cessation of the rains, while the large boat drifted in the open water, a bird was released; it returned since no land was visible upon which it could light. Then another bird and, after a delay, a third bird. The third bird did not return, thereby revealing that finally land had appeared above the water.

It is an interesting fact that flood stories have been a part of the folklore of many nations in the Near East and even in other parts of the Northern Hemisphere. Probably the stories, as has been true of most legends, had a factual basis. In some of the archaeological excavations made in recent years in the Near East, evidence has been uncovered that many years ago, before the Biblical era, considerable flooding did occur; the common assumption of the archaeologists has been that there had been local flooding. But in recent years, science has produced evidence that in about 10,000 B.C., due to the interaction of a variety of climatic factors, there occurred a tremendous amount of melting of the ice sheet which at that time covered a large part of the earth; as a result, a vast amount of water was sent cascading across the land, flooding many coastal areas in its path. It is conceivable that such an event, if it did occur, gave rise to the numerous flood stories. It may be observed in this connection that Plato, quoting what Solon was told by Egyptian priests, wrote that in approximately 10,000 B.C., the deluge occurred that destroyed Atlantis.

The story in Genesis of Adam and Eve, with its sexual symbolism, a story that also occurs as a part of the Yahwist Epic, has an especially ingenious and attractive plot. Although the tale has long been recognized by most Judaic and Christian scholars as a myth, apparently derived from a Sumerian legend that was concerned with the origin of man and his early history, some adherents to both Judaism and Christianity do accept the story as providing a true documentation of events involving the first man and woman on earth. Moreover, some early Christians found deep significance in the reported fact that Adam "sinned," thereby giving rise to the concept of Original Sin, an idea that first appeared in

Christian literature, it appears, in the letters of Paul. The doctrine of Original Sin received strong emphasis in the fourth century A.D., especially in the prolific writings of Augustine. When Adam yielded to the temptation of Eve, according to the doctrine of Original Sin, he sinned the primordial sin, and so was no longer able to fulfill the supernatural state to which Divine plan entitled him. Moreover, the fact that Adam sinned was responsible for causing all his descendants to lose grace. Thus, as a result of Adam's ill-conceived act, those who accept the doctrine of Original Sin believe that sinfulness became a condition of man; they further believe that all the generations of men who have followed Adam, actually as a fact of inheritance, have been plagued with an awful sin for which they must seek redemption. The idea of Original Sin as thus conceived continues to be regarded as fundamental doctrine by some influential Christian sects.

In some parts of the Near East the Muslims, who like the Christians accepted as part of their religious heritage much of the early Judaic tradition, possess religious legends that embroider the story of Adam and Eve with tales of the penance that the Deity required of Adam because of his sin. For instance, one tale is developed around the theme that for a thousand years, because of his sin, Adam had to stand motionless on one foot on a tall mountain.

All the common religious traditions seem to have within their background, usually along with some fact, a substantial amount of myth and legend. Myths found as a part of the cultural heritage of people in quite different societies often are remarkably similar with respect to some of their key elements, even in societies that are separated by vast distances. J. W. Colenso, Englishman who was appointed in 1855 to be the first Anglican bishop of Natal, became familiar with the Zulu language. He was amazed to note the great similarity between some of the stories recited by Zulu religious and the stories found in Genesis. Consequently, he publicly advocated the thesis, regarded as heresy at that time, that the early Books of the Bible, at least in part, were merely Hebrew folklore; certainly, he argued, they were not dictated by God. The fierce theological controversy that followed the pronouncements of Colenso overflowed into the English secular press. Disraeli quipped, "The Zulus have converted our bishops." An item in one newspaper was titled "Moses or the Zulu."

The legends incorporated in the Book of Genesis must have had a strong appeal to the persons responsible for the later canonization of the

Biblical materials. Undoubtedly much of the recognized importance of the legends in both the Judaic and the Christian traditions can be explained by the fact of the great emphasis that they give to the significant role of God in happenings that occur on earth, including its creation. Some of the episodes that are treated in the legends ultimately took on important symbolic significance in the folklore of many of those who subscribed to Judaism, and certain of the episodes were given symbolic meaning in the writings of some Christian ecclesiastics.

Most modern Judaic and Christian scholars are not disturbed by assertions that the Book of Genesis and some other parts of the Bible contain a substantial amount of legend, for they know that one must accept as fact that the Judaic Bible is a literary creation of man. In truth, the development of the Biblical text had a long and fascinating history. Actually, the Judaic Bible is the product of a very long evolutionary process, and inherent in the process, to which innumerable poets, singers, writers, and editors contributed, is the evolving story of the development of a culture, a culture with a distinctive religion at its heart.

Along with its collection of traditions and legends pertaining to the very early history of man, the Yahwist Epic included much other material that ultimately became part of the Torah. For instance, in the epic occurs the story of the nomadic wanderings of Abraham along with a treatment of his patriarchal role in the primal period of the history of the Hebrew people. The epic also told the story of Moses and enunciated the moral and ethical codes, undoubtedly in a very early form, that bear his name; as a part of the story, the epic provided an elaborate account of the dynamic and wise leadership of Moses during the Exodus of the Israelites from Egypt and while they were undergoing the long period of uncertainty and hardship in the Sinai Desert. In addition, such well-known Biblical stories as those of Isaac, Jacob, and Joseph were included. Apparently the epic was also the source of some material that became part of the Book of Judges.

Many Biblical scholars believe that about two hundred years after the composition of the Yahwist Epic another epic poem which treated much of the same material as its predecessor made its appearance in northern Israel. The second epic is commonly designated as the Elohist Epic, a name derived from the fact that in it the Deity is referred to as Elohim rather than Yahweh. Probably the Elohist Epic represented an attempt on the part of the poets and singers who composed it to cast into permanent form for the northern people a documentation of their versions of legends and traditions, including most of those in the Yahwist treatment, that were popular in a large part of the Near East. Ultimately, it appears, the treatments of the Yahwist and Elohist Epics were synthesized, but the synthesis was carried out in haphazard fashion with no great effort to achieve consistency. In fact, the Torah appears to be a conglomerate of materials from the Yahwist and Elohist Epics and from other sources. Undoubtedly the present Torah, revered by all followers of Judaism and accepted by Christians as fundamental to their faith, represents a considerable expansion of earlier versions of the work as well as the fact of much rewriting and extensive editing.

When, after the time of Solomon, Israel was dissolved into two segments, the part inhabited by the northern tribes became known as the Northern Kingdom. The other segment, with its capital at Jerusalem, became known as Judah, the name of the more influential of the two tribes that remained loyal to the old monarchy. Only infrequently did the two new political entities find it possible to cooperate. The Northern Kingdom, from its very beginning, was beset by internal dissension, and soon it was suffering from almost continuous pressure from outside adversaries. The people had become very uncertain in regard to their allegiances and their beliefs, and they seemed to have lost their sense of destiny. Baal worship was more common than the worship of Yahweh. The conditions that existed and continued to exist for many years provided a perfect setting for the exhortations of some of the best known prophets of Judaic history; the first was the great crusader Elijah, a person for whom great reverence is shown in Judaic literature. Among Judaic faithful, Elijah seems to be accepted generally as the most influential, next to Moses, of those men who were basically responsible for their religious tradition. Moreover, Elijah has been acclaimed by some Christians as one of the truly great figures of the early part of their own religious history, adopted and adapted from Judaic history, and his purported ascent into heaven when his life was terminated on earth has been regarded by some Christians as foretelling the purported ascension of Christ. In the Middle Ages, Moses and Elijah were often portrayed in Christian iconography along with Jesus in view of their special status provided by Biblical accounts that the two men had experienced the presence of God.

It is commonly believed by Judaic historians that the forceful pronouncements of Elijah, a man of dominant personality, were responsible during the critical times in which he lived for some resurgence in support of the basic ideologies of Moses. Elijah was such a powerful and determined advocate of Yahweh that his opponents could not withstand the "thunder" in his arguments; it has even been suggested, although Elijah persuaded many people to renounce their pagan ways, that the forcefulness of his contentions and his domineering mannerisms in debate so antagonized some of his opponents that the already existing schism in the populace of the Northern Kingdom between Judaic believers and nonbelievers was magnified.

Elisha, who followed Elijah and who has often been described as having inherited Elijah's mantle, actually became involved in revolutionary plots to eliminate individuals who advocated ideas which he regarded as contrary to those promulgated by Moses. But Elisha's method in dealing with his opponents differed considerably from those of Elijah; Elisha employed subtle methods, and historians have described him as a shrewd diplomat.

Amos, who lived early in the eighth century B.C., was undoubtedly of humble background. Yet, his words of wisdom expressed as he carried his message to the people in both the Northern and Southern Kingdoms mark him as one of the most important among the prophets of Judaism; the nature of his influence supplemented that provided by Elijah and Elisha. In an age when the Judaic religion was rapidly becoming synonymous with ritual, Amos emphasized that Judaism must be interpreted as representing a way of life; man is judged by his deeds, the prophet asserted, not by the extent of his participation in formalized religious activities. Amos emphasized, by contrast with the ideas of some of his contemporaries, that Yahweh is the God of all men, and He is concerned with the welfare of all people, irrespective of their ancestry or other aspects of their background. The words of Amos had great influence upon the thoughts and actions of a tremendous number of people.

Hosea, often characterized as the prophet of love, succeeded Amos in a prophetic role in the Northern Kingdom; he, like those prophets who were his contemporaries, focused strongly upon the wicked behavior of the people. He ascribed the serious moral corruption of his day, which was rampant, to widespread neglect of the true essence of Judaism. He accused the people and their rulers of such great wickedness that the fall of the nation was inevitable; Yahweh, he insisted, would not tolerate continued disobedience to His commands. But Hosea seemed to profess ultimate hope for the Hebrew people if they would repent and would demonstrate loyalty to God, which involved the making of a serious attempt to accept God's desire that each man should display loving kindness toward his fellowman—principles that were regarded as inherent in the teachings of Moses. Almost a millennium later, Jesus, according to Matthew 9:13, supported his own advocacy of the importance of the same ideas by quoting Hosea.

In 721 B.C., the Northern Kingdom, formed when the original kingdom of Israel was partitioned after the reign of Solomon, fell before the armies of Sargon the Assyrian. The turbulent and unhappy history of the Northern Kingdom was at an end. The efforts by such great prophets as those just named to save the nation and its people from what often appeared to them to be an inevitable fate would seem to have been in vain. In fact, outside of the contributions of its few prophets, the Northern Kingdom produced little of lasting significance for the development of the Judaic faith. Now Judah, with Jerusalem as its capital, became the guardian of the distinctive religious and cultural tradition for which Moses was so strongly responsible. The religious leadership of Judah may have been strengthened by some individuals of great competence who had fled south when the Northern Kingdom was invaded. The king of Judah at that time was Hezekiah.

Since Hezekiah was much concerned by the fate that had befallen the Northern Kingdom, he moved quickly upon both the political and military fronts to strengthen the position of his nation from the threats of those who had overwhelmed the people of the north. Moreover, Hezekiah, convinced that the people of the north had been punished by God for their transgressions, initiated a reform movement in his country that was designed to bring the people back to a way of life that would be pleasing to Yahweh. Hezekiah had as his personal adviser the great prophet Isaiah, and within a short time Micah joined Isaiah in providing leadership to a nation struggling sincerely to make a return to the principles enunciated by Moses. The evidence is strong that there were two Isaiahs. The ideas of the first Isaiah seem to have been influenced in some important respects by those expressed by Amos.

The first Isaiah, it is believed, was born into an upper-class family, so it is likely that he was able to exercise influence upon some segments of the population of Israel to which Amos had been able to make little appeal; there was much similarity, however, in the message of the two men. The lengthy utterances of the first Isaiah, appropriately described as sermons by some commentators, were filled with indignation in regard to the injustices and the low state of morality which Hebrew society was tolerating. He emphasized repeatedly, as he assumed the role of spokesman for the Lord, that Yahweh was weary of the spectacle of men giving lip service to His will while they ignored the tremendous amount of social injustice that was everywhere apparent. Isaiah taught that Yahweh stands for a concept of holiness that is virtually beyond man's understanding; nevertheless, he insisted, Yahweh demands that man must attempt constantly to approach the ideal which He represents; this means a total consecration of man to the finest in life. In truth, Isaiah proclaimed, the people of Israel had been designated by God to be the particular people of whom each one was expected to serve as a model for the kind of life that the Lord advocated. The first thirty-nine chapters of the Book of Isaiah provide the texts of some of the "sermons" delivered by the first Isaiah; through the centuries they have served as models for the messages of many spiritual leaders of both Judaism and Christianity.

In Isaiah 2, the prophet revealed his belief that a day is coming when the way of the Lord would receive widespread acceptance, when people who ignored the commandments of the Lord would be ostracized, when peace and happiness would prevail. In Isaiah 9, as the author further developed such a theme, he prophesied that an individual yet to be born would appear to lead the people into the new era; the anticipated individual would sit "upon the throne of David." The great king, Isaiah asserted, would be a Prince of Peace; he would have the blessing of "the mighty God, the everlasting Father." In succeeding centuries, as life for the Hebrew people continued to be very difficult, Isaiah's prophecy of the coming of a great king, armed with the wisdom and authority of God, was heard more and more in the teachings of the spiritual leaders of the Hebrews. The anticipated great king, the hope of the people, was and still is designated in some writings as the Messiah, and the prophecy of his coming has often been described, especially by Christian ecclesiastics, as "Messianic prophecy." The word "Messiah" comes from the Hebrew *mashiah,* which means "one who is anointed." *Christos* is the Greek term for the Hebrew *mashiah.* The use of the title arose from the early practice of the Hebrews of anointing their prophets, priests, and kings. The act of anointing involved a solemn ceremony. In the course of time, the title was attached to only a very few important offices. Later, the title was restricted to the future deliverer, the ideal king, the expected redeemer. Through many centuries, the anticipation of the ultimate and, at times, the early arrival of the great leader often strengthened the determination of many Hebrew people to try to maintain the way of life that was the ideal of the Mosaic tradition in spite of bitter discouragement and persecution. Even now, the anticipation remains undiminished for some followers of Judaism that some day, some time, their God-designated leader will appear to fulfill the old prophecies.

Many variations are to be found in the collection of prophecies and other Judaic writings pertaining to the circumstances surrounding the arrival of the anticipated great leader, his characteristics, and the nature of his earthly assignment. Some Judaic sages expressed the belief that his arrival among the Jews would be accomplished by cataclysmic events. Other wise men seemed to believe that he would appear without great fanfare while revealing himself as one who possessed great natural power in his influence upon the political and religious scenes. Some of the prophecies anticipated a person who would astound his followers by his performance of miracles. But the prophecy that ultimately seemed to supersede the others prepared the Hebrew people for a great king who would come from the House of David; he would have the personal attributes that one would expect of such an individual; moreover, he would be an invincible political leader who also would be a just administrator as he demanded obedience to the laws of Moses.

During the first part of the first century A.D., the politically turbulent period of time in which Jesus lived, there was much talk about the Messiah, the great king of prophecy. It was not unusual for an individual to make claim to the title "Massiah," and then place himself at the head of a small group of followers from whom he expected obedience. Also, rumors became common that the Messiah had appeared, possibly in some out-of-the-way place. There is little doubt, in fact, that members of the Jewish community were often confused and the Judaic leadership was disturbed by the frequent rumors and the conflicting and fraudulent claims.

Micah, already mentioned as a contemporary of the first Isaiah, ministered to the simple folk. His message, similar to and probably influenced by that of Isaiah, was cast into the language of his special audience; his ability to speak in meaningful terms to people with limited educational background has won the acclaim of both Biblical scholars and literary critics. Some of the words of Micah (note Micah 5:2) have been interpreted by many students of the Bible as prophesying that the anticipated Messiah would come from Bethlehem. To have the Messiah born in Bethlehem would be consistent with the view held by Micah and others that the great king would be of the House of David, for it was commonly believed that the family home of David was in Bethlehem.

It is likely that the messages of Isaiah and Micah provided the people much hope and encouragement in view of the intense fear of invasion that constantly gripped the public. In fact, it appears that the reform movement of Hezekiah was making pronounced progress before his sudden death. But, unfortunately, his immediate successor, Manasseh, whose rule was considerably simplified by the fact that outside pressure on Judah was eased somewhat by a combination of military and political events, chose not to push the reforms that Hezekiah had initiated. For over half a century, during the long reign of Manasseh, although the nation made progress on the political front, Judaism slowly became diluted by other beliefs and practices. Within a short time after Manasseh died, however, his son, who is believed by some to have held views similar to those of his father, was assassinated, and Josiah was elevated to the throne.

Josiah proved to be singularly well-equipped in temperament and in understanding to provide the spiritual leadership that the Hebrew people of Judah needed at that time. The new ruler readily accepted the previous warnings of the prophets that the nation was headed for anni-hilation unless the people repented and returned to the way of God as enunciated by Moses. Then the voice of a new prophet, Zephaniah, caused people to tremble as he portrayed in vivid, evangelical terms the ultimate consequences of their sinfulness. Zephaniah was so forceful in his pronouncements that his listeners could not ignore his denunciation of the injustice and the immorality that had become common. It is probable that Josiah heard Zephaniah and was duly alarmed, for he took urgent steps to cleanse the Temple; he also issued directives to eliminate many of the practices of the people that he regarded as unacceptable to the Lord. Judaic scholars generally affirm that under Josiah's leadership the Hebrew people developed a new appreciation of the meaning of Judaism, as it could and should be translated into a way of life. The mood of the people seemed to reflect their genuine desire to try anew to build a kind of life that would be acceptable to the Lord; the Mosaic code became accepted, as probably never before, as something immutable and as the standard promulgated by God.

It was during this time that a brilliantly conceived new book was discovered, supposedly in the Temple, that provided a new rendition of Mosaic concepts. The work was hailed as coming directly from God. The new book, generally known among Judaic scholars as Deuteronomy

since later it provided the core of the content of the Book of Deuteronomy in the Judaic Bible, is widely regarded as having provided much
of the motivation as well as the inspiration for the later canonization of
the Torah. Josiah proclaimed that the newly discovered work was fundamental to life in Judah, and he made a covenant with the people of the
nation pertaining to what he regarded as a proper recognition of its
contents.

The reform movement introduced into Judah by Josiah received additional support when the great prophet Jeremiah appeared on the scene.
Jeremiah, like Zephaniah, denounced the apparent deterioration in the
attitudes, the beliefs, and the behavior of his fellow countrymen; he was
greatly concerned by the growing lack of appreciation by the people of
their religious heritage. The Book of Jeremiah that records his vigorous
pronouncements during that period of time reveals the great depth of his
emotions as he observed that the people of Judah were seemingly
unconcerned as they, in a manner similar to that of the people of the
Northern Kingdom, moved down the road to tragedy. The writings of
Jeremiah make intensely interesting reading for students of literature as
well as of religion, for in his personal crusade to try to awaken the people
of Judah to the dangers that they faced, he revealed the powerful personal
resource possessed by the man who is a master of the use of language.
Jeremiah has been described as "the Golden tongue among the prophets." His exhortations were necessary, he obviously believed, as an
attempt to save Judah from the fate that had befallen the Northern
Kingdom.

But Judah did fall. Although the nation, with Jerusalem as its capital,
survived for 136 years after the fall of the Northern Kingdom, it finally
succumbed to the military might of the Babylonians. After the conquest
of Judah there were two unsuccessful attempts by its former inhabitants
to regain control of their country. Such efforts finally led Nebuchadnezzar and his Babylonian legions, in 587/586 B.C., to crush the defenders of Jerusalem in a massive military action; many of the inhabitants of the city were massacred, others were taken to Babylon as captives,
and the great Temple built by Solomon was destroyed. The Babylonian
Captivity that followed, which is memorialized in many Jewish and
Judaic writings, has been regarded generally by the Jewish people as a
very sad episode in their history. According to some traditions, it was
during the Babylonian Captivity that many of the Hebrew people learned
Aramaic, which during the latter part of the B.C. period essentially

replaced Hebrew as the common language among the Jewish people of Jerusalem as well as the neighboring areas of Palestine.

Even after Jerusalem fell, Jeremiah continued his strenuous efforts, although by that time he was an elderly man, to provide guidance to his countrymen, and his words of encouragement are given great credit by historians for maintaining the spirit of the Jewish people during the early days of the Baylonian Exile. "The Lord," Jeremiah proclaimed (note Jeremiah 23:5–6), "will raise unto David a righteous offspring, and he shall execute judgment and justice in the earth. In his days Judah shall be saved, and Israel shall dwell safely."

Some Christian scholars of the Middle Ages believed that in the life of Jeremiah they observed a prefiguration of Jesus; thus often he was represented with a cross. The manner in which Jeremiah admonished the Hebrew people to forsake their evil ways, his presentiment of personal disaster that seemed to be involved in some of his utterances, and the supposed agony of the death to which he was finally condemned all seemed to some Christians, especially of the Middle Ages, to foreshadow the life and Passion of Jesus.

It appears that as a young man, Ezekiel was among those taken to Babylonia after Judah was conquered by Nebuchadnezzar. Shortly thereafter he revealed his bitterness over his conviction that the heathenism that had permeated his homeland had made its conquest inevitable. In fact, he denounced the leaders of Israel who for so many years had done so little to encourage his countrymen to return to the teachings of the Lord; hope for the future of Israel, he asserted, must come from those who had become exiles from their country, many of whom seemed to be developing a new appreciation of their heritage. Ezekiel, who had tremendous influence on his fellow exiles and who has had a pronounced effect on the thought of many later generations of Jews, was, it appears, much more of a mystic than was true of the other prophets of whom we have knowledge. Upon occasion, the evidence seems to reveal, he actually passed into a state of trance; his interpretations of his visions when in such a condition impressed his associates as bearing the stamp of God. Through Ezekiel's messages to the Hebrew people, sometimes expressed in poetic form, runs a central theme: The God of Moses is supreme and will tolerate no rival; pagan peoples must ultimately pay a severe penalty for their false notions of Divinity; likewise Israel must suffer and suffer for its many years of disloyalty to the Godhead of the nation.

Chapter Four

AFTER THE BABYLONIAN EXILE AND BEFORE THE TIME OF ROMAN CONTROL

In 538 B.C., Cyrus, King of Persia, conquered Babylon. The event inaugurated a new and important epoch in Jewish history and in the evolution of Judaism. During the somewhat more than five centuries that remained before the start of the Christian era, a series of events took place that were of great importance in the developmental process that produced Judaism as we now know it and in the later development of Christianity.

Chapter 1 of the Book of Ezra of the Judaic Bible reports that "In the first year of Cyrus the King" he issued a decree "concerning the house of God in Jerusalem." "Let the house be builded," Cyrus proclaimed. Consequently, history reveals, the great Temple was rebuilt and was dedicated in 516 B.C. Chapter 7 of the Book of Ezra tells of other gracious offers of Persian royalty to assist the Jewish captives in Babylon to renew their life in Judah and in its capital, Jerusalem. It appears, however, that not all the Jews wanted to return to Judah; among them probably were a number of those upon whom, according to Ezekiel, Judaism of the future had to rebuild. In fact, at about the time of the inauguration of the Christian era, descendants of the Hebrews who did not return to Judah may have played a significant role in making Antioch a dynamic center of Judaism and later of Christianity.

Freedom to worship in their own way, granted by Cyrus and his Persian successors to the Jews who returned to the new Judah, to be known as Judea, was a strong factor in the general satisfaction of the Jews with Persian rule. There is little doubt that Judaism in Judea achieved new vitality during the Persian period; in truth, Judaism undoubtedly benefited from some of the ideas and practices advocated by the Persian religion, some of whose adherents possessed a tendency toward the acceptance of monotheism.

The latter part of the Book of Isaiah reveals that the second of the Isaiahs, whose actual name is unknown, but whose prophetic mission took place during the time of Cyrus, was a well-educated man who expressed his ideas with great eloquence. The prophet insisted that God was responsible for the opportunity given to the Israelites to return to the home which rightfully belonged to them as a result of His promise to Abraham, and thus the return would certainly inaugurate for them a new life of greater satisfaction and happiness than they had ever known before. But he constantly reminded the Israelites that his optimistic view of their lot for the future was premised on the assumption that they would not lose their faith. In common with some of the other prophets, the second Isaiah emphasized that the Lord is concerned with deeds, not with adherence to religious formalisms.

When Ezra, a priest with a distinguished Judaic background, was given the letter of authorization by Persian royalty to institute the Mosaic code as the official law of Judea, there was rejoicing in the land; the action seemed to reveal that it was Persia's desire that Judea should undergo a national rebirth within the religious tradition established by Moses. Ultimately, in fact, under the guidance of Ezra and with Persian approval, Judea was organized as a theocracy; thus the high priests, within the framework of overall political control exercised by the Persians, were given the responsibility for the administration of both the religious and the civil laws.

Some historians believe, however, that the reorganization of the government developed by Ezra was disapproved by some of the Judaic faithful in view of the fact that it made no provision for the anticipated great king who was to come from the House of David; thus for those who were the dissenters, Ezra's reorganization of the Government did not seem to conform to prophecy. Consequently, during the time of the theocracy, there may have been the earliest indication of what became a major disagreement within the community of Judaic believers during the later Hellenistic age of Jewish history. That disagreement pitted the pro-Davidic followers of Judaism against those who were pro-Levitic. The pro-Davidic people could not agree with any scheme of government that seemed to ignore prophecy pertaining to the future king from the House of David. The so-called pro-Levitic people, on the other hand, emphasized that Moses made no mention of David, who lived many years after the time of Moses; rather, Moses designated Levi, a priest, and his descendants as the ones who would be responsible for the maintenance of "the Laws."

It appears that one of the early actions initiated by the key people in the new theocratic government was the organization and canonization of the Laws, that is, the Torah. Much of the content of the ultimately canonized Torah was a part of the oral tradition of the Hebrew people, but by the time of Ezra a large part of the so-called oral tradition had been compiled, apparently in several versions. It appears that Ezra and some of his priestly associates decided that the time had come to determine that part of the extensive written and oral tradition associated with the name of Moses, as it existed in various versions and forms, which should be retained as truly representing the word of God; the part not receiving such recognition should be regarded as having a different status and thus should be omitted from the officially approved text of the Torah that was to be developed. The representatives of Judaism involved in making the necessary decisions were faced with an awesome task; they were confronted with the problem of considering a large mass of information that had been handed down through the ages; included in the material was the haphazard synthesis of the Yahwist and Elohist Epics.

Predominant among the materials available to the priests involved in the task of developing an authoritative version of the Torah was the important Book of Deuteronomy, an early version of which, as already indicated, was introduced to followers of Judaism during the days of Josiah. Deuteronomy was recognized as significant both because of its content and because of its literary excellence. There is general agreement that the influence of the Book of Deuteronomy on the attitudes of the priests and on the standards of judgment which they employed in their work of organization and canonization of the Torah was substantial; moreover, the very nature of Deuteronomy, both its content and its style, had obvious effects on the future development of the Biblical text. The Book of Deuteronomy possesses literary qualities that were imitated to some extent by later Biblical writers and editors. In fact, some of the Books of the Prophets in the Judaic Bible, a collection of books that in the course of time was introduced into the Biblical text immediately after Genesis, Exodus, Leviticus, Numbers, and Deuteronomy, the five books that constitute the Torah, clearly reflect the Deuteronomic influence.

Undoubtedly the great effort involved in the canonization of the Laws was accepted as a great challenge by those who were involved in the endeavor. Apparently they were motivated by a sincere belief that the time had come to scrutinize the tremendous mass of religious materials that had been accumulated over a time span of many years; it was necessary, they believed, to make a determination of those materials that had true significance as revealing the will of God. The Torah when completed was to be universally recognized as the word of God and as such it would provide a basis for the kind of life that would be acceptable to God. With the canonized ‚Torah available, people could have a true understanding of sin and a new appreciation of the meaning of repentance. (There is a school of thought within Judaism which accepts the point of view that much of the work of developing the new version of the Torah was essentially accomplished during the Babylonian Exile.)

It has been said that the task of canonizing the material of the Torah required approximately thirteen years. Apparently the work was completed about the time that Nehemiah, highly respected Jewish political leader (note the first six chapters of the Book of Nehemiah), became prominent in Judea, and the accomplishment profited greatly from the endorsement that Nehemiah gave to it. While the work of canonization was under way, Ezra educated a collection of expositors, called interpreters and recruited chiefly from the Levite priests, who would have the assignment of explaining the finished work to the people. Finally, according to some historians, it was on Rosh Hashanah, in the year 444 B.C., that the completed Torah was read in Jerusalem before a tremendous throng. As the great work was read and its reading was supplemented by comments made by interpreters, many of the people wept and trembled. They were convinced that they were hearing the reading of God's word. The importance of finally having available the Torah in documented form cannot be exaggerated; the monumental Biblical work was now available to all the people, although it must be admitted that for a very long period of time copies of it would not become common. Before the act of canonization took place, most of the people knew of the Torah's words of wisdom only as the priests revealed them and explained them. Clearly, the completion of the process of canonization of the Torah along with its public announcement must be regarded as one of the most momentous events in the history of Judaism and, in fact, in the history of Christianity and of the world. A strong element of stability had now been introduced into the still evolving Judaic tradition, and the availability of the Torah as it had been canonized facilitated the spread of knowledge of the kind of ethical and moral society, with its emphasis upon justice and brotherly love, that had received its earliest definition in the Mosaic code.

Many competent Biblical scholars hold to the position, as noted earlier, that one or more later generations of priests provided substantial reediting of the Torah as it was originally canonized. The later priestly efforts, it is believed by many Judaic scholars, involved extensive adjustments in both content and point of view. And it may be true that the priests who collaborated in the work of rewriting and reediting had a tendency, as is unfortunately true of a considerable amount of historical writing, to idealize the past in their portrayal of historical characters and in their depiction of historical events. Undoubtedly, a basic purpose of the various sets of priests as they became involved in reworking the Torah was that of perfecting its presentation of the Law. To determine the source of ideas that influenced the work of the priests as they attempted to accomplish the desired perfection has become an intriguing subject for Biblical analysts. As previously indicated, other peoples of the Near East possessed important legal codes that were available to the priestly editors; parts of those codes were similar in many respects to the ultimate Biblical presentation. It must also be noted that the priestly contributors to later revisions of the Torah undoubtedly introduced changes that had an especial appeal for them, including the addition of much of the material pertaining to ritual. The latter kind of information, a priest would believe, should be regarded as an essential adjunct to the textual material that was concerned with the strictly legal.

The tremendous respect and reverence that the Jewish people have for the Torah is revealed by the fact that upon occasion it is separated from the rest of the Judaic Bible and made available as a distinct literary entity. In fact, in the synagogue, the scroll of the Torah is maintained separately from the rest of the Bible; it is from that particular scroll that the weekly reading of the Torah takes place. But the other sections of the Judaic Bible, as the completed Holy Work ultimately took form, possess their own particular kinds of significance for followers of Judaism. Among the Jewish people, no other Judaic literary work, including the very important Talmud, is ever compared with the Bible as a revered document of the Judaic faith.

During the Persian period, sometime after the canonization of the Torah, pressure developed within religious circles for an expansion of the Holy Work by adding to it other materials that through the years had become significant for the religious life and thought of the Jewish people. There was in existence a great amount of both written and oral information pertaining to the prophets as well as a vast amount of other spoken and written literature that had become invaluable to an understanding and appreciation of the Judaic tradition. So during the next few centuries after the canonization of the Torah, the rest of the Judaic Bible, as we now know it, slowly took form. The reasoning behind the decisions that were made with respect to materials that were added to the Torah can only be a matter of conjecture. From the perspective of the present, there is much about the choice of content for the latter part of the Biblical text that puzzles the modern Judaic scholar. For instance, recent work on the Dead Sea Scrolls and other historical studies reveal that many writings that now seem to be very important were omitted from the final documentation. Moreover, since Judaic authorities at the time the Bible was developed must have regarded the Holy Work as having permanent significance for followers of Judaism, modern students of Biblical history find it difficult to understand why the authors of some of the books included in the Bible merely referred to other works that were extant in their day (for instance, in II Kings 15:11, the assertion is made that additional information about Zechariah appears "in the book of the chronicles of the kings of Israel"); upon occasion Biblical authors quoted from non-Biblical works which are unknown to modern scholars and were probably never available on an extensive basis. Most of the books reveal that numerous persons were involved in their authorship and editing; some books, in fact, are obviously conglomerates of materials drawn from a variety of sources.

What has just been said is certainly true of the Books of the Prophets. In general, the Books of the Prophets refer to events that took place several centuries before their final canonization. Some process of selection must have been followed to determine which ones of the prophets should be memorialized (some were included who have received little or no attention in the present work), as well as what available information, both written and oral, pertaining to each prophet should be perpetuated. Each book of the Prophets included in the Bible has provided a separate and distinct challenge to modern Judaic scholars as they attempt to determine the sources of the contributions made to it and try to assign dates for the composition of both the early drafts and the essentially final drafts accepted for inclusion in the Biblical canon. Probably by the year 200 B.C., essentially final versions of all the books of the Prophets had been introduced into the Biblical canon; some had received approval at an earlier date. The books finally incorporated into the section of the Bible devoted to the prophets, using present Biblical designations, were Joshua, Judges, Samuel, Kings, Isaiah, Jeremiah, Ezekiel, Hosea, Joel, Amos, Obadiah, Jonah, Micah, Habakkuk, Zephaniah, Haggai, Zechariah, and Malachi.

The decision to add the books of the Prophets to the Judaic Bible appears to have been the first decision made relevant to an expansion of the Holy Work beyond the Torah. That decision undoubtedly made it easier for religious authorities to continue during the following decades, well into the hectic political period that immediately preceded the Christian era, to augment further the previously determined Biblical content. One may assume that the chief motivation of those responsible for the expansion of the Biblical text—although it is highly unlikely that anyone ever explicitly stated the purpose as such—was that of attempting to assemble in one literary work, a unique undertaking in human history, a collection of the most significant contributions to the culture, a religion-centered culture, of a particular people, thereby creating for them a truly national literary masterpiece. How much more meaningful is such an accomplishment than, for example, the composition of a national anthem!

Included in the monumental work as it finally took form were accounts of legends and reports of events that were regarded generally as having importance for the Jewish people in enabling them to understand their heritage, a collection of ethical and moral principles and associated behavioral guides that were responsible, even in those early days, for giving the Jewish people distinctive attitudes toward God and man, a documentation of the sayings and actions of some of the sages of Jewish history who had been especially influential in determining the nature of Judaic thought, and a selection of poetry and prose that seemed to epitomize the best in Jewish literary endeavor. All knowledgeable people agree that the Judaic Bible profited greatly from the kind of evolutionary process that produced it. The Judaic Bible is truly a remarkable literary work which has been universally treasured and revered by the members of a close society of people who have been strongly dedicated to the religious faith that has been at the heart of their culture and who have possessed an unusual sense of destiny along with their great respect for their heritage. A person who has had a long association with the Judaic Bible has no desire to quarrel with the position of many of those who subscribe to the Judaic faith that their Bible is an inspired work, that the voice of God may be heard speaking through those who were responsible for bringing the Holy Work into being.

The books ultimately added to the Judaic Bible following the inclusion of the Books of the Prophets were regarded as forming a third section, the last section, of the Biblical text; the section is generally known as the Sacred Writings, the Hagiographa. Within the Writings it is common to identify three categories: the Poetical Books (Psalms, Proverbs, and Job); the

Megilloth (Song of Songs, Ruth, Lamentations, Ecclesiastes, and Esther); and the Miscellaneous Books (Daniel, Chronicles, and Ezra). Later Christian scholars divided Ezra into two books, Ezra and Nehemiah; the Old Testament of the Christian Bible reflects such an action.

The individual Psalms of the large collection that provides the content of the first book of the Writings have often been acclaimed as the most beautiful poetry ever written. Some of them were composed originally to be sung, accompanied by strings; in fact, initially, the Christian psalter was a book of psalms set to music. Jewish psalters were never set to music. The Psalms have always had tremendous significance for the Jewish people, and among Christians no religious writings are more popular. It is likely that the particular Psalms chosen for introduction into the Book of Psalms were drawn from many periods in the history of the Jewish people. It is probable also that the Psalms were composed by a variety of poets and singers, but the actual compilation of the poems and their reediting, which may have been extensive, probably was made quite late in the B.C. era. Traditionally, possibly going back to the time of the writing of the Book of Chronicles, the Psalms have been associated with the name of David; the basis of the tradition is not clear. Jerome, wise and astute Christian scholar of the fourth century A.D., denied that David was involved in composing the Psalms, and most later Biblical scholars, both Judaic and Christian, have been in agreement with Jerome's position.

The two books included in the writings designated as Proverbs and Job are sometimes described as Books of Wisdom. In the ancient Near East, the proverb, a writing of instructions from a respected and wise person of advanced age to a member or members of the younger generation, was common. Many of the proverbs contained in the Book of Proverbs, however, by contrast with those in the literature of ancient Egypt and of old Babylonia, reveal the strong religious faith of those responsible for their authorship. The proverbs of the Book of Proverbs are often associated with Solomon, and possibly some of his traditional wisdom is incorporated in the Book, but it is generally believed that the Biblical proverbs had a long history of development in the folklore of the Jewish people. The Book of Job also has counterparts in the literature of other nations of the ancient Near East. But the Book of Job, which probably originated as a folktale, possibly as early as the sixth century B.C., would seem to be distinctive in its tremendous display of faith by Job in spite of his great difficulties and suffering.

The stories of the Megilloth, so dear to the Jewish people, actually possess an unusual universality of appeal. Probably all the stories were based on folklore that had been popular for many generations. The Song of Songs, a poetic delight, is concerned with the wonders and beauty of human love. Modern scholarship is inclined toward the belief that the Song of Songs is a collection of wedding songs, although the tradition persists among some Biblical students that the story of the Book is that of a country girl who remained faithful to her beloved in spite of the blandishments of Solomon, great and wise king but also one of history's great lovers. The tender story of Ruth is well known. Lamentations, as the name implies, is a series of elegies and dirges, supposedly by Jeremiah, induced by sorrow over the terrible fate that befell Jerusalem when it was conquered by the Babylonians. The suggested identification of the Book with Jeremiah seems to have come from a reading of 2 Chronicles 35:25, but not all scholars agree with such a point of view. Lamentations is commonly read at the annual Judaic commemoration of the fall of Jerusalem. Ecclesiastes is an essay of philosophical reflections in which its author makes reference to his experiences which probably took place near the end of the third century B.C.; it seems to reflect the low state of mind of the Jewish people at that time, for they were beginning to lose hope that God would ever come to their rescue. The beautiful story of Esther probably had a long history of popularity with the early Jewish people; today the story is told and retold in many forms. Many modern Biblical scholars believe that the Book of Esther was the last book inserted into the Biblical text; certainly the date of its introduction in the canon must have been very late, possibly early in the Christian era. The latter suggestion receives some confirmation from the fact that not even a small part of the Book of Esther has been recovered from among the Dead Sea Scrolls whereas many fragments of all the other books of the Judaic Bible have been identified.

The Book of Daniel is generally regarded as a good example of what is commonly called apocalyptic literature, as such literature was conceived by Judaic writers during the period from approximately 200 B.C. to about A.D. 100. The Book of Daniel purports to be the story of a boy named Daniel who was a captive during the Babylonian exile and who remained steadfast in his faith. An apocalyptic writer, as was true of the author of the Book of Daniel, built his plot around an event in previous history although the message being conveyed could and should be interpreted in terms of contemporary people and events. The Book of Daniel seems to have been written during the Maccabean period; references in the plot of the story, which has its setting in the story of the Babylonian Exile, appear to be to certain people and events of the Maccabean era. One may speculate on the reason behind the fact that the Book of Daniel was included in the text of the Judaic Bible whereas evidence exists that a large number of other writings of similar type were excluded; it is conceivable that editors of the Judaic text regarded the Book as a desirable addition to the Biblical content because in a subtle way the theme of the work provided encouragement to the Jews to continue their harassment of the hated Antiochus Epiphanes, mentioned later. The Book of Daniel, it may be noted, is included among the writings in the Judaic Bible, but the Old Testament, the Christian version of the Judaic Bible, includes the book in the category of Prophets.

A Hebrew historian of the third century B.C., known as the Chronicler, developed a history of Israel that seemed to have its origin in a desire to update some of the historical material, chiefly legends, reported in Genesis; the updating would involve a continuation of the historical narrative of the Jewish people as recorded in Genesis to the time of the Persian period. Apparently the Biblical compilers found the work to be interesting and important and thus decided to introduce a substantial part of it into the Biblical text, but the part introduced into the original canon was partitioned into two books, Chronicles and Ezra. The Book of Ezra treated the latter part of the Chronicler's historical exposition. Later Christian scribes when developing their own version of the Judaic Bible, as already indicated, divided Ezra into two books: Ezra and Nehemiah. The Book of Chronicles is of interest to Biblical students because it reveals something of the attitudes and historical insights of a Judaic scholar who apparently lived during the time of the theocracy in Judea.

The Judaic Bible, evolving as it did over a period of many centuries, is truly a literary memorial to the sacrifices, to the struggle to find meaning in life, and to the aspirations of the Jewish people. Over a period of many centuries, the Judaic Bible has provided inspiration and guidance to many millions of readers along with the kind of satisfaction and intellectual stimulation that comes from association with great literature. The Holy Work also reveals, in a remarkable manner, the intellectual insight of the vast number of people who contributed to it.

And, of the utmost importance, although the Judaic Bible is the result of the endeavors of many generations of Hebrew scholars, and although one may assume that its appeal was directed essentially to the Jewish people, many non-Jewish populations of diverse ethnic and cultural background have found solace and guidance in the Judaic masterpiece. The Judaic Bible has had such a pronounced and continuing influence upon so many people and nations that one must conclude that the Biblical text truly provides a meaningful treatment of fundamental concepts and values for which there will always be universal appreciation.

In about 430 B.C., Samaritan religious adopted the Judaic Torah as the foundation for their religious faith. It is believed that the Samaritans, neighbors of the Jews but generally disliked by them because of some of their deviations from Judaic precepts, were the first non-Jewish people to accept a fundamental part of the Judaic Bible as basic to their religious beliefs and practices. In fact, the Samaritans at that early date rigidly accepted the principle—as is true of the very small colony of Samaritans still in existence—that their religious behavior must be consistent with the teachings of Moses, as such teachings are revealed, according to Samaritan interpretation, in the Torah.

The long period of Persian control of Judea finally ended in 331 B.C., when young Alexander of Macedon, later to be known as Alexander the Great, crushed the armies of Darius, King of Persia, in one of the most significant battles of world history. The victory of Alexander initiated what is often known as the Hellenistic era in Jewish and Judaic history. Before his death at the age of thirty-three, Alexander had conquered a substantial part of the Near East and was well on his way toward the realization of his dream of a world empire. Although Alexander was a skillful and aggressive warrior who often displayed primitive cruelty when annihilating his enemies, he had some of the attributes of the scholar, undoubtedly a consequence of the fact that he had been tutored by Aristotle. Alexander was impressed with many aspects of the civilization of the East, so he justified his military conquests on the basis that they were enabling him to create a world state in which the culture of the East would be merged with that of the West. To implement his cultural ideas, he indulged in a variety of strategies, including the issuance of a directive affecting several thousand of his soldiers that they should take wives from among the conquered Eastern peoples. But for Alexander the only acceptable way of accomplishing the actual cultural blending that was his ultimate goal was through the medium of things Greek, including the Greek language; it appears to have been his expectation that the biological and cultural blending of peoples of diverse cultural and ethnic background which he was fostering would yield people of new and strong characteristics but they would still think as the Greeks thought. In the civilization of the vast geographical area conquered by Alexander, the Greek language, Greek philosophy, and Greek customs soon became vital elements. The resulting effects upon the development of

Western culture, we now know, were highly significant. In fact, the influence of the Hellenistic movement initiated by Alexander upon the existing Judaic tradition and then upon the development of the Christian tradition was much greater than some scholars in the field of religion seem to understand. There is substantial truth in the assertion that classical Christianity was Judaism with a Greek veneer; in a sense, however, the statement is incomplete, for Judaism itself had undergone major modifications as a result of the Hellenistic influence. Alexander seemed to respect Judaism and did not interfere with those who adhered to its traditions.

One of Alexander's major contributions to world culture was his creation of the city of Alexandria on the Mediterranean coast of Egypt. Alexandria was designed in such a way that, even though it was in Egypt, it possessed characteristics that were more Greek than Egyptian. The new city, it appears, was established by Alexander as an outpost of Greek culture and authority; following a directive from Alexander, those who designed the city attempted to create a model Greek community. The great city that was the result had magnificent theaters, beautiful art centers, one of the finest universities, museums, and libraries in all of history, and a large and active emporium. Hardly a trace of its early magnificence can be found in modern Alexandria, now the home of a huge mass of struggling and impoverished humanity. Although Alexander was buried in Alexandria, his grave is unmarked and unknown. The great significance of early Alexandria is due very strongly to the fact that soon it featured a tremendous concentration of remarkable scholars and cultural materials; to accomplish such a concentration, an intensive search for distinguished scholars and significant manuscripts was carried out by emissaries of Alexander and his immediate successors throughout the vast area which Alexander ultimately controlled. The great Alexandrian library, often described as the most important ever developed, contained a vast number of original manuscripts of tremendous value; in addition, a stable of scribes was maintained to copy important works that could not be obtained for the library in their original state. Consequently, Alexandria rapidly became the cultural and intellectual center of the ancient world. Alexandrian scholars made significant contributions to literature, to art, to mathematics, to science, to religion, to philosophy. It was in Alexandria that Euclid created his great work on mathematics of which the geometry studied in American secondary schools is only a small part. It was in Alexandria that Herophilus and Erasistratus did their pioneering work in anatomy and that Eratosthenes measured the earth's circumference. For the nearly thousand years that the city lived, especially during the early centuries of its existence, Alexandria provided the environment and motivation for extremely important intellectual endeavors that later became the basis for much of Western man's cultural progress.

Judaic writings, especially the Torah, were very familiar to many persons in Alexandria; the legal and moral codes of the Torah, along with its philosophy and its literary standards, were subjects for analysis and discussion by Alexandrian intellectuals. The many Jews attracted to Alexandria soon after its founding provided a stimulus to the studies of Judaic literature, including the Torah. But it is said that most of the Jews in Alexandria, within a few generations after the creation of the city, had adopted the Greek language and were no longer able to speak or read Hebrew, the original language of their Bible, and they were also unacquainted with Aramaic, which in the latter part of the B.C. era had essentially replaced Hebrew as the common language of the Jewish people in Palestine and as the language in which the rabbis generally carried out their religious obligations.

As a consequence of such circumstances, Alexandrian officials along with Alexandrian scholars decided to sponsor a Greek translation of the Torah. The Greek version of the Biblical work was completed early in the third century B.C.; it was completed at about the same time that Euclid wrote his *Elements,* probably the greatest mathematical work in human history. Over a century later, probably because of a demand in the synagogues for a Greek translation of the Books of the Prophets, a Greek version of the second section of the Judaic Bible was produced. Probably not too much time had elapsed since the section of the Bible pertaining to the prophets had been canonized by Judean scholars in Jerusalem. It is apparent that the Greek translation of the various prophetic books was carried out by different individuals. During a period of more than a century following the development of a Greek version of the Books of the Prophets, Judaic scholars in Alexandria, who apparently maintained a close contact with religious developments as they were taking place in Jerusalem, also translated into Greek the third section of the Bible as well as a large number of non-Biblical religious works then associated with Judaism. Moreover, Alexandrian Judaic scholars made additions to the growing collection of religious writings by originating in the Greek language new materials of special relevance to the Judaic tradition. The completed Judaic Bible in Greek that ultimately resulted from the efforts in Alexandria is commonly known as the Septuagint; the term "Septuagint" is derived from the legend that seventy (Latin: *septuaginta*) scholars were imported from Jerusalem in the early days of the work to assist in carrying out the task of translation.

It is a notable fact that Alexandrian scholars included in the Septuagint more Biblical books or portions of books, actually fourteen more, than are contained in the official canon of the Judaic Bible; some of the extra books had to be translated from the Hebrew, but the original language of the others was Greek. The fact that the Septuagint contained the extra books is not surprising, for the canonization of the latter part of the Judaic Bible had taken place in Jerusalem just a short time earlier and, moreover, the various Judaic sects still had not adopted a unified position upon the books to be included in the official Biblical canon. Widespread acceptance of any particular canonical compilation could not be expected, even among the Judaic scholars in Jerusalem, until after a considerable passage of time. It is not known how the Alexandrian compilers determined which of those religious writings available to them should be included as extra books in their new Greek version of the Bible. But the fact that the Septuagint, as it ultimately became accepted, did contain fourteen more books or portions of books than the original approved Judaic canon has had some interesting consequences. For instance, the Latin version of the Judaic Bible officially adopted many centuries later by the Roman Catholic Church contained fifteen books or portions of books, the fourteen contained in the Septuagint plus one more, that are not found in either the usual standard Protestant Christian versions of the Judaic Bible or in the several versions of their Bible authorized by Judaic authorities. This interesting circumstance resulted from the fact that when the early Roman Christian ecclesiastics approved a Latin version of the Judaic Bible for the use of Christians, the version which they approved was little more than a translation of the Greek Septuagint into Latin. The first Latin version of the Judaic Bible to which reference has just been made was responsible for a considerable amount of Christian tradition pertaining to the Bible that was part of the inheritance of Jerome when in the fourth century he brought forth his highly regarded Biblical work in Latin.

The "extra books," as they appear in some versions of the Judaic Bible, are known as apocryphal books or Apocrypha, a term first employed by Jerome; the term "apocrypha" comes from a Greek word meaning "something hidden." Some Christians have characterized the Apocrypha as spurious religious documents in the field of Christianity, but such a characterization would seem to be unfortunate. An apocryphal book is merely a book that was not included in the original Biblical canon. In addition to the fourteen Apocrypha included in the Septuagint, other books of very great importance within the Judeo-Christian tradition, properly described as Apocrypha, were written at about the same time and many others were composed at a later date. Through the ages, some of the religious works not included in the Biblical canon have been widely read and studied; in fact, a number of them have had a pronounced influence upon both Judaic and Christian thought, and some of them have been invaluable sources of information for both Judaic and Christian scholars. For instance, the First and Second Books of the Maccabees as included in the Septuagint—other books of the Maccabees were not included although they were in existence when the First and Second Books were available—provide an elaborate and, apparently, an essentially authoritative historical account of the turbulent and important era in Jewish history that included the Maccabean period, discussed later; moreover, the Second Book of the Maccabees provides interesting confirmation of the fact that trends existed in Judaic belief and thought at the dawn of the Christian era that must have exercised great influence upon the doctrinal positions of early Christians. Certainly the Apocrypha cannot be ignored by students of religion who are trying to understand the evolution of the Christian tradition.

The organizers of the Septuagint were also responsible for the fact that Christian versions of the Judaic Bible involve a modification of the traditional tripartite organization that characterizes authoritative Judaic texts. The Septuagint grouped the Biblical books according to subject matter, a custom followed essentially in both the later Protestant and the Roman Catholic versions of the Judaic work.

From the point of view of historians of Judaism and Christianity, the development of the Septuagint in Alexandria was a momentous event, for it facilitated the introduction of the Judaic tradition, insofar as that tradition had been cast into written form, to the Greek world. The language and syntax of the literary masterpiece in Greek were substantially those of the Greek-speaking people in the vast empire that had resulted from Alexander's conquests, so knowledge of the Biblical work spread, not rapidly but steadily. The importance for the Western world of the fact that the Septuagint became a part of Greek culture is immediately apparent, for it was from the Greeks that later European civilizations drew a substantial part of their cultural foundation. And, interestingly, although the Septuagint had its origin in Judaica, knowledge of its contents facilitated the later spread of Christianity. The teachings of the Septuagint represented a distinct break with the polytheistic concepts of paganism which were common in that day, and they provided a basis upon which the principles of Christianity, promulgated in the early centuries A.D., could be explained. The development of the Septuagint also benefited the work of much later students of Christianity because of the fact that its preparation served to codify the Greek dialect of its time. Since that same dialect was the one which was widely employed during the period in which much of the original Christian New Testament was written, the Septuagint provided later Christian scholars an important key to an understanding of many passages in early Christian literature, including the New Testament.

But an objective appraisal of the cultural results of the development of the Septuagint reveals some consequences that must be regarded as unfortunate. When a literary work is translated from one language to another, something is always lost; some meanings become changed. The Septuagint was Greek, not Jewish; the content was of Jewish origin but the language, with its subtle meanings, in which that content was conveyed to its readers was a part of the cultural tradition of the Greeks. Moreover, although we have not had access to the Hebrew text or texts of the Judaic Bible upon which the Greek translation was based, evidence increases that the translators along with other contributors to the text of the Septuagint chose to modify some of the source materials, even making deletions and additions, when they developed the new version in Greek.

When Alexander the Great died in 323 B.C., the great empire which he had built suffered almost immediate dissolution as each of his generals moved quickly to obtain a share. Ptolemy of Egypt gained control of a small portion of Palestine that comprised Judea, then a comparatively small area surrounding Jerusalem. After that, Judea remained under Egyptian domination for approximately a century. During that time, Egypt and Syria were almost continuously at war, and frequently Judea served as their battleground. Often the Jews in Judea were divided in their loyalties; some supported the Egyptians and some the Syrians. Frequently at issue insofar as the Jewish people were concerned was the manner in which the high priests should be appointed since, at least part of the time, the appointments were regarded as political prizes.

In spite of the political controversies and the military conflicts that existed in all the parts into which Alexander's empire was partitioned, the Hellenistic influence continued to gain strength; Alexander had built a solid foundation for a growing acceptance of Greek culture. Hellenism in its many forms became increasingly fashionable even among the Jewish people of Judea, especially among the affluent and the politically power-ful. As a result of the trend, some Judaic traditions were being eroded, and, of even greater importance, the high priests, who often were political appointees, began to display weakness in their advocacy of Judaic doctrine as, quite obviously, they were trying to maintain the approval of the Hellenistic political leadership.

In 198 B.C., Antiochus III of Syria, most famous and most competent of a political dynasty established by Seleucus, another of Alexander's generals who had obtained a portion of Alexander's empire when the great Greek ruler died, defeated the Egyptians and then annexed to his realm much of Judea, including Jerusalem. Then Antiochus III con-tinued to add territory to his Syrian Empire before two disastrous defeats by the Romans forced him to discontinue efforts to expand the area under his control. While Antiochus III ruled Jerusalem as a part of his Syrian Empire, most members of the Jewish populace of the City of David found life to be generally satisfactory. But when Antiochus III decided to retire, members of the ruling hierarchy of Syria became involved in vicious political intrigue; finally, Antiochus IV, also known as Antiochus Epiphanes, succeeded Antiochus III as the ruler of the area that included Judea, partly as a result of military victories over Egypt.

Antiochus IV (176–164 B.C.) may be the most hated man in Jewish history; he was and still is utterly despised. When his Jewish subjects ulti-mately rebelled against some of his policies, and when assorted acts of cruelty perpetrated by Antiochus against the leaders of the rebellion did not quell the revolt, the despot decided to resort to repressive measures of a kind that he believed would hurt the most; he attacked the rebels by way of their religion. Circumcision became a capital offense as a result of edict, and religious sanctuaries were desecrated in ways that can only be characterized as vulgar. Apparently the vicious persecution quickly spread to areas other than Jerusalem; there is reason to believe, for example, that the situation soon became just as serious for the Jews in Antioch. The Biblical Book of Daniel reveals the agony and the bitter hatred of the time.

While the terrible ordeal continued, some Jewish residents sought refuge in places where they hoped to find peace as well as the oppor-tunity to continue their religious practices. Among the fugitives was the elderly and influential priest Mattathias and his five sons; they fled to a village a few miles from Jerusalem. Shortly, however, Mattathias dis-covered that he had not escaped the terror, for he was confronted with an official demand that he, as a recognized Jewish leader, must set an example for other Jews by his demonstration of obedience to the religious edicts of the government. The courageous defiance of the government by the aged man of religion is reported in the apocryphal book I Maccabees. "God forbid," he thundered, "that we should forsake the law and the ordinance." Then he and his five sons, joined by a constantly growing band of loyal supporters, fled into the rugged countryside to conduct a campaign of opposition to the oppressors.

Although Mattathias soon died, his sons, one by one, took over the leadership of the Jewish patriots who were determined to rid their country of a despotic government that was equally determined to squelch forever the Judaic movement. The five sons of Mattathias, four of whom ultimately lost their lives in the conflict, are known in Jewish history as the Maccabees, a term which is derived from the fact that Judah, the third son of Mattathias and an extremely popular and competent leader, was surnamed "the Maccabee," a word that in Hebrew may have meant "hammer head." The Jewish people continue to display their tremendous respect for the Maccabees; the ultimate victory of the Maccabees over the oppressors was responsible, many historical scholars are convinced, for the survival of Judaism. And without the survival of Judaism, it is hard to believe that Christianity would ever have come into being.

For thirty years, even after the death of Antiochus IV, the Judean hills and neighboring areas were the locale of the most vicious kind of guerrilla warfare; some of the roughest country in the Near East provided sanctuary for the Jewish loyalists who were defending their traditions and their rights. Rome, which rapidly was becoming a great power and which welcomed opportunities to further its expansionist goals, provided some encouragement to the Jewish patriots and became involved in some of the intrigue which, especially in its later stages, became a factor in the bitter struggle.

Often military action was supplemented by treachery and by political chicanery. That crucial period in Jewish history is so full of political complexities and had so much significance for the future of civilization that the development of its true story is a challenge to historians.

An account of the very important Maccabean period that provides remarkable reporting of the horrors of the persecution perpetrated by Antiochus on the Jews, as well as a record of the tremendous courage revealed by many Jews and the great faith that they displayed in their Judaic heritage, is provided by the apocryphal books First and Second

Maccabees. I Maccabees gives a detailed account of events that took place during the forty years that elapsed from the time that Antiochus IV became the ruler of Syria until the death of Simon, last of the five sons of Mattathias. II Maccabees treats less than half the same period but from quite a different point of view. I Maccabees, originally written in Hebrew, is merely a detailed historical narrative. By contrast, II Maccabees, written in Greek several decades after the time of the events it treats, possesses a strong religious flavor, so in addition to the historical value of the work it contributes to our understanding of certain aspects of Judaic thought apparently accepted by many progressive adherents to Judaism at that time in history.

Actually, the so-called author of II Maccabees, by his own admission, had utilized a voluminous history of the Maccabean period by a certain Jason of Cyrene when he wrote his book. But it appears that II Maccabees was written deliberately in such a way that it treated significant historical events within the perspective of what the author regarded as fundamental Judaic doctrine, at least as it was accepted by him and probably as it was accepted by the Jews with whom he was associated. It is important to note that the exposition of the Book emphasizes the religious importance and significance under some circumstances of martyrdom for one's faith. For instance, the Book tells of an aged man named Eleazer who was ordered by the oppressive government to violate the dietary laws. But, according to II Maccabees 6:30–31, rather than disobey principles that he regarded as fundamental to his faith, he chose death on "the rack," and

> As he was dying under the blows, he said with his last sigh, "The Lord in His sacred knowledge is aware that though I could escape death I now endure terrible suffering in my body under these floggings; yet within my soul I suffer this gladly because of my reverence for Him." In this way he died, leaving in his death an example of nobility and a memorial of valor, not only to the young but also to the great majority of the nation.*

In II Maccabees 7, it is also related that seven brothers with their mother, again because of a refusal to violate the strict dietary laws of Judaism, were subjected to unbelievable torture and death. As one by one they suffered and died, they mocked their executioners with such words as:

*The Second Book of Maccabees, translated by Sidney Tedesche and edited with commentary by Solomon Zeitlin (New York: Harper & Brothers, 1954), p. 159.

> You may release us from our present existence, but the King of the Universe will raise us up to everlasting life because we have died for His laws.

> Do not vainly deceive yourself. We suffer these things because of ourselves, because we sinned against our own God.

> Better is it for people to be done to death by men if they have the hopeful expectation that they will again be raised up by God, but as for you, there will be no resurrection to life.*

The reference to the concept of resurrection in the previous quotation provides interesting confirmation, along with other quite similar references in Judaic literature, that during the Hellenistic era of Jewish history many interpreters of Judaic doctrine, including the Pharisees, accepted the idea that the resurrection of the body after death could and would occur under some circumstances. The significance of this as a factor in the development of Christian doctrine cannot be ignored, for Paul, who created the original, although an elementary, Christian theology, was a Pharisee. Also it may be observed that the particular reference just quoted, especially the part pertaining to the possibility of resurrection, has special meaning for historians of Christianity if, as some astute analysts now believe, the unknown author of II Maccabees was one of the progressive Hellenistic Jews in Antioch, which became an early citadel of Christianity where many elements of Christian doctrine must have been expounded.

In 142 B.C., as victory in the long Maccabean struggle finally seemed to be assured for the Jewish patriots, Simon, the last surviving son of Mattathias, was acclaimed by members of the populace as their new ruler; in fact, he became the chief priest as well as the secular leader. As a result of such actions, the theocratic concept of government established in the days of Ezra and which in some of its aspects had continued to be accepted in a formal way even by Antiochus IV and his successors was replaced by a commonwealth. Simon, it appears, was an unusually competent organizer, and he rebuilt the political system of the nation around a series of courts that was surmounted by the High Court, also known as the Sanhedrin, in Jerusalem. The Sanhedrin in Jerusalem had legislative as well as judicial functions. (Some highly regarded Judaic scholars insist, and with strong supporting evidence, that the courts created by Simon were of two kinds, religious Sanhedrins and civil Sanhedrins; each kind

*Ibid, p. 163.

90

had well-defined functions. Unfortunately, many questions pertaining to the nature of the government in Judea during Roman times have not been resolved in a way that has received general acceptance by Judaic historians.)

After Simon became a victim of treachery, his own third son, John Hyrcanus, took advantage of existing political circumstances to cast himself into the same role that Simon had held; that is, Hyrcanus became both the chief secular officer and the chief religious officer of the nation. Then he moved quickly to strengthen his position by outmaneuvering Ptolemy of Egypt. But still he had to contend with the armies of the rulers of Syria who continued to insist, as they had throughout the Maccabean struggle, that Judea was within the realm of their overall governmental control. Ultimately, following a series of fortunate happenings, Hyrcanus was able to ignore the continuing challenge of the Syrians. Moreover, as a result of successful military campaigns conducted with the aid of mercenaries, he was able to achieve predominance in the political life of a large part of Palestine. Among the nations which he conquered was Samaria, a small political entity north of Judea, and Idumea, a nation to the south that involved a substantial part of the area now designated as the Negev. The conquest of Idumea holds special interest for students of Christian history since Antipater, then a powerful figure in Idumea and soon to be a powerful political figure in Judea, was the father of Herod, who was the nominal ruler of Judea when Jesus was born. There were further conquests in Palestine by Hyrcanus and by his two immediate successors, so Judea, during the early part of the century preceding the time of Jesus, became a powerful nation in the Near East.

The great political and military successes achieved by Hyrcanus led him to announce that he was assuming the title of king. The Pharisees, a Judaic brotherhood described later, which was dominant at that time in determining the nature of Judaic belief and practice, immediately opposed the idea; they did not like Hyrcanus and many of his policies, and, in addition, since the Pharisees were strong advocates of Messianic prophecy, they were concerned that Hyrcanus was not of the house of David. Hyrcanus then threw his support to the Sadducees, another Judaic brotherhood which was less influential than the Pharisees, and he ordered the Jews to ignore the Pharisees and their Biblical interpretations. The country was soon in turmoil. But the Pharisees, in spite of the oppression to which they were subjected, succeeded in preventing Hyrcanus from becoming king.

After his death, Hyrcanus was succeeded by his son, Aristobulus, who immediately assumed the title of chief priest and also proclaimed himself to be king, thereby changing the commonwealth to a kingdom. Again the Pharisees proclaimed their objection, and soon the country was in an uproar. Aristobulus became fearful of anyone and everyone, and he even imprisoned his mother and his brother to thwart any ambitions for power that they might have. Aristobulus died after only a year in his highly controversial position. Then his clever widow, Alexandra, moved quickly to marry Alexander Jannaeus, a brother of Aristobulus. Apparently Alexandra believed that her marriage to Jannaeus would eliminate some of the bitter feeling that existed in the country since Jannaeus, like his brother, was a descendant of Mattathias, and Jannaeus seemed to be more popular than Aristobulus. But Jannaeus continued the program of Aristobulus, so the turmoil within the country became intensified; physical violence became common. The Pharisees suffered greatly; thousands of them were massacred, and, it appears, many of those who survived fled the country. Ultimately Jannaeus crushed his opposition and thus won complete control of the nation; that control lasted for twenty-six years, that is, until 78 B.C. During his long reign, Jannaeus survived several ill-conceived external military ventures along with a variety of plots against his life and his rule. In spite of his many difficulties, Jannaeus succeeded before he died in expanding the territories under his control.

It appears that Alexander Jannaeus, as a device for facilitating an expansion of the political influence of Judea, decided to take deliberate steps to increase the number of people in Palestine who were affiliated with the Judaic faith, for it seems to have been at his initiative that a specific policy was pursued of trying to convert to Judaism the pagan peoples in Palestine. The maintenance of such an active policy of missionary activity was unusual at that time in the history of religion.

Probably, however, the idea of trying to persuade selected pagan peoples to change their religious affiliation to Judaism did not originate with Jannaeus. Starting in about the third century B.C., a new and interesting trend developed in the thinking of the rabbis of Judea; they began to employ a distinctive method of analysis, employing both logic and psychological insight, as they attempted to isolate previously undetected meanings in many sections and phrases of their Bible. The result was a considerable broadening in interpretation and in suggested applications of the Holy Work. The dynamic period in rabbinical study that was inaugurated at that time and which continued for several centuries is often characterized as the Period of Rabbinic Judaism; it was a period of much shrewd analysis of fundamental Judaic concepts and principles, some of which had an effect on early Christian thought. As a result of some of the analyses which the rabbis pursued, it was concluded that a person has the right to change his religious affiliation. No explicit treatment of such a subject appears in the Torah. Obviously then it was an easy step from an acceptance of the idea that a person has the right to make a change in his religious affiliation to an attempt by militant Judaic advocates to urge a person to take advantage of that right.

According to Gospel accounts in the Christian New Testament, Jesus, obviously familiar with Judaic missionary policy which seems to have been well established by the time of the first century A.D., instructed his followers to work actively to convert nonbelievers to acceptance of the religious principles which he advocated. Undoubtedly the Judaic missionary activity that was under way at that time provided a good foundation for the work of the missionaries of Christianity. For the advocacy by Judaism of an invisible God beyond human comprehension along with the rites associated with the worship of that God had an appeal to many non-Jews, especially the Greeks, who possessed a philosophical and mystical turn of mind. The Judaic concept of morality and social justice based on such notions as the brotherhood of man and the fatherhood of God, so important to Pharisaic philosophy, also had a very strong appeal for persons who had no previous experience with such ideas. All of these factors were as applicable to the work of the Christian missionaries as they were to the work of the Judaic missionaries. For many years after the time of Jesus, the aggressive endeavors of some Judaic missionaries provided strong competition to the early Christian missionaries. On the other hand, Christianity profited from the fact that some of the early Christian missionaries had originally been Judaic missionaries, so they continued to practice many of the techniques that had become familiar to them in their earlier role; possibly Paul could be categorized as such a person.

After the death of Alexander Jannaeus, his widow, Alexandra, moved quickly to assume his powers. Since Alexandra, being a woman, could not occupy the position of chief priest of Judea, she appointed her incompetent son, Hyrcanus, to that office. Her other son, Aristobulus, who possessed a keen intellect, became known in the nation as an able military leader, but since he was regarded by his mother as a potential rival, he was deliberately isolated from opportunities that could provide him too much power. Alexandra proved to be a cunning and competent administrator; in fact, she continued to rule the nation, still a kingdom, for nine years. Shortly after assuming her position as ruler of the country, Alexandra took steps to renew the traditional recognition given to the Pharisees, and she released from prison many Pharisees who were held there. Such an action proved to be very important in providing her the kind of public support that was necessary to sustain her in her position.

When Alexandra died, shortly after she had inducted Hyrcanus into the kingship as her successor, alert Aristobulus quickly took command of both the civil and religious structures of the state. At that moment, however, the previously mentioned Antipater, then military governor of Idumea, became a significant character in the plot of the Judean drama that was unfolding. Wise, cunning, and unscrupulous, Antipater soon revealed an amazing capacity to stay out of the limelight and yet be able to manipulate the key people as well as the action of the real-life story that was taking place in Judea at that particular time in history. First, Antipater engineered a civil war between the two factions of the populace, headed, respectively, by Aristobulus and Hyrcanus. At the height of the turmoil, Pompey, one of the generals who were then contending for power in Rome, saw an opportunity to move into the picture, hopefully to win dominion over Judea and thereby gain an important stepping-stone on his way toward his desired conquest of much of the Near East. The tide of battle, which soon involved some of Pompey's legions serving the cause of Hyrcanus, fluctuated from one side to the other. Finally, in 63 B.C., apparently Pompey introduced more of his well-trained legions into the fray, for he quickly terminated the struggle by overwhelming the defenders of Jerusalem. Large numbers of the Jewish inhabitants of the city were massacred by the Roman soldiers, but Pompey ordered that the great Temple be spared. The conquest of Jerusalem by Pompey effectively terminated the existence of an independent Jewish nation. Two millennia were to elapse—until, in fact, modern Israel was formally created in A.D. 1948—before the Jewish people would again have their own independent state.

Chapter Five

JUDEA UNDER ROMAN CONTROL

ITS POLITICAL LIFE

After Pompey had taken control of Jerusalem, thereby making Judea a Roman province, he installed the weak Hyrcanus as chief priest of Judea and as the ethnarch, the chief secular officer, of the nation. According to the political plan created by Pompey for a large section of the Middle East, Hyrcanus had to serve under the general jurisdiction of the Roman governor of Syria. Working behind the scene was the wily Antipater, providing guidance to Hyrcanus in his new responsibility of trying to overcome the fears and concerns of the Jewish populace and of mediating the new political relationships with the governor of Syria and with the authorities in Rome. Some members of the populace appeared to welcome the new political climate under the strong Roman control, for the country was comparatively quiet and the Romans seemed to be tolerant of the religious practices of the inhabitants. But most of the citizens were very unhappy because of the loss of the nation's independence. All of the people of Judea realized, of course, that Hyrcanus was a mere pawn in the political game being played by Roman officialdom.

In 48 B.C., Pompey's armies were defeated by the veteran soldiers of Julius Caesar, the ambitious military genius who rapidly had become dominant in the Roman political hierarchy. Antipater, controlling virtually every move of Hyrcanus, immediately moved to the side of Caesar and won the great respect and admiration of his new Roman superior by providing him invaluable assistance. Consequently, Antipater was officially designated by Rome as prime minister of Judea while Hyrcanus retained the meaningless title of ethnarch; in addition, Antipater was made a Roman citizen. At once, Jerusalem began to receive many favors from Rome; the controlling political interests even put on displays of respect for Judaism; in general, the Jewish population rejoiced at the turn of events. When Julius Caesar was assassinated in 44 B.C., genuine sadness prevailed among the people of Judea.

Shortly after the death of Julius Caesar, Antipater also died, and Herod, his son, contrived to become the head of the nation, ruling through Hyrcanus. Herod undertook his new responsibilities with a severe handicap, for he was already unpopular; probably, in addition, he was afflicted with serious psychiatric difficulties. Certainly the Jewish populace of Jerusalem regarded him as a reprehensible character because of several sordid episodes in which he had been involved before he took over his new responsibilities and because of his earlier leadership of military operations against the followers of Hezekiah, a popular Jewish hero who lived in the rugged country north of Jerusalem. The hapless ruler attempted to ameliorate some of the criticisms that constantly plagued him in the early days of his rule by becoming the escort and finally the husband of Mariamne, a descendant of Mattathias since she was the granddaughter of both Aristobulus and Hyrcanus, but still he was not accepted by a majority of the Judean Jews. In fact, throughout Herod's long rule, which lasted until 4 B.C., he found little peace; he had to face virtually continuous opposition from within and without the nation. When attempting to crush his antagonists, he did not hesitate to indulge in ruthless methods. Several times, in fact, he slaughtered thousands of people. Ultimately, even his wife, the grandfather and the brother of his wife, his sister's husband, and his three sons did not escape Herod's wrath; all were executed. A system of spying on members of the populace was instituted, so the climate of fear that soon existed often caused people to shrink from engaging in conversation or even from indulging in some common activities. It appears that the Pharisees, although still influential with the public, played a somewhat subdued role during Herod's reign, but it may be true that some of the Sadducees catered to the whims of the tyrannical ruler. The complexity of the political situation induced by some of Herod's actions was magnified by intrigue on the part of several surviving descendants of Mattathias. Especially severe complications were introduced into the situation when Herod lost the support of his wife, Mariamne; at her husband's order, she was executed. After her execution, Herod suffered, according to the historian Josephus, from almost unbearable remorse. The Talmud, influential religious work of the Jews, contains a bizarre account of Herod spending much time with Mariamne's embalmed body and actually having carnal intercourse with her corpse, obviously the actions of a person with a broken mind. After Mariamne's death, Herod had to deal with a new collection of bothersome problems caused by the fact that he soon took nine wives; at one time he had all nine of the scheming and jealous women living together in his palace. Herod's sister, the beautiful Salome, added to the tensions in the household by often playing the role of villain. The continuing struggle for political power in Rome was also the cause of many headaches for Herod; he had to step gingerly in determining to whom he should give his allegiance. Several times the problems with Rome involved the behind-the-scenes manipulations of Cleopatra, who was having a love affair with the Roman Antony.

In view of the real and imagined conspiracies with which Herod continually had to contend, which often seemed to pose physical danger for him, he utilized for purposes of safety and relaxation the fortress on Masada, a virtually inaccessible high plateau overlooking the Dead Sea. In fact, Herod was responsible for expanding and perfecting the extensive living facilities and fortifications on Masada, which have been revealed in recent years as a result of excavations directed by Yigael Yadin, distinguished Israeli archaeologist and military genius.

In the early days of Herod's administration he gave unswerving loyalty to Antony, his superior in Rome. This faithfulness was rewarded by Antony at several critical points in Herod's career; in truth, it is likely that without Antony's backing Herod's administration would have been terminated within a few years after he took office. Moreover, it was because of Antony's support that ultimately Herod was given the designation "king," thereby eliminating any possibility that his role in the Judean government would be regarded as secondary to that of Hyrcanus. When Antony committed suicide, following a similar act by Cleopatra, Herod quickly and easily transferred his loyalty to Octavian, Roman successor to Antony.

Octavian was either a great democrat or a master of public relations, for very soon he made the announcement that he was renouncing the great power to which he had succeeded in Rome; in fact, he took the early step of requesting the Roman Senate to restore Rome to its earlier status as a republic, a form of government that seemed to be compatible with the democratic thinking then in vogue among the Romans. A grateful Senate quickly conferred on Octavian the title "Augustus" and actually voted him extensive political control over the Roman empire.

In view of Herod's recognized administrative competence as well as loyalty, he quickly became an invaluable person in the new decentralized political structure that Augustus created for the eastern part of the Empire; actually, a close friendship developed between the two men. This friendship, however, was tested severely in the latter days of Herod's life when a series of sinister machinations engineered by Salome and one of her suitors, with the assistance of Herod's own son Antipater, involved the purveyance to Augustus of false charges against Herod. Nevertheless, Herod survived all plots against him and died a natural but painful death in 4 B.C., just shortly after the probable date of the birth of Jesus.

From an objective point of view, Herod was a very competent administrator; in fact, he has been designated by some historians as Herod the Great. He had an efficient system for the collection of taxes and he eliminated unemployment by means of the development of a vast system of public works. Among the many projects initiated by Herod, the one that was especially successful in winning the good will of the people was the rebuilding of the great Temple. But the work was not completed for two thirds of a century after his death. Only a few years after the completion of the Temple, the great edifice was permanently destroyed by the Romans. The Temple structure that was ultimately constructed as a result of Herod's initiative was larger and more magnificent than the original Temple of Solomon. The new Temple, which apparently was about half completed when Jesus made his last visit to Jerusalem, featured a large façade in Greek style. Between the elaborate façade and the inner sanctuary was a collection of three "courts"; each court was designed to accommodate a particular category of pilgrims or Temple visitors. The inner sanctuary was divided into three sections: the Vestibule, the Holy Place, and the Holy of Holies. The Holy Place was the locale of devotional services that involved large choirs of singers and ensembles of harps, and it was also the place where sacrifices and related ceremonies were conducted by the large number of priests always in attendance. The Holy of Holies contained the Holy Ark of Yahweh; the doors to that most sacred of all places were constantly sealed except on Yom Kippur when the High Priest entered to enact a rite that possessed tremendous significance for the faithful. During the last part of the B.C. period and the first part of the A.D. era, the Temple, although obviously a religious shrine of great meaning for the Jewish people, was, along with its environs, a popular gathering place for local residents as well as for outsiders, including the large number of pilgrims who were visitors to Jerusalem. Consequently, assorted vendors chose the Temple grounds as a desirable location to peddle their wares. It is likely that the commotion in the court of the Temple was often very great as aggressive hucksters solicited customers and as loud haggling took place between hundreds of merchants and prospective buyers.

When Herod died, the large territory which he and his predecessors had acquired was dismembered; each of his three surviving sons became the ruler, known as a tetrarch, of one of the three parts. Archelaus, eldest of the three sons, who clearly had less administrative ability than either of his two brothers, became tetrarch of Judea, which at that time included Samaria to the north and Idumea to the south. Virtually as soon as Archelaus took over his responsibilities, revolt, which had been smoldering throughout Herod's rule, broke out in much of the region under his jurisdiction. It soon became clear to officials in Rome and also to the Roman governor of Syria, who had general jurisdiction over Judea, that Archelaus was unable to cope with the situation. The inevitable collapse of the inept tetrarch's administration was delayed, however, when the governor of Syria sent some of his Roman legions to try to restore order. In an attempt to curb the rebellious tendencies within the populace, some two thousand Jews in Jerusalem and its vicinity were taken into custody by the new contingent of Roman soldiers, acting under the command of the Syrian governor; shortly thereafter, the detained individuals were crucified. Crucifixion, an extremely cruel form of torture and death, was a Roman form of punishment that was regarded by the Jewish people as contrary to the teachings of their Bible and thus was anathema to them. Ultimately Archelaus was replaced in Judea by a new governor who was awarded the novel title "procurator"; thus the new governor became the first in a series of procurators. Pontius Pilate, associated in Christian history with the death of Jesus, was the fifth in the series.

The procurators served within the Roman political tradition of that day, which provided for a considerable amount of self-government. In fact, it is common for historians to comment upon the fact that to a great extent during the time of the procurators the people of Judea were in charge of their own affairs; they faced few governmental barriers when pursuing their commercial, civil, and religious interests. Actually, each procurator, who was responsible only to the Roman Emperor, had vast power, but most of the time he exercised that power in a discreet manner. The High Court, also known as the Sanhedrin and created originally by Simon, was continued by the Romans without any major change. The continuation of the Sanhedrin without any important modification was very important for the Jewish people, since it had come to represent for them an institutional expression of their autonomy. The Sanhedrin functioned independently of the Roman civil authorities when making its decisions upon religious questions and upon local law; it determined the levies needed for the operation of the Temple, and it answered questions pertaining to family life and the calendar. Of considerable importance for the people was the fact that the Sanhedrin determined the punishment, sometimes severe, to be imposed upon persons who had broken the religious law. Originally, the Sanhedrin could invoke the death penalty, but evidence exists that the Romans, starting during the reign of Herod, refused the right of the Jewish judges to impose such an extreme penalty.

But in spite of the privileges granted to the Jewish people in Judea, all was not sweetness and light. Increasingly, as time progressed, the procurators seemed to bypass official procedures through the use of illicit methods; there were rumors within the populace of bribe taking, and there were charges of corruption. Moreover, the high priests who officiated at the rites held in the Temple were appointed by the chief secular officer, who was a Roman. The practice was initiated by Simon, but, in the beginning, the appointing officers were Jewish; now they were Roman. Apparently, a considerable amount of bribery was involved in the appointment of the high priests, but, most important, a high priest, anxious to serve the wants of the particular procurator who was responsible for his holding high office, could usually be relied upon in an important civil or criminal trial to be a willing witness to provide testimony of a kind that would satisfy the ruling officer. Thus political expediency rather than justice soon became the more important criterion for the determination of punishment in cases that were not within the jurisdiction of the Sanhedrin; it became easy for a procurator to make away with a person who provided a challenge to his authority or for whom he had developed a disliking. Many of the high priests, obviously, became despised persons. Moreover, although the Romans were known for their well-conceived systems of taxation, it appears that the procurators learned how, in subtle ways, to manipulate the system of taxation to serve their own purposes. Everything was taxed: people, donkeys and other animals, houses, business transactions, and imports and exports. Complaints about taxation became loud and common, chiefly because the money was used to subsidize the government that occupied the country. The mere presence of large numbers of Roman soldiers continually antagonized the freedom-loving Jews.

As a result, the procurators were plagued with more and more difficulties in their dealings with the populace; in fact, members of the public displayed growing disrespect for their Roman rulers. The turbulent condition in Judea was rapidly approaching a state of civil conflict between the Roman rulers, supported by their legions, and the members of the populace. The turmoil was intensified by the growth in strength among the Jewish people of fanatic dissident groups. Chief among the latter were the Zealots, who have been described by historians in both complimentary and uncomplimentary terms. Probably the Zealots should be regarded as members of a militant Judaic party, possibly a branch of the Pharisaic community; their watchword was "No God but Yahweh, no tax but to the Temple, no friend but the Zealot." The Zealots seemed to have considerable support within the populace as they often indulged in violent tactics to embarrass the Romans who occupied their country. The motivation of the Zealots is unclear. Some students of Jewish history believe that they were attempting to create conditions that they thought would serve to bring about an early fulfillment of Messianic prophecy pertaining to the arrival in Judea of the great and powerful king from the House of David. In addition to the assistance to the nation that such a king would provide, personal salvation, many people had come to believe, depended on his arrival. The turbulent political conditions that existed at that time in Judea caused many fanatical visionaries to believe that the day of the Messiah must be at hand, and, consequently, some of them may have believed that they should do what they could to facilitate his arrival. Some fanatics even went about the countryside shouting, "The world is coming to an end; prepare for the arrival of the Messiah."

Although all the procurators had to contend with serious conditions of unrest within the populace, the situation was approaching a state of crisis during the time of Pontius Pilate. By contrast with his predecessors, Pilate often indulged in displays of the great authority which had been vested in him by Rome, thereby increasing the antagonism of the freedom-loving Jews. The hostility of the Jewish citizens toward Pilate reached a crucial state when apparently he attempted to draw upon the treasury of the Temple to finance a huge aqueduct. Finally, after a decade in his position, Pontius Pilate was removed by his superiors in Rome.

A short interlude of comparative tranquility then followed for the people of Judea when Agrippa, grandson of Herod, became the procurator. Agrippa indulged in tactics that won him much favor from his subjects, and he displayed political sagacity. But his superiors began to have suspicions in regard to his motives, for some of his actions seemed to indicate that he was moving in the direction of reestablishing an independent and strong Jewish nation. Consequently, after only three years, Agrippa's reign was abruptly terminated by Rome.

At once the latent revolutionary forces within the populace were released, and the Jews indulged in every conceivable tactic to harass the Romans. As Roman patience became exhausted, Jewish leaders were crucified on the slightest pretext, and Roman soldiers did not hesitate to torture and kill their Jewish tormentors. Such actions by the Romans, however, only served to stimulate the Jews to further resistance. It became impossible to govern Jerusalem. Simultaneously, the Jewish people became restive and combative in other Jewish centers of the Roman Empire, in Alexandria, in Antioch, and elsewhere. Consequently, through the adoption of new procedures and policies, Rome hardened its attitude toward the Jews generally, thus causing an even greater intensification of the antagonism displayed by the Judean populace. Simultaneously, the quality of leadership provided by the Roman leaders in their governance of the Empire seemed to deteriorate; the wise administrative policies introduced by Octavian generally had been discarded. Consequently, a bloody confrontation between the Jewish people in several localities of the Roman Empire and their Roman conquerors seemed imminent.

In A.D. 66, Florus, procurator of Judea at that time, became the subject of much abuse from the people because of the fact that he took money from the Temple treasury to take care of the substantial arrears that existed in the tax collections; he reacted by slaughtering six hundred Jews. That event was all that was needed to trigger a great rebellion of the Jewish people living in Judea; for four years thereafter the Jews and the Romans would strike at each other with every conceivable kind of savagery, rarely matched in the history of human conflict. During that time a rebel band of Jews captured the Masada, and slaughtered all the Roman defenders. About the same time, three thousand Roman soldiers, who had been rushed to help the Roman defenders of the fortress in Jerusalem, were trapped by the Jewish patriots and were massacred along with the defenders; often trickery was employed by the Zealots and other Jewish rebels to accomplish their ends. Cestius Gallus, Roman representative in Antioch, much disturbed by the turn of events, rushed additional Roman troops to Jerusalem, but, after encountering the bitter resistance that the Jewish patriots offered, they retreated in disarray, leaving thousands of their dead on the battlefield. The victory-maddened

Jews quickly followed through by clearing the Romans from one third of Palestine. The Roman Emperor Nero, now realizing that he must deal urgently and severely with a very real and serious situation, sent the competent Vespasian and 50,000 men to recover the lost territory. Slowly and systematically, although the Jewish defenders fought brilliantly and often desperately, Vespasian's legions successfully subdued all the previously lost area of Palestine with the exception of Jerusalem. The attempt to conquer Jerusalem was interrupted when Vespasian was called back to Rome to become the Emperor, the successor to the deceased Nero.

Shortly thereafter, however, Vespasian decided to complete the task of conquest, so he sent his veteran troops, now under the command of his competent son Titus, to set siege to the City of David. Although some of the walls had been strengthened by Agrippa, he had not been permitted to complete the fortifications which he had planned. So with the great mechanical war machines that the Romans had available, breaches were made in the protective ramparts of the city; shortly thereafter the defenders were overwhelmed, and most of the great city was devastated. Structures of special significance to the Jewish people, including the great Temple, were systematically destroyed. And thousands of residents of the city, men, women, and children—virtually all, apparently, who could not escape—were massacred. The date, A.D. 70, is recalled with infamy in the history of the Jewish people. After the destruction of Jerusalem, some Jewish citizens of Judea, probably including a few who had escaped from Jerusalem, took refuge from the Roman conquerors in the fortress of Masada. There, after holding out for three years against a series of strong assaults by the Romans, all the surviving defenders, approximately one thousand according to Josephus, chose self-inflicted death rather than surrender to the Roman oppressors.

As a conclusion to the tragic events, a Roman garrison was left in control of Jerusalem. Then, in A.D. 132, after an unsuccessful attempt by a new generation of Jewish patriots to reestablish Jerusalem as the heart of a free Jewish nation, the Romans utterly destroyed what little remained of the ancient and Holy City. In fact, a Roman edict ordered all Jews permanently excluded from the city that was originally conceived by David as the citadel of their faith and as the capital of their nation. Moreover, in a gesture of disdain for the Jews and for all that was dear to them, the Romans rebuilt part of the Holy City to cater, apparently, to the worst features of the pagan Roman culture of that day. Although the

Jews were forced out of Jerusalem, many of them continued to live in Palestine.

To a great extent, the events just described signaled the end for many centuries of any serious attempt by the Jews to have their own nation. During the long interlude, however, vast numbers of the Jewish people continued to live with their dream that some day the promises of the Lord to Abraham could and would be realized. Individual Jews and colonies of Jews, descendants of the Biblical Jews or descendants of later peoples converted to Judaism, are found today in most of the countries of the world. Some Jewish colonies, such as the Falashas in Ethiopia, have lived such an isolated existence for so many centuries that, although they subscribe to the basic tenets of Judaism and observe the common Judaic holidays, they have developed other religious practices and ideas that are distinctive within the framework of Judaism. Most Jews, while jealously guarding the fundamentals of their Judaic culture, have made important adaptations and significant contributions to the kind of life maintained by the non-Jewish peoples who have been their hosts, sometimes unfriendly hosts. It is common among the Jewish people to speak of the Diaspora, the scattering of the Jews outside their homeland, to which they have been subjected for nearly two thousand years, actually until the creation of modern Israel provided a new homeland for those Jews who chose to accept its hospitality. The fact that through the long years of the Diaspora the Jews have been able to maintain their integrity as a people with a distinctive culture must be acknowledged to be one of the miracles of history; it was Judaism, candid analysis seems to reveal, that supplied for the scattered Jewish people the necessary powerful bond of unification.

JUDAISM IN JUDEA DURING ROMAN TIMES

In spite of the turbulent political situation that existed in Judea during Roman times, the political period during which Jesus was born, Judaism became an increasingly vibrant religion. Possibly it was partly because of the demoralizing effects on the populace of the existing chaotic political situation that the leaders of Judaism were encouraged to give renewed attention to the meaning for the citizens of Judea of the religion to which most of them professed allegiance. Thus it may have been more than mere coincidence that the Roman era of Judean history included much of the early part of the Period of Rabbinic Judaism, already mentioned, when new generations of well-educated rabbis, many of whom were true intellectuals, discussed and debated traditional Judaic concepts and principles. Although the rabbis who were active in the movement accepted without question the Judaic Bible, especially the Torah, as basic to all their considerations, they recognized that its content should be subjected to careful analysis and that when determining answers to man's problems of an ethical nature even the Judaic Holy Work usually needs interpretation. During the several centuries of intense intellectual activity on the part of many of the Judaic rabbis, Judaic philosophy underwent a considerable amount of modification which ultimately was reflected in significant changes in the rules and laws promulgated to provide guidance to the Judaic faithful.

Any modifications of common Judaic precepts that the scholarly rabbis might ultimately persuade the Judaic leadership to accept, even modifications that might appear to be of comparatively minor importance, could have a significant effect upon life in Judea, for Judaism virtually defined the nature of Judean culture. This had been true for many years, long before the time of the Roman control of Judea. Judaism had become the most important and the most influential factor in determining the day by day elements of life for most of the Jewish people in Palestine. Although the Jewish people had lived through many difficult times since the days of the Exodus, and although there had been numerous and continuing challenges to Judaism from pagan neighbors and conquerors, the Judaic movement had developed great strength and momentum. To a great extent, this was a result of the fact that so many of its adherents were determined to maintain a way of life that would be consistent with the teachings of Moses, teachings which also provided the Jewish people a driving sense of national purpose and destiny.

But in common with all maturing religious traditions, Judaism had become strongly organized and formalized, both with respect to the ideas which it fostered and in its practices. Prescribed patterns of behavior were accepted and followed by a majority of the Jewish people in their religious activities, which reached deeply into virtually every aspect of life. It must be observed, however, that not all members of the Jewish population of Jerusalem and neighboring areas professed unquestioned belief in all the fundamentals of Judaism as usually taught; apparently similar divergencies in attitude toward Judaic doctrine and practice have always been found within the total Jewish community. Perhaps the constant challenge to the tenets of Judaism in whole or in part, as posed by Jewish dissenters, has served through the ages to cause adherents to the Judaic faith to indulge in frequent analytical studies of their position; the probable net consequence of the continuing debates on even some of the basic elements of Judaism has been a remarkable fortification of the Judaic movement against those who would destroy it.

The Judaic tradition emphasized during the Roman period, as is true at the present time, that great reverence and respect must be accorded to the Bible. Children soon sensed from their studies and observations that the Bible is the basic guide to life; they soon learned to accept as an axiom of life that it is through the Bible that one learns the will of God. The Scriptures were studied intensively, and key passages were recited every day. The Bible was regarded as a treasure in every Judaic home, and it was properly safeguarded. In addition, children were taught that man has access to God through prayers. Although a rudimentary form of prayer had been a part of some of the primitive religions, the concept of prayer as we now know it, so important in the Christian tradition as well as in the Judaic tradition, was introduced to man by Judaism. The concept, as noted in the following paragraph, was a product of its own interesting process of evolution.

The early Hebrews, as already observed, adopted as basic to the practice of their faith the pagan notion of sacrifice. Moses, for example, indulged in the practice of sacrifice and the rites associated with it. The great Temple built by Solomon took on its aura of deep meaning for followers of Judaism, at least in part, because of the fact that it was the approved location for the sacrificial rituals. Although Judaism adopted the sacrificial ritual from the pagans, it appears that in the course of time the event took on a meaning for the Hebrews that was quite different from that associated with the event by the pagans. The sacrificial ritual for the Hebrews became their means of sharing their blessings with their God, who, although held in awe, was regarded as their beneficent friend who always remained in close proximity. Probably the liturgy that accompanied the sacrifice was designed to assure God of the respect of those who were the participants in the ritual and to ask God's blessing and guidance. Thus, the Judaic liturgy associated with the sacrifice contained the rudiments of prayer. Even before the destruction of the Temple by Nebuchadnezzar, it had become officially approved practice for a considerable number of the faithful to gather in designated locations other than the Temple to indulge in much of the liturgy of the sacrificial ritual because of the virtual impossibility of attending the ceremonies in the Temple; the outside meetings were held simultaneously with the religious rites held in the Temple. Thus communication with God as an activity that was separated from the actual sacrificial event began to be recognized as approved and as highly desirable practice; the concept of prayer had been born. An edifice in which the faithful met for their prayers, that is, the place where they met to communicate with God, became known as a synagogue, the Judaic predecessor of the Christian Church. Some of the early rabbis are said to have called such a place of worship a *miqdash me'at,* a small sanctuary. During the Babylonian Captivity, of necessity, the edifices designated as synagogues became the chief institutions for the cultivation and the maintenance of the faith. Then when the Persians permitted the Jewish people to return to Judea, many preferred, as previously noted, to go to other parts of the Near East; such people erected synagogues in which to say their prayers.

It is an interesting fact that some forty synagogues from the Roman period have been excavated by modern archaeologists working in Palestine, and each one was built in the form of a Hellenistic-Roman basilica, a structure that possesses great outside pillars. That fact reveals, in part, something of the Hellenistic influence upon Judaic practices during that time in history. The very name "synagogue" comes from the Greek, a word that means "convocation." As the concept of synagogue continued to evolve through the years, its prime function increasingly became that of providing a place where there would be systematic study of the Torah; nevertheless, a synagogue continued to be a place for prayer. On the Sabbath and on festival days the faithful gathered in the synagogue to hear selected readings from the Torah and to listen to interpretations of that which was read.

Prayer, as the concept matured within the Judaic tradition, became an important demonstration of Judaic belief that man has direct access to God; no intermediary is necessary or even desirable. Through prayer, in fact, it was believed that man displays his belief in God. Moreover, to maintain his spiritual life, man should communicate with his God; he must tell God of his gratitude for His blessings; he must beseech Him for further help and guidance; he must experience the closeness to God that prayer makes possible. The true follower of Judaism must pray regularly at specified times and occasions, but, in addition, he is encouraged to indulge in prayer whenever he feels the urge to communicate with his God. Irrespective of circumstances, even for prayers that have been formulated in advance, prayers must come from the heart. Today as well as in Roman times, the Jew, bowing his head only upon a few fixed occasions when he prays, conveys the impression that he is merely conversing with the understanding God who he believes to be very close.

During the Roman period, the Judaic tradition emphasized, as is true at the present time, the importance of family and home; it was regarded as essential that children show proper respect for their parents, and it was stressed that parents must accept certain obligations for the upbringing of their offspring. At that early date it was already a recognized aspect of Judaic philosophy—a principle confirmed in modern times by psychologists—that a child's future habits, his attitudes, and his mental processes are strongly determined by the environment in which he lives during the first years of his life. Thus parents initiated the education of their children when they were very young; much of that education was informal and, when possible, involved participation by the children in regular activities of the family, including the periodic religious observances that were conscientiously carried out in the home. The annual Passover celebration was an event of especial significance, for all the Jewish people held to the belief that they must regard themselves as among those saved from bondage in Egypt; the children soon sensed the importance of the occasion.

Since Judaic philosophy regards the world as capable of sanctification, many of the happenings in the home, even some of the simple events of daily life, became occasions for the giving of blessings and the offering of thanks to the Lord. Inherent in all of the instruction provided for children was the idea that God is to be accepted as a friend, a friend who is always very close and whose guidance should be sought in connection with virtually every kind of human endeavor.

In addition to instruction in the teachings of the Torah and in the wisdom provided by other written as well as unwritten sources of knowledge of the Judaic tradition, children at an early date received assistance in learning the several languages then in vogue and in learning how to handle some of the practical needs of life. In fact, the Talmud, great source book of Judaic wisdom, directs a father to teach his sons a trade; Jesus, according to testimony provided in the New Testament, learned carpentry from his father. Labor itself, the Talmud and other Judaic writings assert, is a religious duty; even Jewish men desiring to become rabbis, who were and are the recognized teachers of Judaism, are enjoined by the Talmud to master a trade even while pursuing their rabbinical studies. Children also learned in the home that procreation is a religious duty.

As specified in the covenant between Abraham and God, each male child was circumcised on the eighth day after his birth, even if the day came on the Sabbath. The ceremony of circumcision was often followed by a festive meal at which a special grace was recited. When a boy reached his early teens, he was expected to assume adult religious duties and responsibilities.

Each child, as a part of the informal educational program of the home, was made aware of the existence of the extremely important dietary laws, as specified by Judaic tradition and as such laws were believed by the Judaic faithful to have been approved by the Lord. Some foods must be rejected altogether. Some other foods and drinks were unacceptable unless they were kosher, that is, unless they were prepared in accordance with a prescribed set of strict regulations. Some of the dietary laws pertaining to foods probably had their origin in experiences that seemed to point to certain foods as the frequent cause of illness. Explanations that have been given of the origin of the majority of the laws seem to many students of Judaism to be of doubtful validity.

For many families within a comparatively large area surrounding Jerusalem the most important event of a lifetime was a pilgrimage to the great Temple in Jerusalem, where it was common to make a contribution to the Temple treasury. Three pilgrimages a year were prescribed for the Judaic faithful, but that was not possible for most people. Apparently the normal population of Jerusalem at the start of the first century A.D. was about 250,000 people, but, according to Josephus, the population often increased to as many as 2.5 million persons during the time of major religious festivals, such as during Passover or the Festival of Tabernacles. Such estimates probably represented exaggerations. The opportunity of visiting the great Temple was a tremendous experience for people from the rural areas. The large and ornate structure was awe-inspiring, and the religious pageantry associated with worship in the Temple was extremely impressive. It is said that on special occasions as many as 20,000 priests officiated at ceremonies within the Temple while huge throngs of people stood outside (and there were no loudspeaker systems). Discussions and debates, when devotional services were not in progress, were common in the Temple; often the debates, which were encouraged, were between those who were learned in Judaic doctrine and practice and those who were novices, including the young, or between those who held to orthodox views and those who questioned some aspects of the Judaic tradition. New Testament writings report that Jesus, at the age of twelve, participated in some of the discussions within the Temple. The annual trips to the Temple also provided opportunities for families to make purchases to satisfy some of their unusual needs. The Pharisees, who were in control of practices followed in the Temple, had strict regulations against money changers operating within the edifice, and even the sale of sacrificial birds and animals was prohibited inside the great structure, but in the court area surrounding the Temple money changers and vendors of every description maintained a thriving business.

Probably the most unhappy part of a pilgrimage to Jerusalem during the time when the Romans were in control, including the period during which Jesus died, was the obvious presence of large numbers of Roman soldiers; they remained aloof from the populace, for they regarded the Jews as hostile and as strange and difficult people. The Romans could not comprehend the arrogant spirit of independence that the Jews continually displayed as well as the pride in their heritage that they constantly revealed.

The organizational complexity inherent in the maturing Judaic movement and the variety of doctrinal interpretations and emphases which were possible within the broad framework of Judaism had, by the time of the Roman period, encouraged the development of a number of religious societies, two of which have already been mentioned. It appears that some of the religious societies should be designated as Judaic sects but probably others should be described as brotherhoods with generally accepted special missions within the Judaic program and organizational structure. The fact that such societies became so important and influential may be attributed, in part, to the Hellenistic influence.

Josephus in some of his writings, when telling of events that took place during the time of Jonathan of the Maccabean period (a century and a half before the Christian era), describes the Pharisees, the Sadducees, and the Essenes as the dominant *haeresis,* "school of thought." But it is known that other religious societies existed at that time, and apparently their number continued to grow. Josephus, from the perspective of the first century A.D., during which he lived, wrote that "the Pharisees are held to be the most authoritative exponents of the Law." Undoubtedly they constituted the largest of the religious societies, and it appears that at that time the Jews generally regarded them with great respect. The religious

110

ideas of the Pharisees, it was acknowledged by most of the Jewish people, were to be accepted as representing an authoritive interpretation of the Law. Josephus wrote, "Whatever the people do about divine worship, prayers, and sacrifices, they perform according to the direction of the Pharisees." The Pharisees, whose name was derived from their original designation as Separatists, probably were given their descriptive title because they actively attempted to separate themselves and those who followed their teachings from what they regarded as "Levitical impurity," which had become increasingly important as a factor in the religious thought of the nation since the days of the theocracy. The condemnation of Levitical impurity by the Pharisees, implied in much of what they did and said, was a consequence of the strong belief of the Pharisees in Messianic prophecy, a much-discussed subject at that time. The Pharisaic brotherhood had great concern that proper interpretations of the Law be made known and that the religious practices which were followed should be in accordance with its own canons of religious teaching. Thus the Pharisees considered it to be a major part of their responsibility to safeguard the sanctity of the Temple. Christianity, as well as Judaism, is indebted to the Pharisees for their preservation of prophetic wisdom with its emphasis on social justice and on the very important factor in Messianic belief that with the ultimate arrival of the Messiah all men would accept the fatherhood of God and the brotherhood of man. The Pharisees believed that man continues to exist in a new form after death; moreover, as already noted, a belief in the ultimate resurrection of the body, at least for some people, was a cardinal doctrine of the Pharisees. It would be a mistake to believe, as has been implied upon occasion by some Biblical students, that the Pharisees were extremely rigid in their viewpoints; much evidence exists that it was not unusual for them to find that Judaic doctrine permitted interpretation in a way that would provide significant assistance in meeting some pressing current need. In fact, it seems fair to say that the Pharisees were often quite liberal in their rendition of Biblical interpretations. Since the Pharisees regarded themselves as religious advocates, not as experts in fields other than Judaism, they took no partisan position on many subjects. The Pharisees gave much attention to the importance of a direct God-person relationship, and, because of that fact, some students of Judaism and Christianity seem to have developed the false belief that the Pharisees minimized the significance of cult and even of formal worship. Each individual, the Pharisees taught, has uninhibited access to God through prayer, and the laws of God take on meaning only insofar as they are accepted by each person as the modus operandi of his life. As one gives close attention to the religious philosophy advocated by the Pharisees, it becomes easy to believe that their ideas provided a favorable religious climate, undoubtedly reflected in the ideas of Paul, discussed later, for the nurture of Christianity.

The Pharisaic leadership believed that the very nature of Judaism is such that it demands continuous study and analysis with respect to its true meaning. During the Roman period, as already noted, many rabbis joined in such a belief. Thus in existence in Jerusalem at the start of the first century A.D., were two especially distinguished Pharisaic academies. It appears that the better known of the two was the one headed by Hillel. Hillel himself had tremendous influence on Judaic belief and practice. He emphasized, for instance, the importance of the Golden Rule; in the wording of Hillel, the Golden Rule was "What is hateful unto thee, do not do unto others." Strongly motivated young men, usually of great ability, came from far and wide to attend the Academy of Hillel; they wanted to sit at the feet of men who were regarded as the greatest masters of the age in their understanding of the Torah and in the manner in which they interpreted the Holy Work. The attempt was made in the school, drawing on the many Judaic resources that were available, to understand God's true meaning when in some manner He made known his wishes to Moses; the Torah, of course, was the basic textbook. Since it was a recognized premise of Judaic scholarship that the Torah is the fundamental source of information about God's designs for man's behavior and thought, the studies in the academy involved discussions of a wide range of subjects. Hillel taught a method of interpreting the Scriptures that was revolutionary. The net result of a person's use of the method was that he could interpret a section of the Biblical text in many ways; he could adapt the content of the section to a variety of circumstances. The young scholars educated in such a manner possessed great flexibility in using the Torah to find solutions to the problems of life.

It is said that Hillel had eighty disciples who were a product of the program of his academy. Some of them achieved great distinction. Most became influential in the religious life of Judea, but some embarked on ambitious missionary programs outside of Judea in behalf of their deeply held faith. One of them named Yohanan, of whom we have considerable knowledge, spent much time in Galilee, where Jesus was born; Galilee was regarded by the Judaic leadership as a fertile area for missionary activities. Galilee still had a heavy pagan population, and even many of those who had accepted Judaism had introduced unusual principles and concepts into their faith, probably arising from their intimate contact with pagan ideas and practices. Some adherents to Judaism in Galilee had become involved in faith healing, and some of them seemed to believe that individuals who were properly dedicated to the Judaic faith should anticipate the common occurrence of miracles. Yohanan, to whom reference has just been made, reported several times upon his utter frustration while in Galilee as he struggled in his missionary endeavors to overcome many strange ideas and to engender in his listeners what he regarded as a true understanding of Judaism.

Of very great importance for followers of Christianity is the fact that Paul, early advocate of Christianity and its greatest missionary, was one of those who underwent the rigorous program of religious instruction at the Academy of the House of Hillel, not the same academy as the Academy of Hillel. At the time when Paul was a student in the Academy of the House of Hillel, it was headed by Rabbi Gamaliel, son of Hillel. Thus Paul was well educated in Judaic doctrine and philosophy, which was apparent in his teachings and in his writings.

In the Christian New Testament, the Scribes are mentioned frequently along with the Pharisees. It is likely that there was a close relationship between the Pharisees and the Scribes (Hillel was a Scribe), but virtually nothing is known about the Scribes or the history of their society. It seems clear, however, that the Scribes were learned men who in the judgment of contemporary Jews had attained a very high level of competence in their ability to interpret Judaic principle and in their capacity to make judicious decisions upon religious and related issues. Certainly the opinions of the Scribes were widely respected; many of them were teachers and some served as judges.

During Roman times, the Sadducees had a much smaller membership than the Pharisees, and it appears that their influence with the populace was considerably less than that of the Pharisees, but the two groups, in some respects, were competitors. The Sadducees had a history of participation in political affairs that often was not popular with a majority of the people; thus they had quite limited support from within the Jewish community. Originally the Sadducees were known as Saddokites; they were priests who claimed to be descendants of the high priest Saddok, who lived during the time of Solomon. Saddok, in turn, professed to be a descendant of Phineas, the recipient, according to tradition, of a promise from God that the priestly dynasty of which he was the originator would have God's blessing and would have great influence upon the affairs of Israel. The Sadducees, whose following seemed to come essentially from the wealthy and the well-placed in Jewish society, were very conservative in their positions on religious subjects; in fact, they were extremely literal in their interpretation of Judaic principle; they resisted innovation. The Sadducees were often very critical of the Pharisees, for the Sadducees believed that many of the rulings of the Pharisees involving an interpretation of Judaic law were based on mere expediency rather than on careful reading and rigid acceptance of the wording of the Law. And some ideas of the Pharisees, including, for example, their ideas on life after death, were regarded by the Sadducees as extremely radical and as contrary to sound Judaic doctrine.

The Zealots, possibly a militant brotherhood of individuals who were also Pharisees, have been mentioned previously. Rabbinical literature conveys the impression that some Jewish leaders of the Roman period in history regarded the Zealots as unreasonable fanatics whereas others regarded them as true patriots and as extremely loyal to their religious traditions. The historian Josephus, not entirely objective in his appraisal, characterized one section of the Zealot brotherhood as Sicarii, which meant dagger wielders or assassins. The Zealots, it appears, did not hesitate to indulge in violence; as already observed, it was common for them to conduct campaigns of terror against representatives of Rome or against any other non-Jewish power that had control over their lives. Certainly the Zealots contributed mightily to the turbulent political situation that existed in Judea during the lifetime of Jesus of Nazareth.

Several monastic sects existed within the framework of organized Judaism during and before the Roman period. The troublesome times that existed provided a stimulus for some persons, especially those who possessed a particular kind of religious dedication, virtually to withdraw from society. Many of those who withdrew believed that the world in which they lived had become hopelessly bad, that it was impure, and that a holy war which would purify man was imminent. The monastic sect that was best known during the latter part of the B.C. period and the early part of the A.D. era was the society of Essenes. Several historians of that period gave considerable attention to the Essene sect, for its members, although accepting the basic tenets of Judaism, differed considerably from other adherents to Judaism in some of their ideas and practices. In fact, some followers of Judaism undoubtedly regarded the Essenes as an irrational force within the Judaic community. Pliny, Roman historian, wrote an interesting description of the Essenes (*Natural History*, 15), which presumably was based on reports that had been provided him by Romans with experience in occupied Judea. Pliny wrote:

> Lying west of the Dead Sea, and sufficiently distant to escape its noxious vapors, are the Essenes, who live apart from the world. They differ in a marvelous way from other people throughout the whole earth, for they have no women among them; they are strangers to sexual desire; they have no money; their only companions are the palm trees. Their number continually increases because of the large number of strangers who join them, driven to take up the customs of the Essenes by the tempest of fortune and wearied by the miseries of life. Thus it is, through a very long period of time, amazing as it may seem, the Essenes have continued to exist, without a single birth taking place within their habitation.

Pliny may have been misinformed when he described all of the Essenes as confirmed celibates; the winning of a wife and having a family were fundamental tenets of Judaism. In fact, recently translated materials that were written by Essenes seem to contradict Pliny's assertion in regard to universal celibacy for the members of the society. Nevertheless, it is likely that the kind of life followed by most members of the monastic sect served to deter women from sharing their life with them. Certainly Pliny's commentary must be accepted as authentic, however, in regard to the apparent fact that most of the Essenes had chosen to withdraw from society to live a quiet monastic life in the extremely desolate and rugged area to the west of the Dead Sea, but it appears that some members of the Essene society did live in towns of the area and others roamed the countryside, probably seeking recruits. Since the programmed activities of the sect were carried out in secret, very little knowledge of those activities is available; it is clear, however, that the Essenes maintained a highly disciplined and regimented kind of society.

The very existence of the Essene sect and somewhat similar sects provides a puzzle for Judaic historical scholars, for Judaism does not seem to be the kind of religion that would provide encouragement to its adherents to become affiliated with a sacred, monastic society. One cannot doubt, however, that the Judaic monastic sects reveal the influence of the Greek culture that had become so important in the life of most of the Near East during the latter part of the B.C. period; there is considerable resemblance, for example, between the kind of life maintained by members of the Essene community and that which was common to the Greek Pythagoreans.

In their quiet environment, the Essenes probably spent much time in study and meditation. And of very great importance, they collected and accumulated a vast library of manuscripts, notably Hebraica and Judaica; the latter were written in the several languages employed at that time in Judea. Moveover, like the Christian monks of the Middle Ages, the Essenes copied and recopied many documents, some of which now have tremendous value for scholars. In addition, some of the creative thinkers of the sect composed new literary works on Judaic doctrine and philosophy and on subjects pertinent to life in their time; the latter are proving to have very great value for students interested in the religious, social, and political environment in which Jesus lived.

The comparatively recent discovery of the Dead Sea Scrolls provided our first true knowledge of the tremendous library collected and maintained by the Essenes. Now the sect's philosophy of life and its works have become a subject for urgent and serious study by many students of both Judaic and Christian history. In fact, because of the availability of the Scrolls, a truly remarkable opportunity has emerged to improve our knowledge of many aspects of the culture of Judea and neighboring areas during and just before the first century A.D.; that knowledge is proving to be very helpful in answering some important questions pertaining to the Christian tradition. The experience of suddenly having available a huge mass of previously unknown materials of obvious value for our understanding of our religious heritage has led to tremendous excitement, to feverish speculation, to new analyses, and to new controversies. Some Biblical scholars have weighed new evidence as provided by the Scrolls and have hardened their already held beliefs whereas other scholars have accepted substantial modifications of previously held viewpoints. It is likely that many aspects of the meaning of the comparatively recent discovery will not be fully understood or appreciated for many decades. In view of such evidence as is already available, however, one cannot doubt that a new era of Judeo-Christian studies has been initiated and that ultimately new determinations of great importance will be made in regard to some of the earliest elements of Christian history.

The story of the Dead Sea Scrolls starts in the spring of 1947. At that time a Bedouin boy who had the job of tending goats in the very rugged country on the western shore of the Dead Sea, along with a companion, made the difficult climb into a previously unnoticed opening in the rock face of a cliff. Inside he found many tall clay jars, some intact, others broken. When he took off the covers from some of the intact jars, he found that they contained dark rounded objects, longer than they were wide and giving off an obnoxious odor. Further examination of the objects revealed that they were long manuscripts, tightly rolled; the rolls had been wrapped in linen and then coated with some kind of black pitch. Some of the manuscripts were in a remarkable state of preservation but others were badly fragmented. Approximately a year after the discovery of the Scrolls, shrewd analysis by experts revealed that passages of one manuscript under examination were written in Hebrew and were actually part of the Book of Isaiah. The discovery caused great excitement, and instantly intense controversy was ignited in some religious circles when it became apparent that the newly discovered text of Isaiah involved minor but nevertheless interesting and sometimes important variations from the text of Isaiah in any one of the several accepted versions of the Judaic Bible now in use. Soon a mad rush ensued on the part of government officials, scholars, and Bedouin plunderers to gain possession of fragments of manuscripts from the vast quantity of materials being removed from the original cave as well as from several other caverns subsequently discovered within the same general area. Nearby were found the ruins of an ancient monastery, obviously associated with the people, soon identified as Essenes, who had deposited the manuscripts, clearly part of a huge library, in the caverns.

A preliminary examination of the tremendous collection of materials already taken from the caves, a considerable amount of which is now safeguarded in a new building especially erected for the purpose in Jerusalem, reveals that some of the manuscripts were written in Greek and some in Aramaic as well as in ancient Hebrew. The assembly of manuscripts, most of which are badly fragmented, contains sections, often with interesting but minor variations from the usual treatment, of all the books of the Judaic Bible except, apparently, the Book of Esther. This fact seems to provide some confirmation of the idea that the Book of Esther was a very late addition to the Judaic Bible. One complete manuscript of Isaiah has been found. In addition, the huge collection contains a large number of non-Biblical religious works, apocrypha, many of which were previously unknown, along with assorted documentary materials pertaining to details of the life of the Essenes and of the difficult times in which they lived. Some of the previously unknown apocrypha seem to have been written specifically for the purpose of supplementing books of the Bible; others provide significant kinds of information upon religious customs and thought of the period in which they were written.

To determine the dates of the manuscripts taken from the caves, traditional historical and archaeological procedures as well as modern methods associated with the decay of radioactive elements have been employed. It is now commonly believed that the Biblical and other materials deposited in the caves were produced during the period of time from approximately 150 B.C., to the latter part of the first century A.D. After the dating of the manuscripts had been accepted, it was realized that those of the newly discovered Judaic materials that were written in Hebrew were very much older than any original Hebrew manuscripts from antiquity previously available to scholars. Since the discovery of the Scrolls, however, some other ancient Hebrew manuscripts, a part of the Pseudepigrapha, discussed later, have been found by historians to be even older than some of the Hebrew materials included among the Scrolls. English translations of many of the Dead Sea Scrolls are now becoming available.

The manuscripts taken from the caves along the Dead Sea, it is already evident, must bring about a new understanding of fundamental circumstances pertaining to the origins of Christianity. It seems likely, in fact, in view of analyses already carried out, that new insights will be provided by the Scrolls into background events within the framework of Jewish life during the latter part of the B.C. period that assisted in producing a Jesus of Nazareth. Although no serious student of Christianity has ever doubted that Jesus was a Jew, the new materials throw new light upon the extent to which he was influenced by his Jewish background.

Studies of the Dead Sea Scrolls also are yielding information that is providing an improved understanding of the origins and development of the Judaic Bible along with a better comprehension of its place in the Judaic tradition. As already indicated, interesting and often what appear to be meaningful differences are being observed between the content of the Biblical texts in use by the Essenes and the content of any common version of the Judaic Bible, including the content of any Christian version. Moreover, the vast number of seemingly significant religious writings found among the Scrolls which were not introduced into the Bible as it has become part of our inheritance—including, for example, a large number of Psalms—gives emphasis to the element of choice exercised by the original Biblical compilers and editors. It is not possible or desirable in this work to provide an extensive treatment of the many differences already identified by scholars between the content of versions of the Judaic Bible commonly accepted today and those of the same books, usually fragments of the books, included among the Scrolls. An extensive literature on the subject is becoming available. It is important to note, however, that two different Scrolls that treat the same Biblical book often are at variance in certain significant respects, for the materials of the Scrolls were the result of much copying and recopying and editing. The Essene copyists who had the responsibility of reproducing the materials were merely human and frequently they made mistakes in copying or, as was true of the Christian monks who were copyists in the Middle Ages, they could not resist the temptation to inject some of their own ideas and phraseology into their copy work. Thus one cannot resist the speculation that some key sections or phraseologies in versions of the Biblical text with which readers are generally familiar actually were introduced into some early versions of the text as a result of error or by copyists who felt impelled to make changes in literary style or who wanted to introduce some of their own ideas.

Many of the variances between the Dead Sea versions of Biblical materials and common versions of the same materials may seem, at least superficially, to pertain to trivial detail; yet even the terminology employed in a particular sentence of a Biblical manuscript found among the Scrolls that differs from the same sentence in common versions now available may throw new light upon the meaning of the sentence as intended by its original author or authors. That meaning may have been a source of puzzlement to later translators and interpreters. The assistance already rendered to present-day Biblical scholars by the Scrolls in providing a better understanding of some sections of the Biblical text has been extremely helpful. Some of the recently concluded revisions of the Judaic Bible, as made by both Christian and Judaic scholars, reflect some of the early findings by scholars who have been working on the Scrolls, but in view of the continuing discoveries that are being made one might wish that there had been a delay in the publication of most of the new versions.

A few very brief comments upon studies of the particular Dead Sea Scrolls that treat the Psalms will serve to illustrate something of the tremendous stimulus to Biblical analysis for which the discovery of the

Scrolls has been responsible. Included among the great number of Dead Sea manuscripts that pertain to the Psalms are many new Psalms never before available; also included are most of the Psalms contained in the Biblical text but often with some changes in content. In addition, works concerned with exegeses of some of the Psalms have been found among the manuscripts. It would appear that the Essenes had very high regard for the Psalms and found in them, as has always been true of Judaic rabbis and Christian clergymen, meaningful applications and interpretations for life in their time. The authenticity of a statement made in one of the manuscripts that David composed 3600 Psalms as well as 450 other songs has been questioned by many scholars; apparently the reputation of David as a songwriter and poet has long been a part of Judaic tradition.

Among the previously unknown Psalms contained in the materials of the Scrolls is one which characterizes wisdom as a woman (the characterization of wisdom as a woman is also found in Proverbs); that particular Psalm contained in the Scrolls has aroused curiosity because it appears to possess elements of eroticism. Two Psalms found among the Scrolls are obviously the basis for a single Psalm in the Septuagint, but that particular Psalm was not included in the Masoretic text, the basic text of the Judaic Bible in use generally by the Jewish people. The nature of the differences between the two Psalms of the Essenes and the single Psalm of the Septuagint as well as the fact of the complete deletion of that specific Psalm from the Masoretic text has aroused considerable speculation. The two Psalms included among the Scrolls appear to reveal in some actions of David an acceptance of the philosophy of the Greek Pythagoreans and of the Greek Orphists pertaining to the great significance of harmony, as represented by music, as a factor in the workings of the universe. Thus David is portrayed as controlling by means of the music of his lyre the behavior of his flocks of sheep as well as inanimate objects in his natural environment. The historian Josephus seems to imply in some of his writings that Essene thought was influenced by the Pythagoreans. It is easy to advance the conjecture, therefore, that Jewish scholars of the late B.C. period, since they were beginning to react bitterly against Greek culture, would have eliminated any indication in their collection of Psalms as well as elsewhere in the Biblical text of any ideas supportive of Greek influence.

As a consequence of such studies of the Dead Sea Scrolls along with the types of analysis that the studies have stimulated, scholars are receiving additional support for the assumption, which some Biblical scholars of only a few decades ago would have found offensive, that a different aggregation of editors and compilers could have and probably would have produced a Judaic Bible that would be different from any version of the Holy Work with which we are familiar today. Such an observation does not detract from the distinctive reputation of the Judaic Bible as a magnificent literary accomplishment, as a very important reservoir of knowledge and information, and as a source of inspiration and spiritual guidance that is unique among the accomplishments of man. The Judaic Bible, as we know it, must add to the admiration by all men of a great and noble people who through many centuries of frustration and hardship have struggled to find and strengthen, while seeking guidance from the Lord, those fundamental attributes within their civilization that would enable them to fulfill the demands of what they regarded as their God-given destiny.

Values of the Dead Sea Scrolls in addition to those just described have become apparent in very recent times. For instance, the very old documents commonly described as Pseudepigrapha, which have been known to scholars for many centuries, have suddenly taken on new significance. Copies of one or more of the Pseudepigrapha, some of which are concerned with life in Judea even before the first century A.D., are found in many of the ancient archives of the world. Most of them are written in such languages as Greek, Latin, Coptic, the ancient Ethiopian languages, Syriac, Arabic, and Armenian, but it appears that many of them are translations; the originals probably were written in Hebrew, Greek, or Aramaic. Although a few Christian scholars in the Near East as well as some Judaic scholars have insisted through the years that several of the pseudepigrapha possess historical significance for Christianity that had been unsuspected by most historians, the tendency among historians of Christianity has been to ignore them. In fact, to indicate their negative attitude toward the old manuscripts, Christian scholars began many years ago to apply to them the term "Pseudepigrapha," which in Greek means "false writings." The judgment implied in the term was based in part upon the fact that some of the documents were attributed to authors who obviously did not write them, but historians in general seem to have ignored the ancient works because of the commonly accepted view that they were mere fiction, probably written in medieval times.

Much to the surprise, however, of some historians of Christianity, fragments of some of the Pseudepigrapha were found among the Dead Sea Scrolls, thus providing confirmation of the antiquity of the originals of the documents in the archives. At Duke University a project concerned with a systematic study of some of the obviously important Pseudepigrapha is now under way. A report from the project made in October 1977, reveals that the scholars involved in the work of the project had at that time accumulated forty-seven manuscripts which, according to evidence regarded as trustworthy, were written during the interval, 167 B.C.–A.D. 135. Now the materials of obvious importance among those which have been collected are being translated into English. As a result of the work that now is under way, the idea that Jesus was truly a product of the Judaic tradition of his time is receiving strong confirmation. As translations in English of the Pseudepigrapha become available, adherents to Christianity must profit greatly from having new understandings of Jesus and of the origins of their faith.

As one paints his own mental picture of a large number of Essenes, hidden away during much of the time of the Roman occupation of Judea in the nearly inaccessible country of the Dead Sea, serenely copying vast numbers of manuscripts and creating new memoirs that would have great historical value, it is hard to realize that just a few miles away life for others of the Jews had become very difficult, almost intolerable. Nevertheless, for the majority of the Judaic faithful who lived in Judea at that time, long established traditions and beliefs continued to remain central to their thoughts and actions. And, ignoring the political turmoil that surrounded them, a number of industrious rabbis continued their penetrating studies of the Bible, seeking subtle meanings that previously had eluded Biblical scholarship. Although the future for all the Jewish people in Judea seemed bleak, and even though tradition had to contend with the exigencies of the moment, most of the Jewish people remained firm in their conviction that God was their guardian and their hope; in fact, they anticipated the imminent arrival of the Messiah. Into such a troubled little world, Jesus of Nazareth was born.

A Brief Note on the Continuing History of Judaism

After the Roman legions under Titus had destroyed Jerusalem in A.D. 70, the surviving Jews sought new homes, often regarded as temporary homes, in many parts of the Near East. Many Judaic intellectuals gathered in existing centers of Judaic scholarship away from Jerusalem or they created new centers. The already active communities of scholars in

Alexandria and in Antioch were augmented by outstanding intellectuals who had fled the chaos in Jerusalem. And apparently a large number of rabbis and other Judaic scholars assembled at the famous Judaic Academy at Jamnia, just south of Tel Aviv. The destruction of the City of David seemed to provide a challenge to Judaic sages in these various centers and elsewhere to intensify their studies of the Torah and other Judaic materials, partly because they believed that they had a new opportunity to instruct the Jewish people in the significance of their religious heritage.

Some of the rabbis continued in an intensive way the analytical work already started; thus some Judaic historians have described the age as the Period of Rabbinic Judaism. Over a period of many decades, they revised and augmented existing rules and laws that pertained to many aspects of life and which must be regarded as applicable to all dedicated followers of Judaism. Ultimately, in approximately A.D. 200, the revised rules and laws were codified and edited by Rabbi Judah ha-Nase to form the Mishnah, which ultimately became an important part of the Talmud.

Moreover, after the destruction of Jerusalem, some influential rabbis decided, in view of the serious need for guidance by the Jewish people, that a particular version of the Torah, probably a version that had been reedited shortly before the Temple was destroyed, had their approval and should be regarded as the official presentation of the Laws. Then, some students of Judaic history believe that a short time later, using the approved version of the Torah as its basis, a new and even more authoritative text of the Judaic Bible was produced, possibly under the leadership of the Judaic scholars assembled at the Judaic Academy at Jamnia. However, information in regard to the development of such a revised text is almost nonexistent.

In view of the fact that so many Greek-speaking Jews were now scattered throughout the eastern Mediterranean area, a demand soon developed for an authoritative Greek version of the Judaic Bible which could be accepted as trustworthy. Thus the so-called version of Aquila Ponticus, in Greek, was produced; apparently it was essentially a translation of the then commonly accepted Hebrew version. The Aquila Bible was used for many years in the synagogues of most of the geographic areas where the Greek language was spoken. Later Greek versions were produced by Theodotion and by Symmachus.

Undoubtedly the work of the rabbis on the text of the Judaic Bible that

123

took place just before and just after the fall of Jerusalem ultimately provided the basis for the conception and development of the well-known Masoretic text of the Judaic Bible, an event of tremendous importance in the history of Judaism that occurred during the eighth and ninth centuries, A.D. The belief is common that the Masoretes, those who labored on the Masoretic text, were especially educated Judaic experts who undertook their task, probably upon assignment, of fixing the orthography and vocalization of the Biblical text so that it would be truly acceptable insofar as it would meet the criteria of the best available scholarship. The Masoretes also accepted the task of creating for future generations of Biblical students and readers a guide to the use of the authoritative Biblical work which they had produced. Thus, in connection with the Biblical text as finally reedited, the Masoretes compiled a collection of notes that were designed to provide for its future users some assistance upon pronunciation, information upon unusual spelling of certain words, and help upon strange grammatical constructions as well as other peculiarities in the text. The remarkable nature of the accomplishment of the Masoretes becomes clear when it is realized that adherents to Judaism continue to the present day to accept the Masoretic text, sometimes as translated into a modern language, as the basic Biblical work for teaching and worship. And for adherents to Christianity, the tremendous importance of the Masoretic text is obvious, for the Christian Old Testament resulted from the translation and editing of the Masoretic text by Christian scholars.

Chapter Six

THE BEGINNINGS OF CHRISTIANITY

JESUS OF NAZARETH

Jesus of Nazareth, a Judaic reformer of simple background, lived in the first part of the first century A.D.; in fact, a date assigned to his birth by early Christians was employed to inaugurate the start of the first century of the Christian era. Shortly after the time of Jesus, some of his followers who believed that he partook of Divinity and that he was the Messiah anticipated in Judaic prophecy were responsible for the creation of a special cult within Judaism that ultimately, as a new religion, Christianity, began to feature its own distinctive evolutionary development. Today, less than two millennia after the time of Jesus, Christianity is universally acknowledged to be the dominant religion in the world. For many centuries, in fact, the culture of a large part of the world has reflected the influence of Christian ideologies. And now, in the Christian world, the name of no historical character is better known than that of Jesus of Nazareth; even in non-Christian societies it is widely acknowledged that actions perpetrated in the name of Jesus and ideas advanced in his name have had tremendous impact upon the history of human affairs.

Yet, in reality, virtually no information which historians would accept as authentic is available in regard to the life and work of Jesus. The so-called four Gospels of the early part of the Christian New Testament treat some aspects of the career of Jesus, but they were written many years after the time of Jesus. Moreover, there is little doubt at the present time that each Biblical Gospel is representative of one of the many differing traditions about Jesus, based essentially on legend and hearsay, that were current in the Mediterranean area for many decades after the death of Jesus. In addition, a careful analysis of the section of the New Testament concerned chiefly with the life of Jesus combined with some understanding of the contexts in which it was written makes one realize that historical accuracy was not a motivating factor in its preparation.

Then, when one seeks information about Jesus from the writings of historians of his age, it is soon discovered that generally he was ignored. For example, in the prolific writings of the Jewish historian, Josephus, who lived during the time of Jesus, one would expect to find extensive documentation of Jesus and his ministry if Jesus had been an influential character in Judea during the early part of the first century A.D. But Josephus in what are accepted as his original writings makes no mention of Jesus. Since the extensive writings of Josephus reveal that he was an astute observer of important people and events of his time, one must conclude that he did not know of Jesus or at least did not regard him as an important personage. In view of implications in the New Testament that Jesus created significant problems for the Roman masters of Judea, it would be expected that Roman historians of that era would have given considerable attention to his activities. But Pliny, when telling of Roman handling of some dissident Jews, makes only a brief comment about a person who, in the view of some historical scholars, may have been Jesus. Suetonius mentions a "Christos," possibly referring to Jesus, when describing Roman actions in dealing with revolutionaries, but the reference could be to a person other than Jesus since *christos*, as noted previously, is merely the Greek word for "anointed." Tacitus, in a very brief comment, apparently does refer specifically to Jesus, using the designation "Christos," as one of those who was sentenced to death by Pontius Pilate.

Upon occasion, the writings of Eusebius of Caesarea have been cited as offering confirmation of some key parts of Biblical testimony pertaining to the life and mission of Jesus. Although it must be acknowledged that Eusebius was a remarkable historical scholar, undoubtedly one of the greatest of all time, and that his writings have been extremely valuable in helping us understand much of significance in the early history of the Christian movement, he was a man of the fourth century A.D. In fact, his magnificent work, *History of the Christian Church*, was completed in approximately A.D. 325, about three centuries after the time of Jesus. Although Eusebius had available for his use many early Christian writings, one must doubt that he was in possession of much if any information that would be accepted by historians as providing independent validation of key elements of the reports made about Jesus by any one of the New Testament writers.

Some apocryphal gospels, which accumulating evidence seems to indicate were written about the same time as the Biblical Gospels, appear to have represented other traditions about Jesus that were current at that time; they differ in interesting respects from the Biblical Gospels.

In view of the almost complete absence of historically acceptable information in regard to Jesus, it is not surprising that upon occasion a student of Christian history has expressed doubt that Jesus ever lived; but such a point of view is hardly tenable. All students of Christian history, however, are virtually forced to accept the position that Jesus was not well known during his time; the "multitudes" of people to whom Jesus was supposed to have ministered upon occasion were probably small gatherings similar to the clusters of people who now listen to street-corner orators in many modern cities. During the time of Jesus, people who lived in areas along the eastern Mediterranean were accustomed to seeing and hearing many traveling evangelists who advocated a variety of novel religious ideas; moreover, it was common for an individual to make the claim of being the Messiah of prophecy.

Since virtually the only information pertaining to Jesus, his life, and his message that is accepted and used by persons affiliated with the Christian faith is contained in the four books in the Christian New Testament known as the Gospels, ("gospel" means "Good Tidings"), it is imperative for our purpose that early attention be given to some of the important background elements which influenced the composition and content of the New Testament, especially the Gospels.

It must be emphasized immediately that the development of the New Testament was not the result of a plan conceived in advance; the assembly of books as finally compiled was partly a product of evolution but, of very great importance, the ultimate choice of books to be included in the collection was clearly the result of a careful consideration of many writings produced by the first generations of Christian authors; one becomes convinced, after considering the available evidence, that the persons responsible for compiling the collection were strongly motivated by a desire to maintain in the final text the doctrinal positions accepted by those who had achieved early positions of authority in the Christian movement. There is widespread agreement that the materials finally included in the New Testament were written over a time span of almost a century, starting with the middle of the first century A.D.

The first unintentional step in the development of the New Testament took place, it appears, when some person or persons began to make a collection of the early letters on religious subjects written by Paul,

127

Hellenistic Jew and a Pharisee, educated, as already observed, in one of the leading Pharisaic academies of the day. Probably slightly more than a decade after the death of Jesus, Paul became a confirmed advocate of primitive Christian principles, and he assumed a position of leadership in a Judaic movement, actually of a Judaic cult, that acknowledged Jesus as its founder. Possibly the individuals who assembled the letters were members of Paul's large company of associates and followers. Paul composed the letters, often by dictating them to a secretary, over a period of several years, starting in approximately A.D. 50, about two decades after the death of Jesus. The letters to the Thessalonians, which are contained in the Christian New Testament, were the first letters written by Paul of which we have any certain knowledge. The letters reveal Paul's desire to maintain a close relationship with and to provide guidance to those persons who had accepted his evangelical teachings pertaining to Jesus of Nazareth. Many of the recipients of the letters were involved in difficult problems associated with the organization of new churches, undoubtedly still described as synagogues, or with the maintenance of the spiritual life of the members of already-established churches. Probably because Paul was such a prolific writer, the evidence seems to indicate that compilers of the New Testament collection of writings made the decision, as the number of letters increased, to add only a few carefully chosen of his later letters to the collection being assembled. And then, as seen in retrospect, of tremendous importance for the growth of the new religious movement and also for the development of its Biblical text, it was further decided to have copyists make many duplicates of the growing collection of accepted letters and to distribute sets of the copied letters to a number of the new congregations established by Paul and probably, in addition, to individuals of importance in the new movement. One may assume that the compilers of the letters believed that the Pauline letters provided significant information in regard to a new and important Judaic movement and that the letters had value as a source of knowledge, inspiration, and guidance for individuals who might seek to know more about Paul's unusual religious ideas. At an early date those ideas became fundamental to the development of the basic concepts and principles accepted by members of the new religious movement.

It may be noted at once, so that there may be some preliminary comprehension of the meaning and importance of several comments made in this chapter, that the collected letters of Paul remain an invaluable resource for study by historians of Christianity, for it is likely that the first-century religious movement, later to be called Christianity, which introduced into traditional Judaism certain distinctive ideas pertaining to Jesus and his mission, would have become quite a different kind of movement or, most likely, would have faded away if Paul at that time in the evolution of Christianity had not assumed a leadership role. The amazingly strenuous endeavors of Paul in behalf of his particular interpretations of the teachings and mission of Jesus, whom he had not known, and of his own distinctive thoughts upon the meaning of Jesus and his death provided tremendous impetus to the development of the Christian movement. Actually, within the content of Paul's letters is found a rudimentary Christian theology. The story of Paul, Christianity's first great interpreter and expositor and its finest missionary, is told in the next chapter.

Every Christian must also honor Paul for the fact that his early followers, undoubtedly subject to his inspiration, made the decision to assemble so many of his writings and then distribute copies of the sets to a large number of the first Christian communities. The significance of the action for the Christian movement becomes clear when it is realized that the collection of letters provided the basis for the concept of the New Testament and also became its nucleus; moreover, the ideas expressed in the particular Pauline letters introduced into the collection undoubtedly had much to do with determining the nature of the content of the total assembly of religious writings that in the course of time became the New Testament. The ultimate act of canonizing the Christian Holy Work, completed sometime during the early part of the second century, involved the addition of other carefully chosen Christian writings to the selected letters of Paul.

The letters of Paul were written in Greek although he was also proficient in his use of Aramaic. During the time of Paul, Greek was the dominant language in the vast area conquered by Alexander some three centuries earlier. For most of the Jews then living in Palestine, however, Aramaic was the common conversational language; nevertheless, the better educated Jews and those engaged in commerce were fluent in their use of the Greek language. In the areas, especially the cities, where Paul conducted much of his missionary work, large numbers of the residents were of Greek origin. The fact that Paul wrote his letters in Greek undoubtedly has significance with respect to an understanding of the background of the persons to whom Paul was making his appeal. Later books that became part of the New Testament collection, it may be observed, were also written in Greek although, as noted by Jerome and others, Matthew when writing the book that bears his name employed "Hebrew characters." Since the New Testament was written in Greek, the Hebrew name of the nominal founder of the Christian tradition, which actually was Joshua, or possibly a shortened form of Joshua, became "Jesus," the Greek translation of the Hebrew "Joshua."

It is generally assumed that the tremendous missionary endeavors of Paul, as well as the activities of other strongly motivated crusaders in behalf of their understanding of the teachings of Jesus and of his mission on earth, soon led to a desire by both new and prospective converts to the novel cult of Judaism for more knowledge of the person of Jesus and his career. Consequently, the Book of Mark, sometimes described as the first of the three synoptic gospels, Matthew, Mark, and Luke, was prepared. (The modifier "synoptic" is employed by Biblical students to indicate that the three works are in essential agreement on their major themes.) It is the belief of many students of the New Testament that the Book of Mark was composed specifically for use by members of the comparatively active Christian community in Rome. Although arguments are common upon the dating of many events in early Christian history, many competent Biblical historians believe that the writing of the Book of Mark, which seems to have been designed as a comparatively simple narrative of the life and death of Jesus, took place sometime during the period, A.D. 68–A.D. 70. So, it appears that the Book was written some thirty-five years after the death of Jesus and approximately seventy years after his birth. It is possible that as a young man Mark, probably a Hellenistic Jew, had a limited acquaintance with Jesus. Apparently at one time he was a friend of Peter, the dominant member of the interesting collection of twelve individuals who, according to New Testament accounts, were the chosen intimates of Jesus. So it may be assumed that the work of Mark does contain some authentic information in regard to Jesus, but that information was undoubtedly diluted with many legends and much rumor that had grown up through the years in regard to Jesus and his mission, especially within the group of individuals who had become adherents to the Jesus Cult of Judaism.

Some thirty years after the preparation of the Book of Mark, thus sixty-five to seventy years after the death of Jesus and approximately a century after his birth, probably in response to a demand by Christians outside Rome for a more elaborate treatment of the life and work of Jesus, other

Gospels were prepared. Among them were the two other synoptic Gospels, one written by Luke and the other by Matthew. It is believed by some students of Biblical history that the Book of Luke was prepared specifically for the Christian community in Achaea and the Book of Matthew for the Christian community in Antioch, thus partially explaining the fact of their differences. It is evident, however, that the authors of the latter two books relied heavily in their literary endeavors upon the content of the Book of Mark and, probably, in addition, upon some of the same resources that provided Mark a basis for his writings. But each of the two authors, Luke and Matthew, must have drawn on some of his own particular sources of information, a considerable amount of which was probably legendary; it is likely that much of the information upon which the authors relied was being transmitted orally. Undoubtedly other gospels, apocryphal gospels, prepared about the same time were developed to serve the needs of members of other Christian communities; for instance, a gospel recently under examination by scientists in the British Museum may have been prepared for use by the Christians in Alexandria.

Probably Luke, author of the Biblical Gospel that bears his name, was a physician who was one of the non-Jews who became early adherents to the new Judaic religious movement that acknowledged Jesus as its nominal founder. It is commonly believed that at one time Luke was a companion of Paul. The Book of Luke reveals the exceptional literary ability of its author; his remarkable use of the Greek language and his talent for using words to portray an image testify to his genius. Some sections of the Gospel of Luke, such as the story pertaining to the birth of Jesus, have been told and retold many times; children of Christian parents usually hear the story at an early age.

Reports of the birth of Jesus, as recounted by both Luke and Matthew, have been the basis for some of Christendom's finest pageantry and for some of its most beloved music and art. Early in the Christian era, especially after the fourth century, portrayals of scenes of the Nativity, derived from the writings of Luke and Matthew and often acclaimed as significant works of art, became common in Christian literature and as decorations for Christian edifices; the manner in which these portrayals changed through the centuries is an interesting subject for study by anthropologists, for they reveal how ideas are modified by changing cultural trends.

Matthew was a Jew, and it is evident from a study of his writings that he was well-versed in Judaic literature and doctrine. Such a study also reveals that he had become convinced that Jesus was the great leader, the Messiah, for whom followers of Judaism had been waiting. Consequently it appears that he felt impelled to denounce the many Jews who refused to accept his point of view that Jesus was the Messiah of prophecy and who generally refused to believe that Jesus had contributed anything of fundamental significance to their religious tradition. Obviously, Matthew's irritation with his fellow Jews was a factor in what has been described by some Biblical critics as an anti-Jewish bias in his writings. It is important to note, however, that the writings of Matthew indicate that he did not reject his Judaic heritage; in fact, several times in the Gospel which bears his name he made an attempt to reconcile events in the life of Jesus with teachings and prophecies of the Judaic Bible. The Book of Matthew is notable for its efforts, using several approaches, to provide an authentic interpretation, as Matthew understood it, of the Jesus message, and he gives great emphasis to the skill of Jesus as a teacher. Many well-known parables associated with the teachings of Jesus are included in the text of Matthew's Gospel. Matthew used words attributed to Peter as his vehicle for the presentation of his conviction that Jesus was the long-awaited Messiah.

The authorship of the Gospel of John, the fourth gospel, is debatable; the Book was written, it is believed by some scholars, to satisfy the needs of the Christian community in Ephesus. The composer of the Gospel of John, probably written shortly after the writing of the last two synoptic Gospels, undoubtedly relied heavily on the Book of Mark and on some of the other source materials employed by Luke and Matthew. But the Gospel of John is fundamentally different in its content and approach from those produced by Matthew, Mark, and Luke. Although the fourth Gospel, as was true of the other three, is basically concerned with Jesus, his mission, and significant episodes in his career, the method of development employed in the Book of John, as contrasted with that of the synoptic Gospels, is somewhat allegorical. Moreover, the author of the Gospel of John approached his subject not as a historian or as a journalist but as a philosopher who was also a mystic; consequently the Book possesses special fascination because of the symbolism that is involved and the seemingly subtle meanings in some of its passages. Close study of the Gospel of John by historians familiar with the times in which it was written reveals without much doubt that its appeal was directed strongly to the Gentile Greeks, especially, probably, to those in the area of Asia Minor in which Ephesus is located. To make a strong approach to the Gentiles must have been regarded as very important, for they had demonstrated more receptiveness than the Jews to the message inherent in the Jesus story, as that story had been interpreted by Paul.

Each of the four Biblical Gospels, Matthew, Mark, Luke, and John, with which Christians are generally familiar, has its distinctive characteristics, as already implied. These characteristics are inherent in the traditional symbols for the authors of the Gospels that seem to have originated during the fourth or possibly the fifth century. The figure of a man or an angel was used to represent Matthew and his treatment of the "human nature of Jesus"; the lion was used to designate Mark who wrote of the "loyal dignity of Jesus"; the ox was used as the symbol for Luke who emphasized "the sacrificial priesthood of Jesus"; and the eagle was used to represent John who "soars to heaven." Probably because the Gospels were designed to serve the needs of followers of the new religious movement in the four very important Christian communities already named, the decision was made at some point to add the four books to the collected letters of Paul along with other selected materials; ultimately the collection of writings that evolved in such a manner became known as the Christian New Testament.

As already noted, a person who attempts to draw upon the four Gospels of the New Testament as a basic resource for the writing of an acceptable biography of Jesus soon discovers that he has embarked upon an impossible task. Gospel authors obviously felt impelled to stress their belief that Jesus was a descendant of David, which was necessary to be consistent with prophecies that had been made pertaining to the Messiah, but the ideas of Matthew and of Luke seem to be at variance in regard to the line of descent which was followed from David to Jesus. Matthew, Mark, and Luke, when treating the theologically critical events at the end of the career of Jesus on earth, record that Jesus was arrested on the first night of Passover, and then was executed the next day; the Gospel of John, however, reports that each event took place a day earlier than the date given for it in all three synoptic Gospels. Many other curious differences in the four accounts are easily discovered.

When attempting to develop an acceptable account of the birth of Jesus from information given in the Gospels, one encounters great difficulty. Matthew and Luke provide the only information in regard to the circumstances surrounding his birth, and they both report that the event took place in Bethlehem; moreover, both authors report that Mary, the mother of Jesus, was a virgin when Jesus was born. But with respect to other aspects of the recorded account of the birth of Jesus there is little resemblance between the content of Matthew's Gospel and that of Luke's Gospel. Matthew describes a visit of an angel to Joseph, father of Jesus; Luke tells of an angelic visit to Mary, his mother. Matthew writes of the visit of Magi to the infant Jesus, a visit that has become the basis of many beautiful Christmas stories; Luke tells the equally beautiful story of the shepherds, also popular at Christmastime.

Obviously the two narratives pertaining to the birth of Jesus in Bethlehem, the one written by Matthew and the other by Luke, were derived from different traditions, based on differing available reports and legends. The story derived from one tradition, probably being transmitted orally, seemed to assume that Joseph and Mary lived in Bethlehem where upon the occasion of the arrival of their firstborn, Jesus, they were visited by gift-bearing Magi, who were guided to Bethlehem by a moving star. Because a cruel king had decided to destroy Jesus, his parents, according to the one Gospel report, had to take their newly born son and flee to Egypt, but ultimately it was possible for the parents and son to return to Nazareth. In Egypt today and in some other parts of the Near East, celebrations of the birth of Jesus give major attention to the flight of Mary and Jesus to Egypt. The part of the story pertaining to the danger to the infant Jesus and the flight of his parents to Egypt may have been modeled by the originator of its probable legendary basis upon the tale recorded in the Judaic Bible of events that occurred in the early days of the infant Moses, the great Judaic leader with whom, in the probable judgment of the originator of the story, Jesus might properly be compared. The other Gospel story of the birth of Jesus, obviously derived from a different tradition, had the event taking place in Bethlehem while Joseph and Mary were on a trip for the purpose of providing information required by a Roman census. Since the parents were unable to find accommodations in the local inn, they slept in a stable—a common practice; there the birth took place. The latter story is provided a dramatic touch by the well-known account of the visit of shepherds to Bethlehem to acclaim the infant Jesus, whose bed was a manger; the shepherds had been notified of the newborn king by a heavenly chorus of angels while they were in the fields tending their flocks of sheep.

A likely key to the fact that Matthew and Luke specified that Jesus was born in Bethlehem even though their source materials may have presented diverse views on the subject is provided by Matthew (Matthew 2).

Matthew refers to a prophecy of Micah (Micah 5), which, as already indicated, has been interpreted by some Biblical analysts as implying that the Messiah would be born in Bethlehem. It may be recalled again that Bethlehem was supposed to be the family home of David. So one may well believe that Matthew as well as Luke, since both men accepted Jesus as the Messiah, who was to come from the House of David, had no doubt that Bethlehem was the birthplace of Jesus. It is clear that the idea of reconciling any treatment of events involving Jesus with the prophecies of the Judaic prophets was regarded as fundamental by many early Christian writers, including the New Testament authors, especially Matthew.

It is likely that neither Matthew nor Luke knew where Jesus was born; as already noted, they wrote their Gospels about a century after the birth of Jesus, and one must assume that they possessed very little if any authentic information in regard to the life of Jesus, certainly in regard to his birth. Some Biblical students believe that actually Jesus was born in Nazareth; he was known generally as Jesus of Nazareth or as Jesus from Nazareth, a common way of denoting the place of a person's origin. There was no reason why a record should have been made at the time of the birth of Jesus pertaining to the circumstances under which the event took place; Jesus was merely the son of a laboring man without acknowledged social or political status.

Through the years, it has become increasingly evident that Jesus was not born during the first year of the Christian era, even though the Christian era was supposed to have been inaugurated by the birth of Jesus. There is considerable belief on the part of modern Biblical scholars that he was born sometime in the interval 6–4 B.C. Thus he was born near the end of Herod's reign of Judea. No information of significance has ever been advanced in regard to the time of year in which Jesus was born. The first specific designation of December 25 as the birth date of Jesus, commonly known as Christmas, from the early English "Christes Masse," seems to have been made by Philocalus when he designed his calendar in the year 354, but there is little probability that Jesus was actually born on December 25. It is likely that the choice of December 25 as the date of the Nativity was related in some manner to the timing of the widely observed Roman festival of Saturnalia, which came in late December. Support for the date of December 25 increased after Anastasius, Roman Pope from 398 to 401, endorsed it. But attempts to achieve any general acceptance of December 25 as the date upon which Jesus was born have had a stormy reception; at the present time the date is not universally celebrated. In fact, the Eastern Orthodox Churches and the Oriental Christian Churches, using the Julian calendar, celebrate Christmas at a later date.

The idea that the mother of Jesus was a virgin even after she was with child is a fundamental tenet within the system of principles to which many followers of the Christian faith adhere. There can be no doubt that the principle of the Virgin Birth was central to the beliefs of many of the early leaders of the Christian movement; testimony to that fact actually seems to be revealed in the choice of materials included in the New Testament. Very early in the Christian era, however, manuscripts were in existence pertaining to the life of Joseph and Mary in which no mention is made of the Virgin Birth; such manuscripts were widely read during the early days of Christianity. For instance, the apocryphal Gospel according to James the Less, which probably was written about the time the New Testament compilation of Christian writings was being completed, was used as a basic Christian text by many Christian communities in the early centuries A.D., but its author reported nothing unusual in regard to the birth of Jesus. The apocryphal work does, however, tell of some curious elements in the relationship of Joseph and Mary that might very well provide the basis for the plot of an interesting work of fiction. The work describes Joseph as a widower of advanced years who already had several children when he was forced by the high priests, apparently as the result of some kind of lottery, to take Mary, a very young girl, as his wife; at least one version of the work indicates that Mary had lived for several years as a ward of the priests. The resulting situation embarrassed Joseph and he is reported to have said, "To have her [Mary] taxed as my wife I am ashamed; and if I have her taxed as my daughter, all Israel knows she is not my daughter." The work of James the Less portrays the family of Joseph and Mary as ultimately including Joseph's children by his deceased wife along with several children by Mary; of the latter, Jesus was the eldest. Many, possibly a growing number, of students of very early Christian literature believe that a substantial number of the early Christian writings that later were destroyed by a self-constituted group of Christian leaders portrayed the birth of Jesus as quite a natural event and described the family of Joseph and Mary as a normal Jewish family.

During the nearly two thousand years in which Christianity has existed as a distinct religion, many persons, including some very thoughtful individuals who desire to be known as Christians, have found it very difficult to accept the principle of the Virgin Birth. For many of such persons, the principle poses a contradiction with other systems of principles which they have accepted and which provide them a foundation for their chosen way of life. In particular, for a large number of persons, an acceptance of the principle of the Virgin Birth represents a negation of their fundamental belief in the validity of the principles of biological science, principles that have made possible for man a rational kind of life on earth and which seem to have fundamental relevance to the wisdom inherent in the universe. For some individuals, acceptance of the idea of the Virgin Birth actually involves a denial of their particular concept of God, a concept which they may have accepted as fundamental to their religious faith after a long intellectual struggle.

Persons who have had difficulty in accepting the principle of the Virgin Birth have found that their problem is magnified when they try to analyze the background of a puzzling statement that appears in the Book of Matthew, whose strong Judaic background has already been noted; in that particular statement, Matthew asserts that he found in prophecy an anticipation of the Virgin Birth. According to the Gospel account written by Matthew, an angel visited Joseph, sometime before the birth of Jesus, to inform him that his wife Mary would bear a son, to be known as Emmanuel, and the birth would be in fulfillment of the words of the prophet Isaiah. The angel is quoted by Matthew as saying (Matthew 1:22–23), "All this took place to fulfill what the Lord had spoken by the prophet: 'Behold, a virgin shall conceive and bear a son, and his name shall be called Emmanuel.' " The reference, according to the contexts in which it is given, is to a prophecy of Isaiah that is recorded in Isaiah 7:14 of the Judaic Bible. In the venerated King James version of the Old Testament of the Christian Bible, that particular prophecy reads: "Therefore the Lord himself shall give you a sign; Behold, a virgin shall conceive, and bear a son, and shall call his name Immanuel." But it is important to note that Isaiah 7:14 in any English translation of the Judaic Bible, including its earliest versions, reads, possibly with minor changes: "Therefore the Lord Himself shall give you a sign: Behold, the young woman is with child, and she will bear a son, and shall call his name Immanuel." The difference between the two quotations, the one from a commonly accepted Christian version of the Old Testament, in which reference is made to a "virgin," and the other from a version of the Judaic Bible approved by Hebrew scholars, in which the same reference is to "young woman," is of tremendous significance for Biblical students and for Christian theology.

A reading of the section in Isaiah from which the quotation was drawn reveals that it was a part of a conversation that Isaiah had with the king of Judah, who was under military pressure from two other kings. Isaiah was assuring the king that before a child, then being born, had an opportunity to grow up, the two oppressing kings would be destroyed. So, in reality, the quotation from the book of Isaiah has no relevance to the birth of the anticipated Messiah.

It appears that most early Christians did not question Matthew's position as he supposedly based it on prophecy, and the same thing has been true of a vast number of later Christians. But the recently issued *Revised Standard Version of the Christian Bible*,* approved in 1952 by a team of outstanding Biblical scholars, including linguistic experts, employs the term "young woman" in preference to "virgin" in its rendition of Isaiah 7:14. At the same time, in the new version, the traditional Christian statement of the prophecy of Isaiah, as it is quoted in the Book of Matthew of the King James version of the Christian Bible, is retained. Thus readers of the new version of the Christian Bible are confronted with a serious inconsistency.

It appears that the discrepancy between the wording in the original Hebrew of Isaiah 7:14 in the Judaic Bible and its wording in some of the first Christian versions of the Old Testament did not go unnoticed by some early Christian scholars, so explanations began to develop. Among them was a Christian legend involving Simeon, one of the learned linguistic scholars who was involved in the attempt to develop an accurate translation of the Hebrew Bible into Greek, thereby creating the Septuagint. According to the story, Simeon wrote down at the appropriate place in Isaiah 7:14 of the first draft of the Septuagint the Greek term for "young woman," not even considering the idea that he should write in the Greek word for "virgin." But at that point, according to the tale, an angel quickly appeared and erased his writing. Two more times Simeon tried to continue his writing as he was determined to make an accurate translation of the Judaic Bible; each time, however, the angel appeared and erased his work. So, the legend concludes, Simeon decided that he must be acting contrary to God's wishes; he was able to continue his work of translation with the apparent approval of God's angel only

*Copyright 1952 by the Division of Education of the National Council of the Churches of Christ in the United States of America (Philadelphia: A. J. Holman Company, 1952).

after he introduced into his translation the Greek word for "virgin" instead of the Greek word for "young woman."

The principle of the Virgin Birth has been chiefly responsible for the fact that the attention of some important segments of the Christian community has been focused very strongly on Mary, the "Virgin." She has been the subject of many legends, often at variance, in regard to her life and death. Roman Catholic Christians have displayed great veneration for Mary almost from the beginnings of the Roman Church. Cyril, archbishop of Alexandria, in a famous sermon at Eastertime, A.D. 429, advocated the doctrine, accepted without essential change since that time by Roman Catholic Christians, that Mary was the mother of both the Divine and the human natures of Jesus, actually the mother of the Word of God. That sermon and other pronouncements at about the same time are usually credited with the inauguration of the Mary Cult. It should be observed, however, that it was not until the twelfth century that great emphasis upon the virginity of Mary and her importance in Christian doctrine became a dominant theme of Roman Catholic theology and practice. Now the life of Mary is commonly regarded by the Roman Catholic faithful as the ideal example of the Christian life.

The growing emphasis by the Roman Catholic Church after the twelfth century upon the virginity of Mary and upon her significance in Roman Catholic belief ultimately was culminated in the enunciation of the Doctrine of the Immaculate Conception. In 1864, Pope Pius IX issued a Papal bull that, in essence, defined for followers of Roman Catholicism the Doctrine of the Immaculate Conception; the Papal bull asserted: "We declare, pronounce, and define that the doctrine which holds that the most blessed Virgin Mary, in the first instant of her conception, by a singular grace and privilege granted by Almighty God, in view of the merits of Jesus Christ, the Savior of the human race, was preserved free from all stain of Original Sin, is a doctrine revealed by God and therefore to be believed firmly and constantly by all the faithful." Even though some students of Christianity, including many who live by and believe in the major precepts of Christian philosophy, may question the acceptability of the Doctrine of the Immaculate Conception, the depth of meaning associated with it by a vast number of Christians, who regard the doctrine as a fundamental expression of Christian truth, is such that undoubtedly in virtual perpetuity it will remain a very important feature of the faith of many Christians.

Testimony to the great veneration and affection that Roman Catholics have for Mary, the Virgin, has been provided through the centuries, especially in the Middle Ages, by the many artists who have memorialized her by means of paintings and statues, known as Madonnas. Upon occasion the memorialization has been in the form of a Madonna and Child, a representation of the Virgin Mary holding the infant Jesus. The concept of Virgin Mary, as portrayed in such art and as treated in much literature, reveals the great symbolic importance as well as the deep personal meaning that it has for many millions of people. One cannot doubt that the concept is an intimate part of the Christian tradition as accepted by a very large number of people in much of the Christian world. Circumstances surrounding the origin of a concept or principle, although knowledge of such circumstances may facilitate some kinds of understanding, often have little relevance to the ultimate value of the concept or principle in human affairs; much of man's activity, often very important and beneficial activity, is based on ideas, often commonly accepted ideas, that may be questioned when subjected to rigorous examination.

Apparently Jesus was the eldest of five brothers, and he had two or more sisters. At least one brother, James, seemed to have developed a strong belief in the fundamental importance of the mission of Jesus; according to Biblical evidence, James attempted to continue the work of Jesus after his death. Although the New Testament virtually ignored the youth of Jesus, enough is said to reveal the belief of the Gospel authors that his kind of life during his early years was typical of that of a boy of that period of history whose parents adhered to Judaism. The Biblical text reports that he learned his father's trade; obviously he was taught the tenets and practices of Judaism, as already discussed. There is some apocryphal literature of the first century, written after the time of Jesus, that purports to give information, but which generally is regarded as fictitious, in regard to the early life of Jesus; in some of that literature he is treated as a frivolous youngster who indulged in magic, who was erratic in his judgment, and who frequently confounded his elders with his strange behavior. A surprisingly large amount of apocryphal literature pertaining to Jesus that was written in the first few centuries of the Christian era was regarded as unacceptable by early orthodox Christians.

The New Testament tells nothing about the physical characteristics of Jesus, the adult man. Since it was contrary to Judaic tradition of that time to produce any kind of an image of a person, no pictorial representation

140

of the real Jesus would have been made. Paintings of Jesus, even by distinguished artists, add nothing to our knowledge of his appearance; each painting of Jesus that has been acclaimed through the ages must be regarded essentially as a reflection of the cultural and ethnic background of the artist and of the mores of the period in which the artist lived. It is likely, in fact, that no portrayal with which we are generally familiar possesses much resemblance to the true Jesus. A few years ago, a Vatican scholar is said to have expressed the judgment, after indulging in certain anthropological studies, that, based on probability considerations, Jesus was about 5.4 feet tall. His weight, therefore, would have been about 135 pounds. It seems likely also, after considering the nature of the racial mixing of populations in Palestine during the first century, that Jesus possessed a dark skin coloration along with dark hair; certainly he was not a blond. Since Jesus was a devout follower of Judaism, and since, in general, Judaism has maintained such a strong negative position on celibacy, some scholars have expressed the judgment that probably he had a wife. Such a point of view, however, is not supported by any specific evidence.

When Jesus died, in approximately A.D. 30, his age must have been within the range of thirty-four to thirty-six years. Virtually all of his ministry, which occupied only a short period of time—probably about a year but at most three years at the end of his lifetime—took place in his native Galilee. The latter fact may be very important when one considers some aspects of the reported ministry of Jesus, for, as observed previously, the people of Galilee were not too long removed from paganism. Many of the Jews in Galilee, according to the Judaic missionary Yohanan, possessed points of view in regard to the very essence of Judaism that were considerably at variance with the teachings of the rabbis in Jerusalem. Yohanan observed at one point that the people to whom he ministered in Galilee expected frequent displays of signs and wonders, and they expected demonstrations of faith healing. Moreover, it appears that the Law, as taught in the Torah, was not as meaningful for the faith of the Jews in Galilee as it was for the Jews in Judea.

Much of the exposition of the Gospels is concerned with the short period of time during which Jesus was involved in an intensive program of taking his message to the people. One can only speculate upon the factors in his life that motivated him to embark upon the strenuous evangelical campaign that finally led to his death. There is too much that we do not know about him. Nevertheless, it is desirable that an attempt be made to isolate some of the probable influences upon Jesus, especially those of the early part of his life, that would seem to have been persuasive in causing him to undertake in the latter part of his career the strenuous endeavors that were terminated by his death on a cross.

Jesus, one cannot doubt, was a natural leader and an extremely sensitive person who believed that he could provide guidance to many other Jewish people in Jerusalem and its vicinity as they struggled to find solutions to the often seemingly impossible social and political problems with which they were continually faced. Although one may question the historical accuracy of the Biblical Gospels, their testimony is unanimous and therefore of very great significance that Jesus believed and emphasized that the answers to the human problems of his day were to be found in the universal acceptance of fundamental Judaic philosophy. In general, the teachings of Jesus may be identified with the basic teachings of Judaism. This long-held belief by many students of Christianity is now being confirmed by recent comparisons of the teachings of Jesus as recorded in the New Testament and those that are contained in the teachings of the Pharisees, the Essenes, and generally in the teachings of Judaic spokesmen as they were recorded, for example, in the recently translated Dead Sea Scrolls and in some of the Pseudepigrapha.

Probably Jesus was raised in a home in which the fundamental Judaic ideal of brotherly love was carefully nurtured. Thus, as an adult, he must have been disturbed by the fact that man's bitterness toward man was so much a part of life during his time. Although that bitterness must have had much of its origin in the increasingly vicious political situation that pitted Romans against Jews and Jews against Romans, it carried over into Jewish society, which had a critical need for a renewal of its faith in traditional Judaic values. Although most of the Jews of the time of Jesus indulged in the formal practices of Judaism, there appears to have been a tendency, noted by Judaic historians of that era, to ignore much of the real essence of Judaism. And probably Jesus believed that the Judaic intellectual leaders of the day spent too much time on theoretical studies. The prophets of an earlier age would doubtless have displayed righteous indignation that so many supposed adherents to Judaism had strayed so far from what they regarded as God's precepts. One may very well assume that the ultimate decision of Jesus to embark, like the earlier prophets of Judaic history, upon an evangelistic crusade against contemporary conditions was in keeping with his character and was a partial consequence of the educational background he received as a boy raised

142

in a devout Judaic home. But it appears likely that other factors drove him to become a crusader for his notions of the true, the right, and the just.

Mark, the author of the first of the Biblical Gospels to be written, which undoubtedly became a resource for the authors of the other Biblical gospels, inaugurates his narrative of Jesus by telling of John the Baptist and of the influence of John upon the young Jesus. Each of the other Gospel authors, who seem to have been similarly impressed with what they had heard about the contribution of John the Baptist to the career of Jesus, also gives significant attention to the evangelical endeavors of John. Mark opened his Gospel with a short prologue containing the assertion that "as it is written in Isaiah," a "messenger" came to "prepare the way of the Lord." Then he wrote, "John the baptizer appeared in the wilderness, preaching a baptism of repentance for the forgiveness of sins." The influence of John upon the populace, Mark reported, was very great; he attracted many people from great distances who came to confess their sins; then they were baptized in the shallow Jordan River. But the evangelist insisted, according to Mark, that "after me comes he who is mightier than I"; the person who would follow him, John the Baptist indicated, would baptize with the Holy Spirit whereas he could only baptize with water. Jesus, in the judgment of the Gospel writers, was the person whom John anticipated in such a statement, so the baptism and associated "conversion" of Jesus by John are described in dramatic fashion.

By contrast with the lack of attention to Jesus, Josephus indicated in his writings that John the Baptist was well-known in Judea during the time in which he lived and that his dynamic preaching made a deep impression upon those who went to hear him; John must have been a very strong person who was not easily ignored. Apparently the Pharisees, properly concerned by the large number of individuals who suddenly were claiming for themselves the distinctive title of Messiah, questioned John closely about any claim that he might have for himself in connection with Messianic prophecy. It appears, moreover, that the Roman civil authorities, concerned by possible political effects that his preaching might have on the populace, gave close attention to John; in truth, ultimately the civil authorities decided that he was a dangerous character, so he was arrested and then, as happened to so many influential Jewish leaders of that time, he was executed, actually beheaded. Because of the powerful impression that John created upon his contemporaries, the early advocates of Jesus obviously found it desirable to establish a strong connection between John the Baptist and Jesus; probably Jesus was given validity and stature in the eyes of some of the first recruits to primitive Christianity by the nature of his association with John.

Part of the appeal of John, it would appear, was due to his convincing insistence that the establishment of the Messianic kingdom, so long anticipated by those affiliated with Judaism, was imminent. Consequently, John argued that the Jewish people must not delay in preparing for the important event; they must repent their sins. Baptism, a rite apparently popularized by John although the practice was not original with him, provided, according to Josephus, symbolic purification of the body, which probably meant that participation in the act created a basis for a fresh start in life, free of the onus of sin. So it appears that cleansing from sin, as symbolized by baptism, was advocated by John as a prerequisite for admission to the Messianic kingdom.

One can easily believe that John's preaching provided substantial guidance to Jesus as he was trying to comprehend his own personal challenge and opportunities. In fact, probably a case could be made for the proposition that the role of Jesus in the evolution of the Christian tradition was that of providing a bond between John the Baptist and the later Judaic sect that was the precursor of Christianity. Communities of people who professed to be disciples of John the Baptist existed for many decades after John's death, and ultimately, it appears, some of his followers became active in the Christian movement. (Note Acts 18:24–25.) The Mandeans, a very old religious sect presently located chiefly in Iraq, continue to venerate John, but not Jesus.

John's style of life, the general area in which he conducted his early evangelical endeavors (in the wilderness area between Kedron and the Dead Sea), the fact that he indulged in baptism, a practice commonly followed by the Essenes but was not associated in a significant way with most Judaic sects, along with some aspects of his message led a few Judaic and Christian scholars several years ago, before the discovery of the Dead Sea Scrolls, to conclude that John was a member of the Essene sect of Judaism or at least that he had been strongly influenced by the Essenes. The number of scholars accepting such a point of view has increased since the Dead Sea Scrolls, associated with the Essenes, have become available for study.

Even before the discovery of the Dead Sea Scrolls the belief also existed among a number of students of the history of Christianity that

Jesus himself was under the influence of the Essenes, and, in fact, some scholars expressed the judgment that probably he was a member of the Essene sect. Such ideas have had even greater acceptance since the discovery of the Scrolls, for analyses of the Dead Sea materials have revealed a strong resemblance between the concepts and principles advocated by Jesus, many of which were adopted by his early followers, and those that were common to the Essenes. It may be true, in fact, that much of the simple religious philosophy of the original Christians evolved out of the Essene tradition.

Many observations may be made in regard to obvious similarities between the simple Essene tradition in religious philosophy and the classical Christian tradition that relied heavily on the teachings of Jesus. Jesus, according to the Biblical Gospels, often decried the widespread emphasis in his day upon wealth and upon the ownership of property. A consequence of his purported ideas on the subject is revealed in the fact that the early Christian communities, somewhat like the kibbutzim in modern Israel, were often communal in nature; members owned no private property but held their possessions in common. Such a point of view in regard to wealth and the ownership of property was also a pronounced characteristic of the Essene tradition. Moreover, the Essenes, as was true of Jesus and the early Christians, emphasized equality among men; they taught that the practical application of the doctrine of brotherly love should be the prime characteristic of any human society that is based on the precepts of God. Essene philosophy, as was true of Christian philosophy, also gave emphasis to the principle that man has a soul which is immortal. In fact, both the Essenes and the followers of Jesus believed that if a person has lived a life of virtue on earth, his soul after his death is provided an everlasting abode in heaven, a place where supreme happiness exists in perpetuity.

It is quite possible, it must be emphasized, that the comments just made pertaining to some of the basic religious tenets to which the Essenes subscribed should also be regarded as applicable to most of the other Judaic sects. Undoubtedly it was true that some of the major ideas just attributed to the Essenes, at least with respect to their essential aspects, were also accepted by the Pharisees. In fact, some present-day scholars are expressing the judgment that the emphasis of very recent years upon the strong influence of the Essenes on Jesus may represent an exaggeration of the probable truth. It is conceivable, because of the sudden availability of the great number of Scrolls, thus providing us ready access to a substantial knowledge of Essene principles and practices, that we actually know more at the present time about many aspects of Essene thought than we know about Pharisee thought.

Nevertheless, the fact remains, of very great interest for students of the Christian tradition, that there is truly remarkable similarity between the language found in Essene writings and the language of many sayings attributed to Jesus in the Biblical Gospels. Likewise, expositions of doctrine found in some Essene literature resemble in a remarkable way expositions employed by Jesus, as they are reported in many parts of the New Testament. Moreover, it must be noted that the Essene *Manual of Discipline,* translated in recent years, which seems to have been a basic guide for members of the Essene sect, could almost be regarded, as many scholars have noted, as a reference work on early Christian ideas and practices. Of special interest for Christians is the fact that the *Manual* refers to a sacred meal which involved the breaking of bread and the passing of a cup of wine; the nature of the repast and the symbolism inherent in it resemble in a way that transcends coincidence the same aspects of the Lord's Supper, traditionally celebrated in Christian churches upon the occasion of Holy Communion. (The Lord's Supper, an event which Jesus is said to have celebrated as a "last supper" with his twelve chosen disciples, is described by Matthew, Mark and Luke. Note, for instance, Matthew 26.) When reading Gospel accounts of the Last Supper, it is important to realize that the descriptions given of the event undoubtedly received editorial attention by Gospel authors so that they would be consistent with its descriptions and interpretations as previously enunciated by Christian missionary-advocates, notably Paul. The interpretations that Paul gave to the Last Supper are still inherent in the dialogue associated with the traditional Christian celebration of Communion.

Part of the exhilaration displayed by many Biblical scholars as they have pursued their studies of the Dead Sea Scrolls has been caused by the fact that analyses of Essene writings are throwing new light on the meaning behind some sayings attributed to Jesus and other early Christian advocates; the analyses are also assisting in providing more satisfactory interpretations of some events described in the New Testament. Probably of the greatest importance, the continuing studies of the content of the Dead Sea Scrolls reveal, as already implied, how strongly the simple philosophy of primitive Christianity depended on Judaic religious philosophy of the first century A.D., at least as it was accepted by some

Judaic sects. Such findings are being reinforced by even more recent studies of some of the Pseudepigrapha. The essence of Christian philosophy as we know it and as it was taught by Jesus was already old when Jesus was born; it did not originate spontaneously with him.

It is so very unfortunate, parroting the words of the modern scientist, that Jesus "did not publish." We have no statement that bears his signature. Much of what is written in the New Testament probably reveals as much about the individuals who were responsible for the writing as they tell about Jesus. Nevertheless, it is possible to conclude from a penetrating study of the content of the New Testament that although Jesus was not a learned man he possessed a mind that enabled him to penetrate the complexities of society so that he could see it as men, working and living together. So religion for Jesus could not possess the characteristics of an elaborate theological discipline. Rather, one cannot doubt that his ideas in regard to religious principles and practices were founded on simple humanitarian truths that have significance in any society. The complex doctrines and the elaborate formalisms, now often associated with the Christian faith, evolved through the centuries after the death of Jesus. Possibly such a development was inevitable, for in philosophical matters and even in patterns of social behavior man seems to abhor the simple.

For Jesus, the God of Moses was his God. And the will of God, he believed, had been expressed in the words of Moses and of the Judaic prophets. But for man, those words could become meaningless symbols or they could be translated into a way of life. Thus, in the thought processes and actions of Jesus, his great love of God and his reverence and respect for the will of God were translated into a feeling of deep compassion for his fellowman. The Gospel of Mark, written so much closer to the time of Jesus than the other Gospels, tells of an interrogation of Jesus by a Scribe. (Note Mark 12:28–32.) The Scribe is said to have asked the question, "Which commandment is first of all?" According to Mark, Jesus replied, "The first is 'Hear, O Israel: The Lord our God, the Lord is one; and you shall love the Lord your God with all your heart, and with all your soul, and with all your mind, and with all your strength.' The second is this, 'You shall love your neighbor as yourself.' There is no commandment greater than these." The theme set forth in the reported reply of Jesus to the Scribe is reiterated many times and in many ways in the Gospel narratives; even the nature of the reports in the Gospels about the miracles which Jesus is said to have instigated along with his varied kinds of involvement with members of the public, including his contacts with tax collectors, publicity seekers, and sinners, seem to supplement and reinforce such a theme. One cannot doubt that the reply of Jesus to the Scribe, as quoted in Mark 12:28–32, represents in a concise way the simple ethical and moral philosophy in which Jesus believed and which he enunciated. It is a philosophy that every sincere adherent to Christianity must acknowledge as basic to his faith; it is a philosophy that every conscientious student of human society must applaud. It points the way to the development of concepts and principles upon which a noble life may be built, and it may be regarded as providing a challenge to every man to use his vast natural capabilities, some would say his God-given capabilities, to improve the society of which he is a part. Of fundamental significance for students of the origins of the Christian tradition, it must be observed that the basic philosophy of Jesus, as it is enunciated in Mark's account of the interrogation of Jesus by the Scribe, received the approval of the Scribe who asked the question, just as it would have won the approval and respect of Hillel and the other great Pharisaic leaders of that day.

Many people who subscribe to Christianity accept as fact that the Christian Bible represents the true word of God. In keeping with the acceptance of such a principle, they believe that the content of the Bible must be accepted as authoritative and as completely valid. One must respect the beliefs of this category of individuals. By contrast, other persons, although possibly perturbed by some aspects of the classical Christian tradition such as the Virgin Birth and the Resurrection, accept the Bible as great literature, the product of Christian scholarship, and they read the Holy Book with great admiration. In the message of Jesus, they find the kind of inspiration, hope, and guidance that they associate with a man who has found truth, even God. Employing that message as the basis for the kind of life which they are trying to achieve, although they realize the great difficulty of the task, they regard themselves as followers of Christianity and they accept the designation "Christian." The beliefs of individuals in this increasingly large class of persons must also be respected. A large number of Christian doctrinal positions is possible within the range included within the two extremes just described; thus a variety of Christian sects has become a part of the many cultures now featured in this very complex world.

According to the Biblical Gospels, Jesus, as was true of the great sages of Judaism, was a strong advocate of the position that the moral and the ethical are inseparable. A study of some of the apocryphal literature of

Christianity also leads one to believe that in his teaching Jesus was unable to ignore the political; in fact, it seems likely that the content of the message of Jesus was much more political than reports contained in the New Testament would imply. Perhaps some political coloration to the message of a sincere crusader for truth is virtually inevitable in all but the most simple of societies.

The Biblical Gospels report that Jesus had serious arguments with the Pharisees; that is difficult for some knowledgeable Christians to understand. Actually, however, such disagreements, as described by Gospel writers, would seem to have been inevitable as Jesus, an outspoken and impatient reformer of strong will, found himself restricted by the interpretations of the Law that had been imposed upon him as a member of the Judaic community. The Pharisees had the traditional responsibility for the maintenance of an orderly and tranquil society that functioned within the Judaic tradition, as they interpreted that tradition; thus it became a task of the Pharisees to so interpret the laws of the Torah that their interpretations would have universal applicability to all followers of Judaism. In general, such interpretations were accepted by the populace, and they provided a guide to the members of the Sanhedrin when that body had the responsibility of determining the guilt or innocence of a person accused of violating the Judaic law. Jesus, the idealist, believed in and advocated the development for each person of a strong sense of ethical and moral responsibility; the Pharisees, by contrast, because of the very nature of their responsibility, enunciated interpretations of the Torah designed to provide a suitable basis for a moral and ethical society. The two approaches, unfortunately, do not always lead to the same end point in terms of a code of conduct which a strong, independent individual finds to his liking. Thus, upon occasion, according to Gospel accounts, Jesus revealed his extreme personal frustrations in the harangues in which he is purported to have indulged with the Pharisees.

Students of Christian history have not been in agreement upon the attitude of Jesus in regard to his personal obligation to evolving Judaism. Specifically, did Jesus believe, as presumably a number of his earliest followers believed, that he had been designated by God to be the Messiah? The question is not answerable on the basis of available information, including that contained in the Gospels, but that fact does not prevent scholars as well as nonscholars from indulging in speculation.

The Gospel of Mark, the first Gospel to be written, appears to play down the idea that Jesus came to earth as the particular individual who was to fulfill Messianic prophecy; in fact, in Mark 12:35–37, as some Biblical students interpret the three verses, Jesus seems to deny that he was a descendant of David. But thirty years after the appearance of the Book of Mark, and some seventy years after the death of Jesus, both Matthew and Luke describe Jesus in their writings as the Davidic Messiah; moreover, they seem to imply in their Gospels that Jesus concurred with such a view. And the author of the Gospel of John portrays Jesus as frequently indulging in discourses about his kingship. Matthew even rephrased a question of Jesus as reported by Mark (8:27), "Who do men say that I am?" to read, "Who do men say the son of man is?" (Matthew 16:13). After reviewing and analyzing pertinent sections of the New Testament, doubt has been expressed by some serious students of the Holy Work that Jesus regarded himself as the great king upon whom Messianic prophecy was focused. But, by contrast, a vast number of Christian ecclesiastics believe sincerely that Jesus regarded himself as the one whom God had designated to be the Messiah of prophecy.

Jesus made his reputation in his native Galilee, the locale of his short ministry. Encouraged by his successes, it was only natural that ultimately he would feel impelled to take his message to Jerusalem, the big city which was the location of the great Temple and was the acknowledged center of Judaic life. But it is likely that Jesus knew that he could not anticipate in Jerusalem the cordial reception that apparently had been his lot much of the time in Galilee where religious, sociological, and political conditions were vastly different from those in Jerusalem. Most important, Jerusalem at that time, as already emphasized, was involved in grave political turmoil. Stern measures were being invoked by the Roman rulers to curb actual and potential troublemakers; in fact, executions, often employing crucifixion, were common. If the content of some of the apocryphal literature is valid, Jesus possessed political ideas that undoubtedly would be a source of trouble with the Roman rulers. Because of the uncertainties and possible personal hazards associated with the proposed trip to Jerusalem, one can well believe that attempts were made by his friends to dissuade him from making the journey.

However, in spite of the problems that might confront him, Jesus decided to attend the forthcoming annual Passover festival in Jerusalem; at that time the city would be crowded with pilgrims, so it would be an excellent time for him to preach and to teach. According to Gospel accounts, undoubtedly based on legends, Jesus rode upon an ass when entering the city, an act which was consistent with some traditions that existed at that time in regard to the arrival of the Messiah. Moreover, Gospel writers reported that there was fanfare associated with the entrance of Jesus; according to the Biblical reports, members of his entourage, probably involving only a few close associates, waved palm leaves and shouted "Hosannah!" It is conceivable that some members of the escorting party, ignoring or not understanding the political implications of their words, let it be known that they were accompanying the long-awaited "King of the Jews."

There is considerable agreement on the part of informed scholars that only a very few of the Jews who lived in Jerusalem ever knew of the presence of Jesus in their city or were even aware of his existence; a yet smaller number of Jews, it is likely, ever knew of his execution. Apparently, soon after the arrival of Jesus in Jerusalem, the Roman rulers learned that a strange person, seemingly with political ambitions, had appeared on the scene, and the word obviously caused them to give close attention to the newcomer and his actions. Probably within a short time some of the major religious leaders also became acquainted with the fact that a new critic had appeared in their midst, for it is a fair presumption, as recorded in the Gospel narratives, that Jesus quickly entered into controversy with some of the guardians of Judaism. It is written in the Gospels that he denounced the Scribes and Pharisees as hypocrites; he decried their emphasis on formal interpretations of Judaic doctrine when, in his judgment, the emphasis should be placed on the responsibility of individuals for the solution of real human problems. Modern scholars who are well-versed in the history and the mores of the era in which Jesus lived are generally in agreement upon the likelihood that most of the Jews with whom Jesus had contact, including Pharisees, listened with interest, as they had listened to the prophets of their history, to the critical ideas that Jesus expressed. It would be foolish to deny, however, that if Jesus employed the kind of aggressive approach described in some of the Gospel reports, some who listened may have become alarmed. For Jesus, in keeping with the apparent spirit of his crusading efforts, is reported to have denounced the various merchants and others who he believed were violating the sanctity of the Temple, and finally in a display of temper drove some of the traders and money-changers out of the court of the Temple. Although the Jews of that time, as is true today, were remarkably tolerant, even while they were critical, of any of their people who possessed unusual points of view upon Judaic principle and practice, Jesus was revealing himself as a troublemaker, not merely as an unorthodox adherent to Judaism. Under such circumstances, some of the wiser and older citizens of Jerusalem might well have considered the desirability of trying to restrain Jesus lest, in the extremely tense atmosphere that already existed in the city, he might indulge in some action that would provide a reason for the Roman legions to instigate a pogrom. There had been several occasions when with little or no justification large numbers of Jews had been massacred; certainly those experiences were recalled with bitterness by many Jewish citizens.

The apparently turbulent career of Jesus in Jerusalem lasted only about a week before he was arrested, tried, and executed. Gospel narratives report that Jesus knew that his end was near when the night before his arrest he celebrated his Last Supper with his chosen twelve disciples; possibly the meal in which Jesus and his disciples were involved was the traditional meal that is a fundamental part of the Passover celebration. The Last Supper is commonly regarded by Christians as having great importance in Christian history. The story of that last night and the arrest of Jesus is given a dramatic touch by the reported denial of Jesus by Peter, a favorite of Jesus among his twelve intimates, and by the purported betrayal of Jesus by Judas Iscariot, another of the twelve intimates. It may be noted in connection with the reported action of Judas that among the early apocryphal gospels that were commonly regarded by first- and second-century Christian congregations as authoritative sources of information upon Jesus was one ascribed to Judas Iscariot; possibly, however, Judas was not the author of the work.

The reports given in the Biblical Gospels, which is the only knowledge that we possess, of events that preceded and occurred during the trial of Jesus have been the subject of a vast amount of discussion and controversy. Some of the controversy has arisen because of differing conclusions reached by Biblical scholars who are well versed in Judaic mores of the time of Jesus and by adherents to Christianity who read the Biblical account in a literal manner. One cannot doubt, in fact, that the differing conclusions have been strongly responsible for producing the traditional schism between many Jews and many Christians. In the Gospel accounts, great emphasis is given to the involvement of the high priests in events preceding the arrest and trial of Jesus and then during the trial itself. When noting this emphasis, it must be realized, as already noted, that the high priests of that time were regarded generally by the Jews as despicable characters and as utterly untrustworthy. Since the high priests received their appointment from the Roman procurator then in power, who at that time was Pontius Pilate, they became agents of the procurator in carrying out his will; moreover, they did not hesitate to provide testimony at civil trials of a kind that would be pleasing to the man who had appointed them. The very fact of their purported strong involvement in the arrest and trial of Jesus seems to reveal to many students of Jewish history that Pilate wanted to eliminate Jesus from the scene. The Gospel narratives provide only limited information in regard to the charges made against Jesus, but enough is said to make it seem clear that the Gospel authors believed the charges to be political, not religious. Several accusers, according to Gospel accounts, stressed current reports, which for the Romans had a critical political connotation, that Jesus professed to be a king, the Messiah. Although the procedures followed after the arrest of Jesus are not clarified by the New Testament accounts, one cannot doubt that it was the Romans who conducted the trial, a civil trial.

In the Gospel accounts of the arrest and trial of Jesus, there are brief mentions of the involvement of *the* Scribes. This is very difficult for informed students of Jewish history to understand, for, as already indicated, it is likely that few of the Jewish people in Jerusalem, including the comparatively large number of Scribes, ever knew of the existence of Jesus; to indict all the Scribes, as the Gospel reports seem to do, must be regarded as unfortunate. Moreover, the Scribes, in general, were intellectuals, and they tended to be objective in the way in which they analyzed political, sociological, and religious issues with which they were confronted; they were tolerant of the views of others. In addition, since the Scribes were rigid believers in the tenets of Judaism, they would not subscribe to crucifixion as a mode of execution, and, in the belief of many students of the subject, they would not subscribe to a trial proceeding that might lead to crucifixion.

After the trial of Jesus, such as it was, was completed, he was turned over to Pontius Pilate for any further investigation that he might care to make and for the passing of an appropriate sentence; such an action was consistent with common procedures of the day. It is likely that the appearance before Pilate was a mere formality; even though the procurator might attempt to convey the impression of giving justice, he usually knew before the trial started how he would have it end. In view of the violent and virtually uncontrollable political situation that existed at that time in Jerusalem, it is clear why Pilate would want to make away with a person who he must have decided was dangerous or at least potentially dangerous. So, after carrying out his investigation, probably of a very superficial nature, he ordered Jesus to be crucified. It was easy to give such an order at that time. Crucifixion, it must be emphasized again, was a Roman form of execution that was anathema to the Jews.

So Jesus died on a cross, one of a vast number of Jews of that time who died in such a manner, victim of Rome's brutal policies of oppression. That same day, other men, convicted criminals, were also crucified.

Professing Christians, when making a study of the Gospels, must understand that undoubtedly the authors of the Gospels were much perturbed and actually embittered by the fact that the Jewish people generally had refused to accept Jesus as the Messiah. Moreover, by the time the last three Gospels were written, recruits to the banner of Jesus were almost entirely non-Jewish, so, virtually out of necessity, the last three Gospels were addressed to such a readership. But at that time, because of military and political actions that Rome had initiated against the Jews (of which the tragic destruction of Jerusalem was a part), the non-Jewish citizens of the Roman world were identifying the Jews with their enemies. As a result, few Biblical scholars would now deny that it was virtually inevitable that the authors of the Gospels, especially of the last three Gospels, would display some prejudice against the Jews in their treatment of events that occurred in connection with the trial and death of Jesus.

Even a slight display of prejudice against the Jews in the highly respected work of literature accepted by most Christians as the Holy Book of Christianity must be regarded as tragic, for Jesus himself was a Jew, the twelve men who were his chosen disciples and closest friends were Jewish, all except one of the Gospel authors were Jewish, and most of his early interpreters, including Paul, were Jewish. Moreover, the message of Jesus can only be understood as a product of his Judaic background. But, unfortunately, in keeping with a tradition that goes back at least as far as the third century A.D., which apparently received support from a reading of the Gospels, many Christians have concluded that responsibility for the death of Jesus must be placed upon the shoulders of the Jews living in Jerusalem during the time of Pontius Pilate. Such a theme was developed in a dramatic manner in the traditional plot of the world-famous Passion Play held in Oberammergau, Germany. It is even true that some Christians have believed that the responsibility for the death of Jesus must be placed upon the shoulders of the Jewish people generally. Slowly, such truly unfortunate points of

154

view are being erased. Recently, serious although generally unsuccessful efforts have been made to revise the plot of the Passion Play at Ober-ammergau to eliminate its unfortunate anti-Semitic elements. Moreover, the Roman Catholic Church has revised some parts of its liturgy that in the past have been responsible, many critics have believed, for stimu-lating anti-Jewish attitudes.

Ultimately, many years after the death of Jesus on a cross and after the religious philosophy and theological doctrines associated with the name of Jesus had taken on a number of distinctive characteristics that could no longer be identified with traditional Judaism, the cross generally became accepted as the supreme symbol of the new faith, Christianity. This does not mean, however, that the use of the cross as a religious symbol originated with followers of Christianity; in antiquity, many pagan peoples had adopted the cross for religious purposes. In the Middle Ages, when in much of the civilized world the Christian Church became a tremendous power in human affairs, religious, sociological, and political, the cross was often endowed with tremendous significance, even mystical significance. Making the sign of the cross became accepted as a salutation to the Lord prior to offering a prayer. Christian places of worship, major and minor, were identified by crosses. And the cross often preceded great armies into battle; sometimes it appeared as a part of the insignia of rulers, and it frequently appeared in works of art, especially religious art. Artisans commonly employed the cross as a symbol of faith when they created configurations for personal adornment.

Not too long after the death of Jesus, some advocates of his religious philosophy began to find fundamental theological significance in his death; in fact, many students of Christian history would agree with the assertion that Christian theology, as distinct from Judaic theology, was born as a result of interpretations of the death of Jesus that soon were developed and promulgated. Jesus, it was argued frequently by some of his early followers, and the same doctrinal belief continues to be ad-vanced today by many, possibly most, Christian theologians, gave his life on the cross as atonement to God for the sins of mankind. Thus, basic to the faith of many Christians, today as well as yesterday, is the principle that Jesus offered himself as a sacrifice to make possible man's salvation. The letters of Paul to members of some of the first congregations in which he had an interest contain many references to the deep meaning which he had found and which others fervently dedicated to the new religious movement should find in the death of Jesus upon a cross.

Mark reported that after the death of Jesus, which according to his source of information, occurred the day before the Sabbath, the body of Jesus was placed "in a tomb which had been hewn out of the rock" (Mark 15:46), and then a stone was rolled "against the door of the tomb." "When the Sabbath was past," according to Mark, the tomb was visited by three women who had followed Jesus to Jerusalem, but, to their consternation, they discovered that the stone had been rolled away and the tomb was empty. A young man seated inside the empty cavity, Mark asserted, informed the amazed and frightened women that Jesus "has risen, he is not here." Then the young man instructed the women to "go, tell his disciples and Peter that he [Jesus] is going before you to Galilee; there you will see him as he told you." (In Mark 13:28 it is reported that at the conclusion of the Last Supper Jesus in a dialogue with his close associates not only warned them of his imminent execution but also anticipated for them his Resurrection and later appearance in Galilee.) Mark, when concluding his very brief account of the purported Resurrection of Jesus and the episode at the empty tomb, observed that the three women who had visited the tomb seeking Jesus were astonished and they trembled. Then, he noted, "They said nothing to any one, for they were afraid." That sentence terminates Mark's Gospel.

In the light of later developments, the abrupt ending to the Gospel of Mark must be regarded as dramatic, for the "Resurrection of Jesus," memorialized by Christians in the celebration of Easter, has received widespread acceptance by Christian scholars as the most fundamental concept in the Christian theology that began to evolve very soon after the death of Jesus. In recent years a Christian clergyman asserted in a sermon to his congregation, "Without the substantiation of the claim of Christ to Divinity as provided by his Resurrection, all of his other teaching would be invalidated, and his death on the cross meaningless." The other Biblical Gospels provide considerable elaboration of the simple report of the Resurrection as given by Mark. Thus it is evident that in the thirty years that elapsed between the composition of the Book of Mark and the writing of the Gospels by Matthew, Luke, and John, the report of the Resurrection underwent much expansion and embellishment. Undoubtedly the report had powerful religious meaning for the early followers of Jesus. During the first years after the death of Jesus, the account of the Resurrection must have been transmitted orally from person to person among his followers, and it was a common subject for discussion by advocates of the new Jesus Cult of Judaism.

The idea of the Resurrection of Jesus, as described by Gospel authors, was not incompatible with the pagan beliefs of many of the Roman non-Jews who were displaying an interest in the novel Judaic cult that was incorporating into traditional Judaic doctrine some of the ideas that were being advanced pertaining to Jesus. Moreover, for many Jews, including the scholarly Pharisees, of whom Paul was one, acceptance of the principle of the Resurrection of the body under circumstances that might seem to be applicable in the case of Jesus was consistent with sound Judaic doctrine. And certainly the report of the Resurrection of Jesus would satisfy the psychological needs of his early followers, for they must have found it virtually impossible to believe that Jesus, whom they accepted as Divine and as the Messiah, chosen by God, could die as would any other man. The report also served in a remarkable way, as already noted, to validate much of the Christian doctrine that was evolving. Undoubtedly the idea that Jesus had been resurrected from the dead became a potent factor in furthering the Christian movement.

Although many professing Christians, chiefly in recent centuries, usually the same ones who have had difficulty in accepting the idea of the Virgin Birth, have also had difficulty, for somewhat similar reasons, in accepting the idea of the Resurrection of Jesus, a vast number of Christians do accept the phenomenon as having a factual basis, and they find in it profound religious meaning. Moreover, since the events associated with the death and Resurrection of Jesus occurred during the Passover season, some Christians have interpreted the happenings as signifying a Divine notification to mankind that Christianity represents a new faith that incorporates within itself the Judaic tradition of pre-Christian times.

It is said that Jesus, after his Resurrection, spent fifty days in Galilee, and after that, according to Christian legend, he ascended into Heaven. But a return of Jesus to the earth was prophesied by some New Testament writers, and such a return is fervently anticipated by many Christians; the return is usually described as the "second coming of Christ." It may be suspected that some early Christians, notably Matthew, were influenced in their advocacy of the idea of the "second coming" by the writings of the prophet Micah. (Note Micah, Chapter 1.)

For many Christians it has become a fundamental principle of their faith that upon the occasion of the prophesied return of Jesus to the earth he will preside as judge of all men who have lived since the beginning of time. In connection with that climatic occasion, Matthew (Chapter 24) revealed his conviction, based on a recorded saying of Jesus, that, in advance of the "second coming," the Gospel "will be preached through-out the whole world." But in spite of the substantial progress of the Christian movement which Matthew seemed to anticipate, he warned that the "second coming" would be preceded by "wars and rumors of wars," "nation will rise against nation," "there will be famine and earthquakes," a variety of cataclysmic disturbances will occur in nature, "false prophets will arise," and those loyal to the name of Jesus will be put to death. Other descriptions of the events which would precede the return of Jesus to earth were promulgated by other Christian writers. Paul and some of the other early Christian missionaries undertook the task of preparing their followers for the anticipated second coming of Jesus, which they seemed to believe was imminent. For instance, in the second letter of Paul to the Thessalonians (II Thessalonians 2), he attempted to calm some fears that apparently had developed in regard to the event by urging readers of his letters "not to be quickly shaken in mind or excited"; then he proceeded to warn the Thessalonians that before the second appearance of Jesus on earth they would need to contend with a dangerous anti-Christ who would ultimately be destroyed by Jesus. In his letter to the Romans (Chapter 11), Paul decried the "hardening" that "has come upon part of Israel," but he expressed the belief that, apparently before the final day of judgment, "all Israel will be saved." Thus Paul seemed to believe that before Jesus again returned to earth all the Jewish people would accept him as their Messiah.

Doctrines pertaining to the second coming of Christ and the final day of judgment continue to be a fundamental part of the teaching of probably a majority of Christian sects. According to traditional Roman Catholic principle, the souls of all men will be reunited with their bodies at the time of the second coming. Then, after Jesus has made his final determination of judgment in regard to the merit of each person's life on earth, all men will be assigned to eternal destiny in either Heaven or Hell.

During the period of the so-called enlightenment in the United States and in parts of Europe, which started in the eighteenth century and lasted well into the nineteenth century, a major debate over Christology raged in theological circles. The debate revealed a tendency on the part of some Christian ecclesiastics to make a distinction between Jesus, the man of history, and the Jesus about whom, at least in part, a religion was constructed. The advocacy of such a distinction is interesting because it is typical of some of the devices that often have been created through the centuries by disturbed Christians to surmount some of the difficulties that they encounter when reading the Biblical Gospels; the acceptance of the distinction enabled some critical students of orthodox Christian belief to be unconcerned by some of the problems that arose for them when considering whether they should or could accept such ideas as the Resurrection and the Virgin Birth. A person accepting the point of view advanced by a large number of ecclesiastics during the Enlightenment probably would take the position that, in the real world of experience, the so-called miracles reported in the New Testament, including the Resurrection and the Virgin Birth, did not occur. But, even while taking such a position, probably the same person would concur with the idea, strange as it may seem to many Christians, that the Resurrection and the Virgin Birth, along with all the ramifications associated with them in Christian literature, in Christian art, and in other aspects of Christian culture, are a significant part of the Christian heritage.

Chapter Seven

THE BEGINNINGS OF CHRISTIANITY

PAUL OF TARSUS

A trustworthy account of events that took place during the first years after the death of Jesus and which led to the development of what has often been described as the Jesus Cult of Judaism, later to evolve into a distinctive religion known as Christianity, is impossible to write. It is likely that New Testament writers, as already has been emphasized, possessed little authentic information upon which to base any of their writings; in fact, probably they were forced to contend with conflicting reports and legends when they wrote their accounts of the activities of the followers of Jesus during the first years after his death. And recognized historical sources contribute virtually no information of value to students of the history of Christianity to assist them in resolving their many questions pertaining to events and people immediately after the death of Jesus.

It is the judgment of some careful students of the history of the Christian tradition that most of the followers of Jesus, including his chosen twelve, returned to Galilee shortly after he was crucified. Although Jesus may have attempted to prepare his friends for his probable arrest and even his possible death, the actual occurrences probably caused great dismay and disbelief on the part of his very close associates. Even after a considerable period of time following the death of Jesus, who may have been a person of such strong personality that he exercised almost hypnotic powers over his close associates, his attitudes and ideas must have persisted as a dominant force within the company of individuals who had been his friends. That very fact continued to provide the former intimates of Jesus an identity and a bond of unity that was not easily destroyed. In the course of time, in fact, a number of the followers of Jesus returned to Jerusalem; probably they were drawn there by a common desire to revisit the locale of their last memorable days with Jesus. In Jerusalem, undoubtedly they continued their traditional religious practices as required by their adherence to Judaism, but some of their attitudes and points of view had been modified so that they were a reflection of those of Jesus. Moreover, it appears that the idea that Messianic prophecy had been fulfilled in the person of Jesus had become a key element of belief for most if not all of the followers of Jesus who had returned to Jerusalem from Galilee.

It is believed by many knowledgeable scholars that the disciples of Jesus who returned to Jerusalem organized their own synagogue so that they could more easily maintain their common interests and sense of purpose. In spite of the probable smallness of the group, it rapidly became known as a distinctive and actually as a troublesome clique within the larger community of Jews in Jerusalem. The Book of Acts, which usually is regarded as essentially trustworthy with respect to the major elements of its presentation if not in its details, recalls episodes involving harangues by a few members of the new synagogue that took place before Judaic audiences. The treatment of the Book of Acts seems to confirm the probable fact that several of those who belonged to the new synagogue and who professed to be followers of Jesus took full advantage of the freedom of expression provided by their Judaic faith, in the synagogue and elsewhere, to present the cause of Jesus and to assail those who did not agree with their points of view. Peter, acknowledged spokesman for the twelve men whom Jesus chose to constitute his inner circle as well as the most aggressive among them, was the original leader of the new Jesus Cult in Jerusalem, which quickly became known as a dissident Judaic faction. Often Peter was personally involved in controversy with some members of the Judaic faith who disliked the manner in which so many adherents to the Jesus Cult were diluting traditional Judaic doctrine. During the time of Peter's leadership he won a number of converts to his ideas pertaining to Jesus; it is recorded that he was successful in persuading one of the first if not the first non-Jew to accept the novel religious tenets for which he had become a crusader.

Although relations between the new Judaic congregation headed by Peter and the larger Judaic community in Jerusalem were continually subjected to strain, probably the most critical problems that had to be faced by the dissident group were a consequence of internal dissension and disagreement. For instance, since within a short time a few non-Jews were being attracted to the Jesus-oriented variety of Judaism advocated by Peter and his associates, the question had to arise and be debated in regard to the eligibility of such persons to affiliate with a Judaic synagogue in view of the fact that they had not been circumcised. Even more serious, as the number of recruits to the Jesus Cult increased, was the development of at least two contending factions within the congregation itself; one large faction was composed of Aramaic-speaking Jews and a smaller but very aggressive faction was composed of Greek-speaking Jews, usually described as Hellenistic Jews. The Hellenistic Jews, in their behavior and in their mental processes, were a product of Greek culture. Evidently an extremely serious situation soon developed. The author of the Book of Acts, Chapter 6, noted that "the Hellenists murmured against the Hebrews because their widows were neglected in the daily distribution." Presumably the Hellenistic Jews believed, rightly or wrongly, that because of their minority status they were not receiving their fair share of the benefits, including food for widows and alms for the poor, that were commonly allocated to individuals in need who had an affiliation with the dispensing synagogue. Consequently, seven "over-seers," including the militant and fiery Stephen, were chosen by the Hellenists, with the approval of the leadership of the synagogue, to represent their interests within the community of the synagogue. But the split within the little community could not be resolved so easily, for it appears that most of the difficulties which had arisen actually possessed an ideological basis. The Hellenistic Jews were a freewheeling lot; al-though they were nominal adherents to Judaism, often they found it impossible to accept some commonly accepted interpretations of Judaic doctrine and law; they were almost eager in their receptivity of novel ideas. By contrast, members of the majority within the Peter-led congre-gation were, in common with most followers of Judaism, essentially traditional in their approach to their interpretation of Judaic teachings; they would not permit their acceptance of Jesus as the Messiah and their concept of his mission on earth to jeopardize their adherence to long-established Judaic principles and practices. Judaic law, as given in the Torah, remained the keystone of their beliefs.

Finally, it appears, the situation reached a state of crisis when Stephen began to indulge in harsh debates with influential members of the Jewish community in Jerusalem. Undoubtedly some members of the synagogue with which he had an affiliation did not escape his bitter tongue. The passion that would engulf Stephen during his arguments led him, ac-cording to the Book of Acts, to make irrational statements and to indulge in stinging denunciations of those Jews, (the majority) who would not accept his unusual ideas pertaining to Judaic history and doctrine as well as his beliefs in regard to Jesus. He advanced the idea that the Jews were an undeserving people who throughout their history had never given proper recognition to the will of God; upon one occasion, reported in the Book of Acts, he even warned that Jesus would return and destroy the Temple, the holy edifice that was the physical focus of the Judaic faith and which was held in tremendous reverence by all adherents to Judaism. One cannot doubt that Stephen's strong condemnation of his Jewish listeners and the vigorous nature of his attack on their traditions and their deeply held beliefs stirred them to a frenzy, especially since some of his charges seemed to smack of blasphemy. So Stephen was taken before the Judaic authorities in Jerusalem, probably before the judges of the Sanhedrin, for examination. When concluding his testimony, Stephen cried out, according to the Biblical record, which must be regarded as an edited paraphrase of Stephen's words, "You stiff-necked people, uncircumcised in heart and ears, you always resist the Holy Spirit. As your fathers did, so do you. Which of the prophets did your fathers persecute? And they killed those who announced beforehand the coming of the Righteous One, whom you have now betrayed and murdered."

Such vitriolic words, which were made especially unbearable by the fact that they came from the lips of a Jew tainted with despised Hellenism, went beyond the tolerance of many members of the Jewish population of Jerusalem, and possibly of the judges of the Sanhedrin. A mob took over, and Stephen was stoned to death. (Possibly the action was prescribed by the Sanhedrin; stoning to death was an acceptable form of execution for extreme violators of Judaic law.) So in Christain society Stephen is often described as Christianity's first martyr; it must also be said that he indulged in tactics that could not fail to stir the most extreme passions of Jews who were dedicated to the Judaic tradition as they understood it and respected it.

The episode involving Stephen and, in fact, the general behavior of the Hellenistic Jews who were members of the congregation that espoused the Jesus Cult of Judaism must have served to increase the tension that existed in Jerusalem between those adherents to Judaism who also professed to be followers of Jesus and the larger Judaic community. It is probable, in fact, that at that moment the very future of the religious movement that ultimately became Christianity hung in the balance. Consequently, Peter was replaced as leader of the particular Judaic congregation in Jerusalem that espoused, along with the usual Judaic doctrines, the novel ideas being advanced by Peter and others pertaining to Jesus and his mission. The successor to Peter was James, brother of Jesus. The conjecture has been advanced that Peter, who was himself an ardent crusader, was temperamentally unable to resolve the issues that had developed among those who had accepted his leadership. Or it is possible that he was unwilling to make certain decisions that had become necessary to solve the critical problems that had arisen. One may well surmise that James, apparently a conservative in his interpretation of the Judaic tradition, decided that a successful future for the religious movement initiated by his brother depended on having the continued strong support of the majority of the group which he now headed; the Hellenistic Jews must be eased out of the decision-making process. (If the previous statement is a valid interpretation of the position taken by James, history reveals that he was mistaken.)

In the meantime a small community of persons attached to the Jesus Cult of Judaism had been formed in Antioch, already referred to as the locale of a dynamic center of progressive thought within Judaism—a kind of thought, it is becoming increasingly clear, that provided a fertile environment for the development of primitive Christianity. Antioch is often described by historians of that era as the Queen City of the East. Its modern name is Antâkya, which is located in what is now southeastern Turkey. Antioch, originally laid out by Alexander's representatives in imitation of the plan conceived for Alexandria, became within a couple of centuries after its creation virtually a miniature Alexandria with cultural resources within the Greek tradition that were excelled only by those of Alexandria. Many, possibly most, of the Hellenistic Jews in Jerusalem who had become followers of Jesus may have emigrated to Antioch after James succeeded Peter; the liberal and dynamic atmosphere that existed in that city would have been very much to their liking. According to tradition, members of the Jesus Cult of Judaism in Antioch, who in the beginning were mostly, possibly entirely, Hellenistic Jews, were the first followers of Jesus to adopt the designation "Christian"; for many decades, however, even those who regarded themselves as Christian, characterized by the Romans as Nazarenes, continued their allegiance to Judaism. Since members of the Judaic community in Antioch affiliated with the Jesus Cult gladly accepted non-Jews within their ranks, the question of circumcision arose. But apparently there was no tendency to insist upon the traditional importance of the practice; rather, baptism, a rite practiced regularly by the Essenes and popularized by John the Baptist but which seems to have received only limited attention on the part of the first followers of Jesus, became acceptable as the symbolic act of a person announcing his decision to partake of "a new life" among

164

"the chosen of the Lord." It appears, in view of the initiative taken by members of the Jesus Cult in Antioch, that other congregations affiliated with the same cult, especially those giving emphasis to the recruitment of non-Jews, soon began to replace circumcision by baptism as the accepted ritual for symbolizing a person's affiliation with the new cult of Judaism and for the acceptance of all that such an affiliation implied. Such a trend obviously represented a truly radical break with the Judaic tradition and reveals something of the liberal spirit of the Hellenistic Jews, especially those in Antioch. In truth, the people in Antioch who affiliated with the Jesus Cult adopted a very liberal attitude toward many aspects of traditional Judaism.

The synagogue affiliated with the Jesus Cult in Antioch, which soon may have had a membership composed of more Greek Gentiles than Greek Jews, has often been described as "the mother of the Gentile churches." Although it appears that the relationship of the members of the Jesus Cult in Antioch with those who belonged to the Jesus Cult in Jerusalem remained fairly cordial, it is easy to believe that strong differences in ideology between the two groups began to develop. When Jerusalem was destroyed by the Roman legions in A.D. 70, Antioch became the citadel of the Jesus Cult. The future of Christianity would now be determined by Hellenists, not by the followers of Jesus who were a product of the cultural climate of Jerusalem. The sponsors of the new religious movement would be strong men who never knew Jesus; it was inevitable that they would enunciate their own interpretations, often novel interpretations, of Christian doctrine. They would remake Christianity in their own image of what they thought it should be. Although the simple but powerful humanitarian philosophy of Jesus continued to be the basic ingredient of the philosophy of Christianity, much primitive Christian doctrine would now reveal the ideas developed by Paul, a Greek Jew, and to the kind of Hellenistic thinking found within the Christian community of Antioch. For the first few centuries of the Christian era, with only a few interruptions in the trend, the stature of Antioch as a dynamic stronghold of Christianity continued to increase.

Although the evidence is limited, it appears that after Jerusalem was destroyed in A.D. 70, some of the members of the Jesus Cult who had lived in the great city prior to its destruction, including virtually all of the persons who had been acquaintances of Jesus and who had survived the massacre, succeeded for a while in clinging together to the north of Jerusalem, possibly in the small community of Pella, a short distance south of the Sea of Galilee. Virtually no information is available in regard to the group or its activities. Suffice it to say, the group had no further influence upon the development of the Christian tradition.

After the headship of the congregation of the synagogue in Jerusalem that was affiliated with the Jesus Cult was shifted from Peter to James, Peter's position in the new religious movement apparently was no longer one of dominance. For a time, however, he actively pursued his missionary endeavors; he was often involved in controversy and even in personal danger. According to Biblical references and apocryphal literature, several of the other intimates of Jesus—John is mentioned frequently—also engaged in missionary work in behalf of the religious concepts and principles that had become basic to the beliefs and practices of the Jesus Cult. But the personal leadership of the new religious movement was beginning to pass to a new generation of crusaders, notably to Paul of Tarsus.

There can be no doubt, however, that Peter continued to be accepted throughout the first centuries of the Christian movement as the most glamorous character of the early Christian drama; probably even today he is the most honored of those, other than Jesus, who were closely associated with Christianity in its infancy. In the early days of Christianity, elaborate romances were woven about Peter's supposed wanderings, which were the subject of many fanciful legends. Such legends captured the interest of many Christians, especially during the second, third, and fourth centuries. One legend pertaining to Peter, commonly accepted as fact by most persons affiliated with the Roman Catholic Church, at least since the fourth century, designates him as the founder of the Christian Church in Rome, where, according to the same legend, he died a martyr's death in A.D. 67. Thus it has become a part of the tradition of the Roman Church that Peter was its first Pope. Hard historical and even Biblical evidence to support the legend of Peter's association with the Roman Church is virtually lacking although Roman Catholic ecclesiastics have advanced many arguments in an attempt to provide validation to the legend.

When Stephen was stoned to death, the mob in Jerusalem, one may surmise from the Biblical account, also vented its rage upon other members of the Jesus Cult of Judaism. Probably several members of the congregation associated with the Jesus Cult were injured and some may have been killed. Among the leaders of the mob, or possibly *the* leader of the mob, was a Judaic Pharisee named "Saul who is surnamed Paul."

166

Under such circumstances Paul is introduced in the New Testament as a character in Christian history. Paul's aggressive actions as one of the leaders of the mob testify to the fact of his deep hatred of the new Jesus movement and of all those who were associated with it; Paul was a passionate believer in Judaism, and he could not possibly tolerate any saying or action that violated his notion of what constituted truth. Yet, if Jesus is omitted from the consideration, that same Paul was the man who made more contributions of greater and lasting significance to Christianity, as it developed into a major component of the cultures of a large part of the world, than any other person in history.

But who was Paul? It appears that Paul was born in about A.D. 10; thus as available data have usually been interpreted, he was born about a decade and a half after the birth of Jesus. The place of his birth was Tarsus, a city located on the Cilician plain in what is now southern Turkey, approximately one hundred miles west of Antioch. Paul, as noted earlier, received a superior systematic education as a student in Jerusalem; moreover, of very great importance, his intellectual background was nourished by the kind of life that he led in his early years. Tarsus, where Paul was born, was strategically located on the land bridge between Europe and Asia used in the first century by a great variety of travelers. So Paul, who has often been described in Christian literature as "the world apostle," was raised in a community that possessed an international flavor; as a young man, moreover, he traveled extensively in Asia Minor. His intellectual development undoubtedly profited greatly from his contacts with many people who possessed diverse backgrounds and who held varied points of view; his mental processes and ideas were also influenced by the several cultural environments in which he spent time. But Hellenism had penetrated strongly into every aspect of life in the area with which Paul was closely identified, especially the cities, so he was chiefly a product of Greek culture and was fluent in the use of the Greek language. Moreover, Paul spoke Aramaic, the living language of the majority of the Jewish people of that period of history.

As is true of Jesus, no image of Paul exists. Legends imply that he was not an imposing man in stature or in appearance; it appears that he suffered severely from ill health. The apocryphal book, Acts of Paul, tells a beautiful story of Paul and of his affection for an attractive young lady named Thecla; the tale was popular in some of the early Christian communities although much of its content must have been fictitious. During the telling of the story, Paul is described as a "man of little stature, going bald, crooked in the legs, but powerfully built, with eyebrows joining, and nose somewhat hooked." It is widely assumed that such a description is essentially accurate, for the Acts of Paul has won favor among many scholars. A reading of Paul's letters reveals that he was a sensitive scholar and that he possessed unusual literary ability.

Paul was a Roman citizen, but he was also a Jew of the tribe of Benjamin; King Saul was of the same tribe. Obviously the stern upbringing in Judaism to which Paul was subjected as a youth was accomplished, at least in part, through the medium of the Septuagint; so his religious philosophy was influenced to some extent by the Hellenistic coloration that the Septuagint possesses. Ultimately Paul became a Pharisee. Then, as noted earlier, since he seemed to develop an intense interest in his religious heritage, he went to Jerusalem to study the Law in the Academy of the House of Hillel, a Pharisaic academy. Although the program of studies offered to its students by the academy was centered on Judaic Law and doctrine, the coverage of the program in terms of content was actually very broad. When Paul went to Jerusalem, the head of the academy was Rabban Gamaliel, son of Hillel. Paul wrote that he "was brought up . . . at the feet of Gamaliel." Because of his determination to become well educated as a Judaic scholar, he threw himself with great determination into the intensive and systematic program of study that the academy maintained. Possibly because of his complete immersion in his Judaic studies, Paul became almost fanatical in his devotion to his religious heritage; several years later, in a letter to the Galatians (Galatians 1:14), he recalled those days by saying of himself, "I advanced in Judaism beyond many of my own age among my people, so extremely zealous was I for the tradition of my fathers."

Although Paul was a contemporary of Jesus, there is little likelihood that they ever met; in truth, it is probable that Paul knew nothing of Jesus while Jesus lived. The career of Paul preceded the writing of the Gospels, but it is probable that ultimately he became familiar with some of the reports about Jesus, mostly oral, that at a later date provided part of the foundation for the writings of the Gospel authors. It is most likely, while Paul was studying in Jerusalem, that he became aware of some of the more controversial ideas being promulgated by members of the new Jesus Cult. One may assume, in view of the troubles that the new cult was causing within the Jewish community in Jerusalem, that Paul, a militant religionist, soon sought occasions to indulge in debate with Stephen and other members of the cult. The initial result of his experiences with those who were affiliated with the Jesus Cult and with their ideas was that Paul developed a passionate hatred of the cult and all that it stood for. As an ardent Pharisee, he was stirred to anger by the bitter and often unjustified attacks that a few of the more zealous members of the cult were making on the Pharisees and on many aspects of the religious tradition that for Paul gave meaning to life. When Stephen was stoned to death, Paul, as already noted, was a leader or possibly the leader of the mob. Then fired by a desire to destroy the blasphemous movement completely, he hastened north toward Damascus to lead an action there against a new congregation of people professing adherence to the despised cult.

On the road to Damascus, Paul underwent a truly remarkable experience that involved a complete reversal of his point of view in regard to some of the most basic tenets of the Jesus Cult; in the terminology of the Christian evangelist, Paul was converted. Although such a phenomenon has not been unusual in the history of the great leaders of mankind, its occurrence in the case of Paul is difficult to explain. He had been a passionate advocate of Judaism; in fact, he had been one of the stalwarts of the Judaic community in Jerusalem. His Judaic faith had not been an element of his life that could be accepted or rejected; his religion had been his life.

Three accounts of Paul's conversion are given in the Book of Acts, and several times in his letters to Christian communities Paul described his personal experience as he traveled to Damascus. From being a bitter crusader against the Jesus Cult of Judaism, Paul, the Pharisee, suddenly became an equally ardent crusader in behalf of the cult and its tenets. Apparently basing his ideas on such information as he had been able to glean from comments made by members of the new cult—and probably that was the only initial information that he possessed about Jesus and the cult that accepted Jesus as the Messiah—Paul developed his own interpretation of the Jesus concept; then he became so completely dedicated to that interpretation of Jesus and his mission that he actually began to believe that Jesus "lived in him."

Any attempt to explain Paul's conversion, of such tremendous consequence for the future of the Christian movement, must involve conjecture. But suggestions have been made that would seem to have considerable validity in explaining the significant change in Paul's life. Modern Judaic scholarship has found that even among some of the most devout among the Jews of the first century there was a pronounced tendency to dilute the traditional substance of Judaism with mystical elements; the trend, it is generally agreed, revealed the influence of Hellenistic culture. For some Jews like Paul who were products of Hellenistic culture, the trend must have taken on intense personal meaning if and when they came under the influence of the Jesus Cult, for inherent in some of its novel ideas were mystical elements that the traditional teachings of Judaism, with their emphasis on the Law, could not provide. The idea of the Resurrection of Jesus must have aroused much interest on the part of Paul. He may have decided while on the road to Damascus, the result of a sudden burst of enlightenment, that the principle of Resurrection, which was fundamental Pharisaic doctrine, had been fulfilled in the case of Jesus. Paul's later utterances seem to reveal that the reported Resurrection of Jesus was a major factor in his decision to accept the Christian faith. Thus Paul, in spite of his previous strongly negative attitude toward Jesus and the Jesus Cult, suddenly found himself impelled to rethink his ideas about Jesus, thus leading to his truly remarkable decision to accept Jesus as the Messiah of prophecy.

Undoubtedly the conversion of Paul on his way to Damascus was the result of factors involved in the workings of his mind that were much more complex than implied in previous suggestions. But of the greatest importance for students of the history of Christianity is the fact that from such mental processes came the realization for Paul that the Jesus Cult's portrayal of Jesus as the Messiah, as the designated intermediary between God and man, and as the Son of God who rose from the grave provided for him, perhaps as a happy culmination to many years of philosophical meditation, a desirable kind of completeness to the prevailing Judaic notion of the God-man universe. But when Paul adopted in essence the strange but intriguing ideas about Jesus that were being advanced by members of the Jesus Cult, one must not assume that he abruptly gave up his Judaic faith; rather, he had made a discovery that for him made his faith more complete and more meaningful.

So Paul, obviously a man of great courage, changed from being a prosecutor of the Jesus Cult to being a defender and an advocate. But even after Paul had spent many years as a dynamic crusader in behalf of the special tenets of the Jesus Cult, it appears that he remained deeply dedicated to Judaism, the faith of his fathers. A reading of Paul's letters to the Romans, written many years after he had accepted the basic principles of the Jesus Cult, provides a glimpse of Paul's pride in being a Jew and of his pride in his Judaic heritage. Nevertheless, Paul had decided, as revealed in his letters, that Jews who refused to accept Jesus as the

Messiah and as their Saviour no longer had adequate spiritual nourishment to sustain their Judaic faith; they could be likened to branches of an olive tree that had been broken off from the trunk of the tree and, consequently, had been separated from the roots that had provided them nourishment. He reminded such Jews, "remember it is not you that supports the root, but the root that supports you." (Romans 11:18.) Probably Paul would have been dismayed if he could have foreseen that his own religious activities would serve to provide part of the basis for the ultimate separation of Christianity from Judaism.

Following Paul's "conversion," he actually took over the disorganized and imperfect ideas of the Jesus Cult and assumed for himself the task of being the cult's spokesman and interpreter as well as the person with the responsibility for perfecting and synthesizing its principles and concepts; he also became its most dynamic advocate. Seemingly he became convinced that Jesus was using him to provide authoritative elaborations and interpretations of the philosophy which he had espoused and, as well, to provide a systematic organization of the ideas that the Jesus Cult was promulgating pertaining to Jesus, his mission, and his death. The humanistic philosophy of Jesus, later to be reflected in the religion named for him, may have benefited greatly from Essene and Pharisaic ideologies, but Jesus did not and actually could not bequeath to his followers a systematic organized religion; that was the contribution of Paul, a contribution that probably revealed the influence on Paul of the rigorous education that he had received in the Academy of the House of Hillel.

The tremendous courage and determination of Paul, as they were soon expressed in his physically strenuous crusade for his new cause, are without parallel in the history of Christian missionary endeavor; the physical demands which Paul made upon himself would be regarded by most people as beyond human endurance. The preaching and writing in which Paul soon indulged, based strongly on his own analyses, extensions, interpretations, and perfection of the ideas that he had received from members of the Jesus Cult, provided much of the theological foundation as well as associated precepts of classical Christianity, and they were responsible for giving great momentum to the Christian movement.

Apparently Paul, the crusading Pharisee with a new vision of his own identity and of his destiny, was in very poor health when he embarked upon his strenuous campaign to win recruits for his understanding of the message and of the mission of Jesus. Nevertheless, he traveled thousands of miles and visited scores of cities as well as small communities. He taught and debated in Jerusalem, where he was arrested, and probably he spent considerable time with Church leaders in Antioch, where much of his thinking may have been shaped, and he visited some of the other previously organized Christian communities, which at that time were few in number. But Paul is best known for his crusading activities in many parts of the Roman Empire where the name of Jesus was unknown and where Roman paganism prevailed. By foot, by boat, and by donkey, Paul carried his message to listeners in virtually all the major seaports along the eastern shore of the Mediterranean and along its northern rim as far west as Rome; he also visited most of the larger islands in that sea. In addition, it appears that he made long overland trips to settlements almost as far north as modern Ankara on the Anatolian Plateau in Turkey, and he traveled to isolated localities in the interior of Greece and in modern Albania. It is common knowledge, because of the letters which are credited to him and which were included in the New Testament collection, that Paul visited Rome, Corinth, Galatia, Colossae, Philippi, Thessalonica, and Ephesus, but a vast number of other communities were included in his itinerary. Upon occasion he spent several months in a locality, teaching, explaining, debating. In some communities he attempted to develop an organization that would survive and would continue his work when he departed. In a few of the larger cities, such as the great seaport Ephesus, where a huge amphitheater was available, Paul probably had opportunities to speak to several thousand people in a single audience; many times he was involved in bitter and rough controversy as local characters, including idol makers, discovered that their economic interests were being jeopardized by the ideas that he was promulgating.

During his extensive travels it was common for Paul to suffer from hunger, from thirst, and from extreme weariness. And more than once he was shipwrecked, and on several occasions he was thrown into prison; he was not popular with Roman officialdom. In truth, it is likely that he was very unpopular with a majority of the Roman citizens in the communities where he visited; there is much evidence that most Roman citizens were not easily persuaded to give up their pagan gods. In his writings, Paul reports that five times he received thirty-nine stripes; three times he was beaten with rods; and once he endured a vicious stoning. In spite of such acts of violence against his person, Paul did not falter in the pursuit of his goals. Finally, in approximately A.D. 62, when Nero was the Roman Emperor, he was executed in Rome after a long and cruel ordeal in prison; soon other active leaders of the new Jesus Cult would suffer the same fate at the hands of the Romans.

Gradually, as Paul expanded his missionary endeavors, he was able to assemble a substantial group of fellow workers to help him. In fact, it would appear that he possessed some of the attributes of an organizational genius, for there is little doubt that he had secretaries, a staff of teachers, and emissaries who helped him maintain contact with the various communities of Jesus Cult members in which he had a special interest. Barnabas, apparently Paul's first close friend, probably shared with him much of the responsibility for the organization and conduct of the elaborate missionary program that soon evolved, but other individuals provided invaluable assistance upon a variety of occasions. The letters of Paul name a number of his associates, some of whom suffered imprisonment with him. During the time of Paul's ministry there were other active missionaries for the Jesus Cult who maintained evangelical programs that were essentially independent of Paul's endeavors, but it was the Paulist company, with Paul as commander, that provided the vanguard of the new religious movement and actually defined it. The work of Mark, who followed his own independent course of action during most of his missionary career, receives brief attention later in this chapter.

Much of our information about the crusading career of Paul is provided by the Book of Acts (of the Apostles), apparently composed about thirty years after Paul's death and then included in the New Testament collection of writings. The author of the Book of Acts may have been Luke. The intent of the author of the Book, it seems clear, was to compile available reports that provided a record of the slow and often painful growth of the new religious movement initiated after the death of Jesus. In addition to its treatment of Paul's missionary endeavors, the Book gives considerable attention to the experiences of Peter, who after the death of Jesus suffered persecution because of his efforts to teach the message of Jesus in Jerusalem and in neighboring areas. Some of the episodes associated with Paul's missionary work, as they are recorded in the Book of Acts, provide great insight into his courage and, in general, into the kinds of problems faced by all those who were early missionaries for the new religious cult; the Book provides especially important insight into the problems of the missionaries that resulted from the growing antagonism toward the Jesus Cult displayed by Roman civil and military authorities.

To learn of Paul's ideas that became fundamental to the primitive theology associated with the new religious movement, one must read those of his letters that were included in the New Testament canon. In addition to the letters to the Thessalonians, which were, insofar as we know, the first letters that Paul wrote, the letters attributed to Paul that were included in the Christian Biblical text, using the designations employed in the typical New Testament index, were Romans, I and II Timothy, I and II Corinthians, Galatians, Ephesians, Philippians, Colossians, and Titus. There is reason to believe, however, that the books known as I and II Timothy along with Titus were prepared after the death of Paul; possibly they are heavily edited versions of letters originally due to Paul. Even the letter to the Ephesians, usually accepted as one of Paul's epistles, may have been written by another person, possibly one of Paul's disciplines; the author was obviously familiar with Paul's ideas and style. Unfortunately, as previously indicated, the letters of Paul introduced into the Biblical text do not represent a complete collection, which probably was very large, of the letters which he composed for members of the new religious congregations; some of his letters were either lost or, for any one of a number of reasons, were discarded. The early compilers of the New Testament canon, it is clear, were quite choosy when making their selection of materials to be included.

It is tremendously important for students of the history of Christianity to realize that when studying the letters of Paul, which probably were not subjected to much critical editing, it is possible to observe his mind at work, shaping both the form and the substance of primitive Christianity. Paul accepted the idea that Jesus was the Judaic Messiah, but, of the utmost importance, Paul's thinking, writing, and teaching were focused upon the spiritual Jesus. Much Christian phraseology originated with Paul; some Christian doctrine was given its first enunciation by Paul or was given validity by the authority of his statement. Several Christian practices were given acceptability as a result of Paul's advocacy or endorsement, and the totality of Paul's writings, as already noted, provided the rudiments of a Christian theology. Because of the teachings and writings of Paul, Jesus became much more in the thought processes of many of his followers than the man-God accepted by some persons as the

Davidic Messiah; he became the Son of God, chosen by God as His spiritual representative on earth. Jesus, in the view of Paul, had been anointed by God, not man, and thus was uniquely entitled to the designation "Christos" or "Christ," a descriptive term ultimately accepted as the appropriate designation for Jesus by vast multitudes of people.

The God of Abraham, of Moses, of David, and of the prophets was Paul's God. But, for Paul, it had become a fundamental element of the new religious philosophy which he had accepted that the necessary communion of any man with God, an essential aspect of Judaism, could only be attained by developing an intimacy of fellowship with Jesus the Christ; by establishing a proper relationship with Christ, he emphasized, it becomes possible to establish communion with God. Thus, although Paul continued to affirm his faith in Judaism, the enunciation of the principle that Jesus can and does serve as an intermediary between man and God represented one of several distinct and fundamental breaks that Paul made with traditional Judaic doctrine. Judaic doctrine specifies that man, through prayer, has direct access to God; there can be no intermediary. Moreover, Paul insisted, it is through Jesus the Christ that man obtains salvation. Paul, mystic that he was, was able to enter into an idealized relationship with his concept of Christ in such a manner that he believed that Christ was living in him and was working through him. As a result, he believed that his utterances had special significance and validity for mankind because Christ was speaking through him; upon occasion, with an assumption of an aura of authority that Christians generally accept as appropriate, he spoke of personally bestowing upon someone the "blessing of Christ" or the "riches of Christ."

Some of the letters that Paul wrote were essentially for the purpose of communicating with his friends; he wrote of many things and he provided instruction on many subjects. Other letters seem to have been written, especially when he was in prison, for the purpose of providing an outlet for his meditations. Several of his letters are remarkable literary productions, often of considerable profundity; one would judge that some of them represented laborious effort on the part of Paul to present his carefully considered ideas in such a way that they would have maximum and permanent significance for his reader audience. To attempt any kind of summary of the content of those letters of Paul that were assembled in the New Testament would be unfair to his genius; a reading of the entire collection is essential for the person who seeks a true knowledge of Paul's expressed thoughts upon Jesus and his mission, the earliest pronouncements by any man upon Christian concepts and principles that are readily available to us. But the quotation of selected passages from Paul's writings may provide a glimpse of some of the major elements of Christian belief and practice which he advocated.

Paul's concept of Jesus Christ, Philippians 2:5–11: . . . Christ Jesus, who, though he was in the form of God, did not count equality with God a thing to be grasped, but emptied himself, taking the form of a servant, being born in the likeness of men. And being found in human form he humbled himself and became obedient unto death, even death on a cross.

The importance of man becoming identified with Christ, 2 Corinthians 5:17–20: . . . if any one is in Christ, he is a new creation; the old has passed away, behold, the new has come.

The original sin of man, but man redeemed through Christ, Romans 5:12: Therefore as sin came into the world through one man [i.e., Adam] and death through sin, and so death spread to all men because all men sinned. . . . Romans 5:18: Then as one man's trespass led to condemnation for all men, so one man's act of righteousness leads to acquittal and life for all men.

The love of Christ, Romans 8:35–37: Who shall separate us from the love of Christ? Shall tribulation, or distress, or persecution, or famine, or nakedness, or peril, or sword? As it is written, "For thy sake we are being killed all the day long; we are regarded as sheep to be slaughtered." No, in all these things we are more than conquerors through him who loved us.

Brotherly love, often known as The Song of Songs on Brotherly Love, I Corinthians 13:1–3: If I speak in the tongues of men and of angels, but have not love, I am a noisy gong or a clanging cymbal. And if I have prophetic powers, and understand all mysteries and all knowledge, and if I have all faith, so as to remove mountains, but have not love, I am nothing. If I give away all I have, and if I deliver my body to be burned, but have not love, I gain nothing.

Christ belongs to all men, Colossians 3:11–13: Here there cannot be Greek and Jew, circumcised and uncircumcised, barbarian, Scythian, slave, free man, but Christ is all, and in all.

Paul's ministry to the Gentiles, Romans 15:15–16: . . . on some points I have written to you very boldly by way of reminder, because of the grace given me by God to be a minister of Christ Jesus to the Gentiles in the priestly service of the Gospel of God, so that the offering of the Gentiles may be acceptable, sanctified by the Holy Spirit.

The relation of Jesus to Judaic law, Galatians 3:16–25: . . . The promises were made to Abraham and to his offspring. It does not say, "And to his offsprings," referring to many; but, referring to one, "And to your offspring," which is Christ. This is what I mean: the law . . . does not annul a convenant previously ratified by God. . . . Why then the law? It was added because of transgressions, till the offspring should come to whom the promise had been made. . . . Is the law then against the promises of God? Certainly not; for if a law had been given which could make alive, then righteousness would indeed be by the law. But the scripture consigned all things to sin, that what was promised to faith in Jesus Christ might be given to those who believe. Now before faith came, we were confined under the law, kept under restraint until faith should be revealed. So that the law was our custodian until Christ came, that we might be justified by faith. But now that faith has come, we are no longer under a custodian.

The significance of baptism, Galatians 3:26–29: . . . In Christ Jesus you are all sons of God, through faith. For as many of you as were baptized into Christ have put on Christ. . . . And if you are Christ's then you are Abraham's offspring, heirs according to promise.

The resurrection, one of the many references: I Chronthians 15: 12–17: Now if Christ is preached as raised from the dead, how can some of you say there is no resurrection of the dead? But if there is no resurrection of the dead, then Christ has not been raised; if Christ has not been raised, then our preaching is in vain and your faith is in vain. We are even found to be misrepresenting God, because we testified of God that he raised Christ, whom he did not raise if it is true that the dead are not raised. If Christ has not been raised, your faith is futile and you are still in your sins.

The second coming of Christ. I Thessalonians 4:16–18: . . . the Lord himself will descend from heaven with a cry of command, with the archangel's call, and with the sound of the trumpet of God. And the dead in Christ will rise first; then we who are alive, who are left, shall be caught up together with them in the clouds to meet the Lord in the air; and so we shall always be with the Lord.

The preaching and teaching of Paul were founded on the concept of Christ exalted on the cross. But at the same time, he gave much attention to the living Christ; he taught that through the medium of the living Christ every man possesses the potential for personal enrichment "in all utterance and in all knowledge." For Paul, the necessity for each person to accept the ideas which he advanced pertaining to the significance of Christ in his or her own way of life was of fundamental urgency because he was convinced that the concept of the Kingdom of God, as he understood it, was about to be fulfilled; such a sense of urgency undoubtedly provided part of the great driving force behind Paul's tremendous missionary efforts.

It is likely that the "churches" that Paul and the other missionaries created were still commonly regarded as synagogues associated with a particular Judaic Cult. In general, they were loosely organized. The "elders" chosen by each congregation were the nominal leaders of the congregation, but as one would expect, the actual leadership was usually assumed by men of strong will. By contrast with what was true of congregations associated with the traditional synagogues, many of the Christian communities sponsored by Paul and some of the other early missionaries maintained a semicommunal way of life. The semicommunal mode of life was supposed to be consistent with the interpretation given by Jesus to the idea of brotherly love, and it was also consistent with the teachings of the Jesus Cult. Thus, many of the earliest Christian communities indulged in extensive sharing of personal resources; poverty was regarded as a necessary characteristic of the individual members of a Christian community. The traditional Judaic policy of giving careful attention to the needs of widows, of orphans, and of the sick was maintained by the early Christian Churches. And there was no deviation from the traditional Judaic custom of offering prayer at three specified times during the day. The early Christians, moreover, adhered rigidly to the Judaic celebration of the Sabbath; in fact, virtually all of the traditional Judaic practices were maintained. As scholars have had more and more access to very early Christian manuscripts, it has become increasingly clear that, insofar as much of their content is concerned, it is difficult to distinguish them from manuscripts acknowledged to be Judaic. Many students of the history of Christianity now believe that early Christianity, at least in its practices and in most obvious respects, did not deviate too much from traditional Judaism until well into the second century, and even later. Apparently, moreover, the first Christians made no abrupt changes in Judaic liturgy; for many years, the Judaic Bible was the basic religious reference work employed by Christians for study and for use during services of worship. By the end of the first century, a variety of writings about Jesus, undoubtedly including one or more of those later designated as Biblical Gospels, were available for reading in a few Christian communities; moreover, somewhat earlier, some of the letters by Paul and other Christian advocates were being circulated in a few Christian congregations.

In many if not most of the early Christian communities, all the members indulged upon a regular basis in a special meal that possessed very simple characteristics and was almost ceremonial in nature. Originally, it appears, the meal was initiated by the saying of grace and by the breaking of bread; the breaking of bread was and still is an intimate part of the Judaic tradition. But when Gospel reports pertaining to the life of Jesus became available, it became known that Jesus gave a distinctive meaning to the breaking of bread upon the occasion now known as the Last Supper. So probably within a short time, the practice of breaking bread during the special meal in which the early Christians indulged began to have a particular symbolic meaning, which included the idea of the close presence of Jesus. In such a way, in the view of some historians, did Holy Communion, the most important rite of the Christian Church, became a factor in Christian worship.

In view of the poverty of the first Christians, it was not common to have wine with their meals. But if and when the early ceremonial meal of the first Christians ultimately became the Christian ritualized celebration of the Lord's Supper, the present conception of which is probably due to Paul, wine was regarded as an indispensable element. Paul wrote in I Corinthians 11:23–26, "For I received from the Lord what I also deliver to you, that the Lord Jesus on the night he was betrayed took bread, and when he had given thanks, he broke it, and said, 'This is my body which is for you. Do this in remembrance of me.' In the same way also the cup, after supper, saying, 'This cup is the new covenant in my blood. Do this, as often as you drink it, in remembrance of me.' For as often as you eat this bread and drink this cup, you proclaim the Lord's death until he comes."

The doctrinal significance that Paul found in the words attributed to Jesus upon the occasion of the Last Supper, an event probably described in the Gospels in such a manner that its description was consistent with the ideas previously expressed by Paul, became very influential in establishing the fact that Holy Communion did become the most important rite of the Christian Church. The dialogue associated with Holy Communion has been prescribed through the ages in terms that employ testimony introduced by Paul. The classical interpretation of Paul's words in regard to the Holy Sacrament, an interpretation that is still accepted by the Roman Catholic Church and essentially so by most orthodox churches, was that during the celebration of Holy Communion, as a result of the process known as Transubstantiation, the bread and wine employed in the Sacrament actually become transformed into the body and blood of Christ. A different and more recent view of the Sacrament, one generally accepted by Protestant denominations, is that the bread and wine employed in the rite merely serve the purpose of symbolizing the body and blood of Christ. The difference inherent in the two interpretations has been the subject of many debates, and there has been much play by theological semanticists upon the shades of meaning that may be associated with the terms employed in describing the nature of the Sacrament.

Mark, the author of the Gospel of Mark, had an early association with Paul, but at some point, apparently, the two men decided that each one should maintain his own distinctive program of missionary endeavor. So, during the latter part of his career, Mark, probably after discussions with Paul, developed his own itinerary of missionary travels within the Roman Empire. In fact, he moved into some areas, notably Egypt, that were not included by Paul in his travels. The Coptic Orthodox Christian Church, still a very important cultural factor in the life of several million people in parts of Egypt and the Sudan, especially in the Nubian area, and a few other sections of the Near East, regards Mark as its founder and as its first Patriarch; upon occasion Mark is also described as the first Pope of the Coptic Orthodox Church. According to Coptic legend, Mark arrived in Alexandria in Egypt as a missionary in A.D. 40, a date that appears to be acceptable. The present Patriarch of the Coptic Orthodox Church is designated as the 117th Patriarch in the two-thousand-year-old religious dynasty that, according to Coptic tradition, originated with Mark.

Almost from its beginning, the Christian movement in the part of the Mediterranean world where Mark pursued his missionary endeavors took on some distinctive characteristics that set it apart from much of the rest of evolving Christendom. Many of the theological pronouncements of Paul that became strongly embedded in Western Christianity never had much impact upon the Coptic Church and upon such churches as the Ethiopian Orthodox Church that were derived from it. The Christian sects which had their origin in the missionary work of Mark, even today, remain theologically simple; at the present time, the churches of such sects are often described by persons who visit them as seeming to be representative of a special sect of Judaism. Even the edifices maintained for worship by some of the sects derived from the classical Coptic Church resemble the Judaic synagogues of the first century.

Many self-constituted Christian leaders in the area of the Mediterranean that had been subject to Paul's missionary efforts seemed to believe that they must follow the lead of Paul in his demand for rigid adherence to the doctrines which he had enunciated. Thus they introduced a policy of outlawing authors and writings that took positions on Christian belief and policy that seemed to be inconsistent with Paul's teachings. By contrast, the leading churchmen in Egypt seemed to encourage diversity in reading and in study. As a result, while Christians in Egypt were comparatively free to read any Christian literature of their choice, Christian authorities in much of the Roman world, during the early years of the Christian movement, exercised a careful watch over the kind of reading in which Christians indulged. In fact, during the early years of the Christian movement, the censorship and even the destruction of Christian writings regarded by some Christian authorities as heretical became comparatively common in most of the Mediterranean areas where Paul had left the mark of his influence. Unhappily, over a time span of several centuries, the campaign against heresy by the Christian leadership in much of the Roman world continued to increase in intensity. Now, students of the history of Christianity shudder with dismay as they read about the destruction of historically valuable materials and the severe persecution of scholarly authors during the fourth, fifth, and even later centuries. In 325, at the first Nicaean Council, those in attendance made a decision on the acceptability or unacceptability of available books. Any slight deviation in the content of a book from acceptable Christian doctrine as that acceptability was determined by those in attendance at the Nicaean meeting was sufficient justification for having the work destroyed and possibly for threatening the author with death. To try to complete the act of safeguarding Christian readers from any contact with unacceptable ideas, Pope Gelasius issued a decree in 494 which specified that the reading of any one of a list of sixty-one books, including some very important gospels, was prohibited. The decree initiated an orgy of destruction of prohibited works; only a very few copies survived. As a result, some of the earliest Christian works, some of which probably predated the Biblical Gospels and may have contained important information on the life of Jesus, were cast into the flames. Some of the works that were destroyed, we now know, provided a picture

181

of some of the events in the early days of Christianity and in the life of Jesus that was quite different from the traditional picture.

While the tragic programs of censorship were being conducted in much of the Mediterranean area, Christians in many communities of Egypt and in neighboring regions often were studying and deriving great satisfaction from books that in many parts of the Christian world had been banned. Such a state of affairs continued for many decades. Undoubtedly the early difference in permissible reading habits between Christians living in Egypt and in neighboring areas and those living in much of the rest of the Mediterranean world was responsible for the development, even while the Christian movement was very young, of significant differences between the two groups in points of view pertaining to Christian doctrine and philosophy.

Historians have been much interested in and excited by the fact that as time passes a significant number of early Christian manuscripts that were censored and then destroyed in much of the original Christian world are being recovered, sometimes well preserved but often in fragmentary form, from ancient desert depositories, even under the sand, in northeastern Africa. During the early centuries of the Christian movement, in addition to the New Testament Gospels of Matthew, Mark, Luke, and John, there were many gospels that, where they were available, were studied intensively by Christian congregations. Among such writings were Gospels ascribed to Judas Iscariot, to Thomas, and to James the Less, all of which have already been mentioned, and to Philip, to Bartholomew, and to Peter; parts of most of the Gospels just named have been recovered. The Gospel of Thomas is considerably different from the other Gospels, for it is essentially a large collection of sayings, including parables, attributed to Jesus. The Gospel is arousing increasing interest among Biblical scholars in view of the apparently growing belief that the work was written before some of the Biblical Gospels; if so, there is little doubt that it provided the basis for some of the parables in the Biblical treatments. According to evidence now becoming available to us, a number of other early Christian Gospels in addition to those just named, works which seem to have completely disappeared, had tremendous influence on some segments of the early Christian movement; among such works was the *Gospel According to the Hebrews*. Christian historians dream of the day when copies of the lost Gospels may be recovered, possibly from under the sands of the Sahara or in old burial sites. Dr.

Montague James, in his introduction to *The Apocryphal New Testament,* wrote: "Many a book, like the venerable *Gospel According to the Hebrews* which we should dearly have liked to possess for the light it would throw on primitive Christian history, has perished in consequence of their [certain early Christian scholars] unfavorable verdict."

After Mark, in A.D. 40, introduced the Christian faith to the people of Alexandria, it spread remarkably fast across a large section of North Africa to the west of Alexandria, across the Nile into the Negev east of Alexandria, and even into the Nubian country in the Upper Nile Valley. The latter area still possesses a substantial Christian population. The people in Egypt and neighboring areas were proving to be receptive to Christian teachings. Within a few decades Egypt became a very significant area within the Christian movement. Although, as already indicated, interesting differences soon became apparent in points of view and in practices between the Coptic Christians and most of the other Christians of the Roman world, the members of both groups lived under the rigid control of the Roman government; all lived under the watchful eye of Roman soldiers. Moreover, all Christians became victims at an early date of the distrust and actual hatred of Roman officialdom. Thus probably the political element was a very significant factor in bringing all Christians together in the early development of many common interests and in the creation of many common enterprises. The Christians in major Christian centers of the Roman world, probably out of necessity, seemed to develop a communication system, probably highly informal, that enabled them to keep in touch with each other, exchanging information on many subjects, including reports upon experiences.

Chapter Eight

THE CHRISTIAN MOVEMENT IMMEDIATELY AFTER THE TIME OF PAUL

THE STRUGGLE FOR DEFINITION AND FOR SURVIVAL

Mark provided a singularly important contribution to the development of Christianity in its earliest days. But from the perspective of those who are a product of Western culture, it was Paul who gave form as well as substance to the new movement within Judaism that soon would become known as Christianity. Moreover, it was Paul who was personally responsible for organizing a large number of the first Christian communities in a substantial part of the Roman world, except in northern Africa. In addition, missionaries whom Paul educated created other centers of Christian activity. As a result of such efforts combined with those of Mark and his associates, the start of the second century A.D. saw the Mediterranean Sea encircled by a sizable number of dynamic centers of Christian activity. Among the cities and provinces which may be named as being strongly identified with that early era of Christian life were Rome, Achaea (including Corinth), Bithynia (including Nicomedia), Pergamum, Smyrna, Ephesus, Antioch, Caesarea, Alexandria, Carthage, and Apollonius. Other cities and even a greater number of smaller communities could be named. There is no implication in such a statement, however, that the total number of Christians in the Roman Empire at the start of the second century was large. The Roman Empire was still substantially pagan, a fact that was an important factor in the grave difficulties encountered at that time by members of the Christian communities.

At the start of the second century A.D., the dominant characteristic of each one of the various Christian congregations was a desire on the part of its members to live a kind of life, featuring the idea of brotherly love, that would be acceptable to Jesus. Nevertheless, in the procedures of worship which they followed and in most of the basic religious principles which they accepted, the Christian congregations adhered closely to the traditional Judaic. Most of the practices and many of the tenets that today are associated generally with Christianity were yet to be introduced. In general, at the start of the second century, there was much uncertainty in most Christian communities in regard to many aspects of church policy and procedure, for there were no traditions and no acceptable models to provide guidance. Consequently, lively debates upon comparatively simple issues were common. As is true now and always has been true of most organizations, the obtaining of competent leadership for each congregation was a problem; the problem was magnified by the fact that much doubt existed in regard to the duties and responsibilities of the several designated congregational officers.

Even greater doubt existed in regard to the proper position that an individual Christian should take on the many principles and concepts with religious connotations that frequently were under discussion in the Christian communities. A majority of the members of most of the early Christian congregations had been raised in pagan environments; they were individuals who had been converted. Thus, for such people, many of the tenets of Christianity as advocated by Paul, for example, seemed somewhat strange, and often they were the subject of passionate debates. Some of the theological pronouncements of Paul, it must be admitted, were not easily understood, a fact to which even modern scholars will attest, and some of Paul's statements can be interpreted in a variety of ways. Consequently, in some congregations the diversity of opinion that existed on some religious issues produced schisms.

Unfortunately, after the death of Paul, Christianity did not possess a leader who was widely recognized as an authority; there was no one to whom leaders of individual congregations could appeal with confidence for help and guidance. Early Christianity did produce some outstanding scholars, but, in general, their influence at the time in which they lived seems to have been quite limited. There is little doubt that some of the key persons of the Christian community in Rome played significant leadership roles in the early days of the Christian movement, but it seems to be the judgment of most knowledgeable non-Roman Catholic scholars that many years would elapse—a subject discussed later—before the Roman Church and its leaders would be accepted as occupying a preeminent position in Christendom.

To add to the complexities of life for the earliest Christians, they were surrounded by hostility. Roman citizens generally regarded the members of the new religious sect with disdain, and Roman officialdom despised the sect and its members. It is recalled that in A.D. 62, Paul was executed by the Roman Emperor Nero. Other violent actions by the Roman government in its attempt to curb the progress of Christianity were becoming common. Yet, such events, awful as they were, were merely harbingers of the terrible persecution of Christians, often approaching the status of a massacre, that would begin within a short time.

Christianity needed a new and dynamic leader, someone who would be respected and who could guide the new Christians through the maze of uncertainties which they were experiencing. The needed leader should possess the personal qualities demanded of a true leader, and, of prime importance, he should be regarded widely as a man who possessed a sound understanding of the basic tenets of Christianity, thus being able to help others distinguish between true and false doctrine.

Such a leader, in the judgment of a large number of his Christian contemporaries, appeared suddenly early in the second century A.D., in the person of Marcion. Marcion, according to tradition, was the son of the Christian bishop of Sinope in Pontus. Apparently early in life he developed some very positive ideas about Christian principle and philosophy. It has been said that he discussed his notions with Polycarp, bishop of Smyrna, but Polycarp rejected them. So he went on to Rome in the hope of having a more receptive audience. Ultimately he parted company with the Christian leaders in Rome; nevertheless, his points of view rapidly attracted much attention both in Rome and outside Rome. In fact, within a very short time, Marcion's ideas seem to have attracted a receptive audience in a substantial part of the Roman Empire, an obvious indication of the fact that the new Christians were hungry for easily understood and authoritative types of information about their newly accepted faith. In view of the need that existed, Marcion and his followers started an elaborate educational campaign within existing Christian communities; moreover, they established their own special Christian congregations, some of which remained active for many centuries. Part of Marcion's appeal seems to have resulted from his obviously sincere attempt to provide simple expositions for the Christian masses of the significance of Jesus, of the meaning of his teachings, of the relationship of those teachings to the tenets of Judaism, and of the real meaning of the teachings of Paul, the great Christian expositor.

Marcion taught that the God in which the followers of Judaism believed was an inferior God whose chief accomplishment seemed to be the creation of the material universe, a universe that was to be ruled by law; man was expected to give obedience to that law. The Judaic God, Marcion emphasized, had to be regarded as a powerful God but He did not deserve the complete respect of man in view of the fact that He seemed to be unable to recognize those essential elements in life, such as brotherly love, that could not be prescribed by law. It is likely that Marcion believed that the laws of Moses deserved criticism in view of the fact that, in line with the wishes of the Judaic God, they were designed to control the behavior of man by law. So, Marcion insisted that Jesus, the Son of the true God, who was the God of Love, had come to tell man about the superior God whom he represented; in fact, Jesus had the task, according to Marcion, of redeeming man from the sins which had been committed by man partly because of the fact that he had been taught a false sense of truth. Christians must learn, Marcion implied in his teaching, that Christianity as taught by Jesus had superseded the more primitive Judaic religious philosophy. As was true of most Christians of that time, Marcion taught that salvation for man came through faith in Jesus, actually in Jesus crucified.

Marcion often expressed support for the teachings of Paul, for whom he seemed to have great respect, but he insisted that generally the teachings of Paul were misunderstood. The misunderstanding arose, Marcion seemed to believe, partly because of Paul's failure to emphasize that Jesus, the Son of the true God, could not be the Messiah. The latter designation for Jesus, in Marcion's judgment, was not possible in view of the fact that the Messiah was a creature of the Judaic God, an inferior God. Since many Christians were giving emphasis to the idea that Jesus was the Messiah, Marcion believed that they were revealing the fact that they had been misled in their concept of the true Jesus. Marcion, it must be observed, actually did not deny anything that Paul taught, possibly because Paul's popularity as a Christian hero was widespread among Christians. But Marcion did attempt in his own strange way to clarify and supplement Paul's teachings.

To provide guidance for his followers and to make available to them an authentic reference work on Christianity, as he understood it, Marcion decided to bring together in one volume a collection of acceptable writings by Christian authors. To find writings that expressed his points of view must have been very difficult. In Marcion's final collection, he included ten of Paul's letters, which he edited in such a way that his own interpretations received full play. In addition, to each of the letters he added a prologue. Then, to the assembly of ten Pauline letters he added Luke's Gospel, which he also modified in several respects. Later, Marcion developed for his followers another work that was to be regarded as a guide to the understanding of the books in his collection of writings. In essence, in the light of later developments in the Christian movement, Marcion had created what must be regarded as his personal version of a Christian Bible. Most of the better-known Christian scholars, irrespective of their location in many parts of the Roman world, observed the actions of Marcion and examined his expressed beliefs with dismay for, insofar as they were concerned, he had introduced some very disturbing elements into Christian doctrine and actually into the Christian movement. Marcion was criticized severely by many Christian leaders, some of whom revealed anger in their comments. In Rome, Marcion was branded as a heretic. But in spite of all the condemnation, the reputation of Marcion seemed in general to remain very high, and in some parts of the Christian world his prestige continued to grow.

To really comprehend some of the strange ideas of Marcion, especially some of his judgments that much in the world is basically wrong, and actually is evil, undoubtedly requires some understanding of Gnosticism. Gnosticism had a strong effect upon religious thought in the Roman World in the second and third centuries and into the fourth century. Persons accepting the strange dogma believed that the world was entirely evil, the result of having been created by an evil God; thus even man's body is evil. But within each person is a divine element, placed there by a good God who had remained aloof from the evil of the world; that divine element had to be recognized and cultivated. We are learning more about Gnosticism in recent years as the result of the discovery in the 1940's of some ancient religious documents in an old burial ground near Nag Hammadi in upper Egypt; the documents are now in the Coptic Museum in Cairo. Study of the documents reveals that Gnosticism drew heavily, but with some strange interpretations, upon some of the content of the Judaic Book of Genesis. Moreover, in the recently-discovered materials are references to Jesus and to early Christianity that are adding to our knowledge of Christian origins.

Whether some of the critics of Marcion were working on their own version of an acceptable Christian reference work at the same time that he was creating his particular version is not known. Certainly, however, the action of Marcion provided strong motivation for a group of Christians who were among his critics to move ahead rapidly on the development of their own version of a reference work, composed of carefully selected writings by Christian authors, which they believed would provide important guidance to Christians. The net effect of such an action, the compilers must have believed, would be that of directing the reading habits of Christians toward acceptable Christian writings and away from non-acceptable, heretical writings.

It becomes mere speculation to attempt to name the organizations or individuals who became involved in the task of selecting from among the Christian writings then available, those works that on the basis of acceptable content deserved inclusion in the proposed authoritative volume. Moreover, no authentic knowledge is available in regard to the criteria that were employed in determining which works should be included. It is the belief of some Biblical scholars that certain selected letters of Paul, possibly those chosen for inclusion in the Biblical text as we know it, provided much of the basis for judging the merits of other Christian writings; if that is true, probably no material was included in the New Testament that seemed to contradict an assertion or a doctrinal pronouncement of Paul. Such a test, however, could provide little basis for determining which of the many available gospels, treatments of the life of Jesus, should be included. Undoubtedly, many criteria were employed; probably some of them were adopted, especially those pertaining to the choice of authors, because of the necessity for producing a work that would be regarded within the Christian community as being authoritative. There is little doubt that many acknowledged Christian leaders were involved in the process of canonization; moreover, it is likely that they were drawn from many parts of the Mediterranean region. Frequently it has been asserted that the leadership for the process of canonization was centered in Rome; that may have been and probably was true.

So, probably shortly before the halfway mark of the second century of the Christian era, individuals who had assumed a leadership role within the Christian movement and who must have been very much concerned by the growing intrusion into Christian thought of such "heretical ideas" as those advanced by Marcion decided to assemble into one volume a collection of Christian writings which, in their judgment, were acceptable and valid and would have value for both professing Christians and prospective Christians. There can be no doubt that inherent in the thinking of those involved in the design of the project was the development of a treatise that would bring together in one work outstanding writings by Christian authors which, after any necessary editing, would purvey the compilers' points of view in regard to Jesus, his nature and his message, and on Christian doctrine as they had accepted it.

As observed previously, the sponsors of the new Christian reference work of accepted Christian writings decided that central to the collection must be a set of the selected letters of Paul; that was to be expected, for it was Paul who had pulled together the basic ideas of Christianity as he understood them, and, in addition, had made some progress in synthesizing them so that they would provide the foundation for the religious faith that the sponsors of the new volume had accepted. Earlier in this work, it was observed that, in addition to the selected letters of Paul, the Gospels of Matthew, Mark, Luke, and John as well as the Book of Acts were accepted for inclusion in the new work that ultimately would become known as the New Testament of the Christian Biblical text. Among the other materials finally introduced into the New Testament assembly of books were three epistles of John; probably they were written by the person who was the author of the Gospel of John. The Book of Revelation (to John), also introduced into the collection, was described by its author as a revelation of Jesus to "His servant John" to "show the things which must come to pass shortly"; probably it was one of the last books introduced into the New Testament canon. It is likely that the latter Book was not written by John; both in style and in content the Book has little resemblance to the other works bearing the name of John. The Book of Revelation, addressed to the then flourishing Christian congregations in southeastern Asia, holds special fascination for Christian scholars in view of the fact that it possessed characteristics commonly associated with what has become known as the apocalyptic tradition, which was concerned with the revelations of prophecy.

Virtually no Biblical analysts believe that I and II Peter, also introduced into the new Christian collection, were written by Peter. Although Peter usually is regarded as having greater intellectual capability than any of the other twelve intimates of Jesus, he was recruited, the Biblical text reports, from among the Galilean fishermen; thus it would seem that he was incapable of writing the letters attributed to him, for they were written in excellent Greek. Moreover, there is little doubt that the content of the letters bearing the name of Peter pertained to events that took place after the time of Peter. I Peter is concerned with the state of the Christian Church at the end of the first century A.D. II Peter, probably the last book introduced into the new collection, was, it appears, written by some leaders of the Christian community in Rome in about A.D. 150; it is likely that the letter was given an association with the name of Peter to gain

190

desired consideration of its contents. Apparently II Peter was written for the dual purpose of reemphasizing Christian notions of truth and of encouraging Christians to remain firm in their faith, especially since it was a common view among Christians during the middle of the second century A.D. that the end of the world was imminent. Apparently the leadership of the Christian Church in Rome thought that the composition of such a letter was urgent in view of the fact that at that time the campaign of persecution of Christians was being intensified by Roman officials. Moreover, grave doubts about many aspects of the religion which they had accepted, even in regard to Jesus himself, continued to be a problem for many Christians, and the doubts were causing strains within many Christian communities.

The author of the letter to the Hebrews, which in a preliminary version appeared near the end of the first century A.D., is unknown. Some scholars attach great significance to the work, for it seems to be concerned with the growing crisis at that time for some individuals who found themselves increasingly under pressure, probably in some cases the pressure of conscience, to make a choice between Christianity and orthodox Judaism; Christianity was still regarded by many persons, both Jewish and Gentile, as merely a Judaic sect that had introduced into traditional Judaism some strange but intriguing mystical ingredients pertaining to Jesus, his message, and his birth and death.

The letter in the new Christian collection attributed to James, the brother of Jesus, clearly was written by a person other than James, probably during the first part of the second century A.D. It may be assumed that James was designated as the author of the work to give authority to its contents. The letter, it appears, was written to condemn the apparent degeneration that had developed in the life of many Christian communities. The letter of Jude, like the one ascribed to James, is concerned with the belief of the author that too many individuals in the early part of the second century who were professed followers of Jesus were indulging in critical deviations from the ideal way of life that Jesus had advocated. The name Jude, or Judas, "the brother of James," was undoubtedly given an association with the work to give authenticity to its message.

The fact that the resulting collection of Christian writings, which actually was the first edition of the Christian New Testament, did not receive early and widespread acceptance would seem to have been inevitable in view of the circumstance that it had its origin with a self-constituted group of Christian advocates. No recognized authority existed within the Christian community in the large to provide the kind of endorsement of the new work that would be necessary for its quick and extensive acceptance. Moreover, many Christians were finding satisfaction and inspiration in Christian writings not included in the new work; persons in the latter category would tend to question the significance of and the justification for the development of the new compilation. So it is likely that any general acceptance of the New Testament collection of writings as the basic text and reference work for the Christian movement evolved very slowly, actually over a period of several centuries. Long after the canonization of the New Testament had been completed, many Christian congregations employed Christian writings other than the New Testament in their study and in their services of worship. Even after the assembly of books had received considerable acceptance within Christendom and probably had received some kind of official sanction, it is likely that only a very few Christians of the first centuries of the Christian era had available for their study and meditation manuscript copies of the complete work. Usually, during those early years, Christian readers regarded themselves as fortunate if they had access to a few of the letters of Paul and possibly all or parts of some of the Biblical Gospels along with some of the better-known Christian apocryphal writings. Before the time of the printing press, all Christian literature as well as other literature was reproduced by pen by copyists; thus copies of books of any kind were regarded as precious. Probably it was many decades, possibly several centuries, after the canonization of the New Testament before persons in most Christian communities in the Mediterranean area even had the gratification of knowing that a complete copy of the work was available in the local parish church.

Through the years since its recognition generally by Church Fathers as an acceptable, and even as an authoritative account, of the life and mission of Jesus and of the early days of the religious movement which he initiated, the New Testament has come to be revered and respected by Christians as the most important of all Christian writings. Certainly the Holy Work, as it has been described frequently by many Christians, must be regarded as a very important resource, although not the only resource, for the person who desires to learn of the early development of Christianity. The New Testament provides information on primitive Christian ideas and practices, and also offers expositions of some of the fundamental principles of Christian doctrine as conceived by some of its most important initial advocates. And of very great importance, the text of the New Testament contains interpretations by Paul and others of Jesus, his mission, and his message along with accounts of his reported sayings and actions; such accounts, the sponsors of the work must have believed, would provide inspiration and guidance for many Christians. It also must have been the hope of the early compilers of the New Testament that the work would have value in persuading potential Christians to accept Jesus as the Davidic Messiah and as their spiritual ideal. Over a time span of nearly two millennia, that hope has been realized for a vast number of people, many of whom have been dominated by the idea that the persons who were associated with the development of the Holy Work were inspired by God.

The fact that the Christian Bible as finally approved by early Christian believers was created by merely joining the New Testament to the Judaic Bible, with the latter becoming known to Christians as the Old Testament, must be regarded as very important and as having fundamental significance. The act of accepting the two great religious works as parts of a whole must be interpreted as meaning that the early Christians who made the decision to join the two did not regard the Christian tradition as being independent of the Judaic tradition. In truth, the early decision to create a Christian Bible by joining the newly created New Testament to the Judaic Bible must have been motivated by a desire to provide adherents to Christianity an understanding of the continuity that existed in the development of their religious tradition from that associated with Judaism of the pre-Christian era. Within a comparatively short time, however, after Christianity was well embarked upon its own course of development, a tendency developed within the community of persons identified with the new faith to regard the particular part of the Judaic tradition that was represented by the content of the Judaic Bible as belonging uniquely to their own religious heritage. It has been common, in fact, for Christian analysts to read into events and sayings reported in the Judaic Bible the foretelling of key elements in the life of Jesus. Moreover, it has not been unusual for some Christian ecclesiastic to announce that he has discovered that some doctrine conceived by Christian theologians pertaining to Jesus and his mission had its basis in certain sayings and events recorded in the Judaic Bible. The extent to which Christians have adopted, adapted, and interpreted the Judaic Bible for their own specialized purposes has been a most remarkable aspect of the history of Judeo-Christian relationships, and even of the history of religion.

A continuing source of embarrassment for early Christian leaders when they attempted to recruit new members to Christianity was the fact that the Old Testament of their Bible makes it very clear that the Israelites are God's chosen people. A basis for resolving the difficulty, one that proved to be useful to many later Christians, appeared in the writings of Paul. For it appears that Paul in his pioneering missionary endeavors when trying to convert non-Jews to Christianity became aware of the fact that he must contend in a reasonable way with the Biblical specification that the Israelites are the chosen people of God. Consequently, in his letter to the Romans (Romans 9:6–13), Paul argued that "not all who are descended from Israel belong to Israel." To support his point of view, he called attention to the fact that of Isaac's two sons, Esau and Jacob, Esau, who was born with physical disfigurement, was disliked by God but Jacob was loved. Thus Paul insisted that ethnic background is not even the major factor employed by God in His determination of those individuals who are to be His chosen people. Since Jacob was loved by God, Paul argued, Jacob should be identified with Israel, the chosen people, whereas Esau could not be identified in such a manner. (Also note Galatians 3:26–29.) Such a clever argument provided the basic theme for many future discussions of the issue by Christians. In later years, after the Jews had been dispersed and were undergoing much suffering, some persons who professed to be Christians insisted that, through the fact of the extreme difficulties experienced by the Jews, God had revealed that He no longer regarded them as His chosen people. As a result of that kind of rationalization, the definition of the "chosen of God" accepted even today by some nominal Christians virtually excludes the Jewish people.

In addition to the books brought together in the New Testament, some other very important writings by Christian advocates who lived during the early years of the Christian era are still in existence. Mention has already been made of a few such early Christian works, including several which were written within a century after the death of Jesus. But there were other works deserving of mention that exercised great influence upon Christian thought and practice during the formative period of the Christian movement. In fact, during those early years, many competent persons of Christian persuasion, some of whose writings are still available, gave serious attention to the doctrinal and organizational base of the Christian movement. Some very able contributors to the cause of Christianity attempted to extend and perfect Paul's Christian theology, and others became involved in the resolution of numerous conflicts and controversies in regard to many difficult questions pertaining to Christian principle and even to Church organization. Actually, some of the most competent scholars of that era of Roman history were Christian scholars; they often displayed fiery zeal and wrote with great intellectual power. The fact that a large number of such scholars were prolific writers and that they revealed great imagination in the ideas that they expressed must be regarded as truly remarkable in view of the very difficult conditions, even personal hazards, under which they did their work. In the next few pages, brief attention is given to a selected few of the Christian advocates who contributed greatly to the development of the Christian movement during the first two centuries after the death of Jesus and whose writings, including letters, must be regarded as possessing fundamental significance for historians of Christianity. The choice made of authors and writings was based to great extent on a desire to provide a fair portrayal of the nature of the interests and problems of thoughtful Christian leaders of that particular period of Christian history.

Clement of Rome, designated at a later date by the leadership of the Roman Catholic Church as the third Pope of the Roman Church, is widely regarded as one of the earliest Christian authorities on church practice and on acceptable Christian doctrine. Some of his ideas were expressed very clearly in a letter which he wrote to the church in Corinth in A.D. 96, little more than a half century after the death of Jesus. In the letter he denounced the "few impetuous and headstrong fellows" in the Corinthian church whose actions were causing an "unholy schism" to exist and thus, he charged, were responsible for the fact that the church in Corinth had "fallen into the gravest ill repute." The schism to which Clement referred was due, apparently, to competition between contenders for high office in the church. The fact that as early as A.D. 96, a leading churchman in Rome adopted such an authoritative stand upon the problems that existed in a Greek church has been mentioned frequently as an indication of the early dominance of the Roman Church in the Christian movement.

Apparently Ignatius of Antioch, one of the earliest Christian martyrs, was one of the large number of persons in Antioch who accepted paganism in early life but who were converted to Christianity. Upon occasion he has been described as the first great ecclesiastic of the Christian movement. Ignatius became so concerned early in the second century with the fact that so many problems were arising in most of the

Christian Churches that, like Paul, he tried to help in resolving the difficulties by writing a series of letters which were widely distributed. Ignatius was truly disturbed by the lack of unity of purpose in many of the churches. In one letter he emphasized the impossibility of achieving necessary unity of purpose by the membership of any church unless there was proper respect for the authority of the bishop, the key person in each congregation, who, Ignatius insisted, should be regarded in the same light as one would regard "the Lord Himself." "Let the bishop preside in God's place," he wrote. In the same letter, Ignatius also gave explicit instructions pertaining to the role of the chosen officers in the program of any church. In particular, he asserted that the deacons have the fundamental task of carrying on the "ministry of Jesus Christ." Ignatius condemned severely those professing Christians who at the same time tried to remain adherents to traditional Judaism. For him, Judaism had become a religion without significant meaning. As was true of many of the leading Christian churchmen of that time, it became common for Ignatius to criticize in bitter terms the various types of "heresy" that were causing consternation and doubt within the Church memberships. It is an interesting fact that he felt obliged so early in the Christian movement to defend vigorously such fundamental tenets of Christian doctrine as the idea that Jesus could and did live as a man, although he was the Son of God, and that Jesus was resurrected from the dead after his crucifixion.

An analysis of the Christian writings of the primary years of the Christian era reveals that many early Christians like many later Christians found it very difficult to accept the idea that an individual who lived as a man and then was crucified was also the Son of God. The nonacceptance of the idea was regarded as heresy by those Christians who accepted without qualification the teachings of Paul. The simultaneous application to Jesus of both the terms "human" and "divine" was and probably always will be a source of controversy. The term "heretic" was also employed to describe those individuals who questioned the Resurrection of Jesus and also to those who questioned the Virgin Birth. In addition, it was common to accuse a person of heretical leanings if he expressed the belief that Mary did not continue to be a virgin after the birth of Jesus or that after the birth of Jesus she had other children, with Joseph as the father. Very early in the history of the Roman Church, certainly before the time of Jerome, A.D. 340–420, it became widely accepted Christian doctrine that Joseph had practiced celibacy all his life and that Mary was always a virgin; a large number of Christian writers had their works destroyed because they ran afoul of this doctrine. As Christian theology evolved, other controversial issues were introduced, thus making it possible to accuse an even greater number of persons of indulging in heresy. Christianity, by contrast with Judaism, has never been a religion that was truly characterized by freedom of speech and of thought.

Polycarp, a contemporary of Ignatius and a long-term bishop of Smyrna, located in Turkey, was a person to whom many Christians, including Ignatius, turned for spiritual guidance. Polycarp became known and was widely respected in Christendom as a dynamic and brave Christian leader in his advocacy of the Jesus message. Apparently he had received his initial indoctrination into Christian principle by some of the Christian advocates who lived very early in the Christian era. Both the aggressiveness of Polycarp and the content of his preaching so antagonized the Roman authorities that ultimately he was executed; the execution took place shortly after he, then an elderly man, had gone to Rome. During his long career, however, he achieved the reputation of being a true authority upon Christian doctrine and practice; his disagreement with some of the ideas of Marcion was mentioned earlier. Polycarp, in agreement with Ignatius, believed that much greater care had to be exercised than was true at that time in the selection of the officers of Christian congregations. He emphasized in one of his written works that the presbyters of a church, chosen by the church congregation, should be compassionate; they should "turn back those who have gone astray." Moreover, Polycarp asserted, the presbyters must always give thought to "what is honorable in the sight of God and man." Polycarp, one notes with interest and possibly with some amusement, emphasized that wives should be faithful to their husbands and should cherish them; moveover, widows should refrain from gossip and should not display a love of money. In his teachings he gave much attention to the proper education of children, who, he said, should be educated in the fear of God. Upon occasion Polycarp's criticism was bitter of those Christians who were deserting what he regarded as fundamental Christian belief to become associated with some particular "heretical" movement. Persons who refused to accept the "testimony of the cross" were described in one of his writings "as of the devil." And those who denied that the Resurrection actually took place were portrayed by Polycarp as the "firstborn of

Satan." The evidence is strong that Polycarp's influence on the evolving Christian movement in its earliest days was a major factor in maintaining it on the path of belief as enunciated by Paul.

Over a period of several decades during the first half of the second century, a collection of Christian scholars, probably drawn from several localities, compiled, undoubtedly after much discussion and debate, a manual of instructions for professing Christians; the work is known as the *Didache* ("Doctrine"). The manual, which according to some legends was supposed to represent a compilation of the teachings of the twelve disciples who were designated in the Bible as being especially close to Jesus, was designed obviously to provide practical assistance to churches and to individual church members faced with a variety of puzzling problems for which available Christian literature provided no generally acceptable solutions. There is little doubt that the *Didache* contributed strongly to the institutionalizing of Christianity, and soon its precepts were recognized generally in many parts of the Christian world as supplementing in a practical way the Christian Bible and other acceptable works of Christian literature in providing knowledge of the will of God.

The *Didache* provided information and guidance upon a multitude of subjects; only a small sample of its contents can be treated here. Each Christian, the work specified, is expected to pray three times a day, using the Lord's Prayer as his model. Very complete instructions were offered for carrying out the ritual of baptism. Wednesdays and Fridays were designated as days of fast. By contrast with the emphasis that traditional Judaism gives to the importance of certain dietary restrictions, the *Didache* warned only against eating food that previously had been offered to idols. Careful and rather elaborate prescriptions were provided for the proper administration of the sacrament of Holy Communion, including the phraseology to be employed by the person presiding over the ritual; baptism was specified as a prerequisite for participation in the ceremonial event. In regard to the Sabbath, the *Didache* emphasized that all Christians should assemble on that day to worship the Lord by breaking bread together and by giving thanks. But two persons having had a serious disagreement must achieve reconciliation of their differences before joining together for their celebration of the Sabbath.

The *Didache*, one notes with interest, gave considerable attention to the necessity for making a distinction between true and false prophets. Apparently the churches were plagued by itinerant evangelists; some of the evangelists were genuine advocates of Christian doctrine, but others, mere charlatans, professed to be exponents of Christian principle so that they could obtain hospitality in the homes of parishioners. Among its several criteria for making the necessary distinction between true and false prophets, the *Didache* made the unqualified statement, "If he stays three days, he is a false prophet."

Presumably a major concern of the early Christian churches, as is true of contemporary churches and will be true of future churches, was the selection of bishops and deacons who possess appropriate qualifications for their positions of leadership in the church community. Apparently the election of church officers was often accompanied by much controversy and even bitterness. So the *Didache* urged church congregations to choose men to be their bishops and deacons who are known to be faithful, who had previously demonstrated capability, and who are a credit to the Lord. Church members must realize, the *Didache* further emphasized, that the ministry provided by church officers should be of such a high quality that it may properly be equated to that provided by the prophets of earlier days. Instead of indulging in destructive controversy and criticism, church members were admonished by the *Didache* to say their prayers, encourage sinners to repent, indulge in charity, and, in general, to follow the example of Jesus as portrayed in the Gospels. The second coming of Christ, according to the *Didache*, must constantly be in the forefront of Christian thought and action. "Be ready," the Christian guidebook warned, for "you do not know the time when the Lord is coming."

Along with the Christian writings which have survived from the early decades after the death of Jesus there are several early Christian prayers and hymns that apparently were popular. Some of the hymns seem to reveal the influence of certain kinds of pagan music. Among the hymns there is one by Clement of Alexandria that is of considerable historical interest; probably it was composed shortly after A.D. 200. Both prayers and hymns, it may be observed, reveal some interesting trends that distinguished them from the prayers and music of Judaism.

To strengthen Christianity as an institutionalized religious discipline, Justin, Roman Christian scholar who adapted Platonic and Stoic philosophy to Judaic and Christian theology, made additions, in approximately A.D. 150, to current precepts upon important aspects of Christian worship. Hippolytus, in about A.D. 217, formulated elaborate instructions, that soon were followed in many congregations of the Christian world, pertaining to the ordination of bishops, presbyters, and deacons. Tatian the Assyrian produced in the middle of the second century a harmony of the four Gospels that was read in Syrian churches for nearly three centuries.

Irenaeus, who was bishop of Lyons during the latter part of the second century, may have been introduced to Christianity by Polycarp when Irenaeus was a young boy in the Near East. But he spent most of his life in the vicinity of Lyons. In the area in which he lived, he was known as an aggressive but a generally-popular advocate of the Christian faith. Nevertheless, in spite of his popularity, ultimately he would suffer martyrdom at the hands of Roman authorities. Among the writings of Irenaeus, one treatise is especially well-known. In that work the author indulged in extensive refutations of the major "heresies," including Gnosticism, that were plaguing the Christian movement at that time. Until recently, most of our knowledge of Gnosticism came from the writings of Irenaeus. Probably of the greatest ultimate importance, the works of Irenaeus gave favorable attention to ideas and principles that later would become basic to Roman Catholic belief. Through close study of both the Old and the New Testaments, which Irenaeus seemed to accept as essential parts of a whole, he determined that for persons who are truly Christian it is necessary that their lives be based on faith. A life based on faith, in his judgment, is the only kind of life that is complete and unified. As a result of his studies of the New Testament, Irenaeus developed the interesting and very important idea that a policy of providing for a definite succession from generation to generation without break in the designation of those individuals who become bishops must be accepted as sound Christian policy; such a policy, Irenaeus seemed to believe, was the intent of God. Thus, it appears to some historians that Irenaeus was responsible for the later adoption by the Roman Catholic Church of a procedure, now well-known, for the maintenance of the succession of individuals chosen for the top position within the Church hierarchy. In general, one cannot doubt that the influence of Irenaeus upon Roman Catholic belief and procedure was substantial. The point of view exists among some church historians that the Gospel of John, which, as already noted, differs considerably from the other Biblical Gospels, was hardly accepted by most Christian ecclesiastics as a proper part of the New Testament before the time of Irenaeus. But Irenaeus provided substantial status to the book in view of the fact that he found in it much support for his ideologies and points of view. Irenaeus also gave much attention to the development of a

Christian theology that apparently he thought was needed in his own missionary endeavors. The result is regarded as important, but, in actuality, the theology that he created seems, to great extent, to have been a popular restatement of the essence of the epistles of Paul, for whom Irenaeus had great regard and respect.

In the middle of the third century, Origen of Alexandria, a prolific writer, exercised strong and lasting influence upon many aspects of Christian worship and doctrine and, of even greater importance, upon the attitudes and beliefs of many Christians of that era and of later years. Without doubt, Origen was one of the greatest Christian scholars of all time, and he has also been characterized as the greatest systematic theologian, with the possible exception of Augustine, of classical Christianity. He was a product of the intellectual climate that still existed in Alexandria; thus, as was generally true of Alexandrian scholars, he was well-versed in Greek philosophy. In addition, and of very great importance insofar as his future scholarly work was concerned, he was a talented student of linguistics and possessed an exceptional knowledge of the Hebrew language. For the first twenty-eight years of his life, he maintained a program of research and writing, as well as teaching, in Alexandria. During the middle years of his career, he traveled to many of the outstanding Christian centers of the day where he lectured and met with students. In the latter days of his life, he created in Caesarea a major center of Christian studies. Probably few Christian teacher-scholars in history have attracted a following of young students who were more loyal to the ideals of their teacher than was true of those who sat at the feet of Origen. Many of those students became crusaders for Origen's analytical methods and for his points of view; thus the influence of Origen upon the development of Christianity in its primitive stage was magnified.

It appears that Origen became involved initially in the Biblical studies for which he became famous when he attempted to develop a reconciliation of some of the competing versions of the Old Testament then in existence. This work led him into extensive exegetical studies of books of the Old Testament; references to his unique points of view as developed in his commentaries upon the Old Testament are common in the writings of modern Biblical scholars. After Origen had spent many years on his studies of the Old Testament, he moved on to somewhat similar studies of the New Testament. In his treatment of the Scriptures, he developed penetrating interpretations of many parts of both the Old and New Testaments. His interpretative endeavors were important in their own right, but, in addition, they provided him a foundation for the development of his religious philosophy, a philosophy that seemed to evolve slowly and which ultimately became so profound in many of its aspects that it puzzled a large number of his contemporaries just as it has puzzled many later Christian philosophers. Origen was a generalist in his intellectual background; he believed that a true Christian must have strong familiarity with the secular. In fact, Christian understanding, in his view, had great value for a person who seeks to understand the secular; moreover, a substantial knowledge of the secular assists in giving meaning to Christian belief. As he developed unusual points of view on many subjects, both spiritual and secular, he indicated his belief that he had derived support for his work from the spiritual power of Christianity. In all of his writings, which number in the thousands, his expositions reveal the fact that he possessed distinctive and carefully developed conceptions of the moral and the spiritual, assisted by his strong background in the area of the historical. Obviously, Origen was influenced in his thought processes by Neoplatonism, but he seemed to realize its weaknesses. The latter part of his work, in the view of some scholars, seems to provide some of the basis for later Stoicism.

Origen was so outspoken as he voiced some of his views that much of the time he flirted with personal disaster, especially since the Roman persecution of Christians was increasing in intensity. And, unfortunately, he also had to contend with the personal antagonism of many Christians. Some of that antagonism would appear to have been inevitable, for Origen's philosophy was very difficult and was easily misinterpreted. But, in addition, at times Origen did reveal, at least from the perspective of some of his critics, a strange lack of propriety in his choice of illustrations and analogies; probably this was due to the likely fact that he felt that he was forced to indulge in various kinds of oversimplification when developing some types of expositions. Upon one occasion, when discussing the Virgin Birth of Jesus, he compared that particular event with the legendary report that Plato had a mortal mother but had the God Apollo as his father. Undoubtedly the intention of Origen when making such a comparison was of the best; certainly he was a devout Christian. But because of his remark about the Virgin Birth, as well as other poorly conceived comments, a number of influential critics of his day accused him of heresy. Consequently, a vast number of Origen's works ultimately were destroyed because of the charge that they advocated false ideologies or that they made dangerous statements. Nevertheless, a large number of his works are still available, at least in translation.

In spite of the fact that many Christian scholars of both yesterday and today have found a variety of reasons to criticize Origen's remarkable contributions to Christian thought, others have found in his analyses a sound foundation for their own studies. Many attempts, usually unsuccessful, have been made by some later Christian scholars to imitate a novel method employed by Origen in his exegetical studies of the books of both the Old and New Testaments. But other scholars have not been impressed with the method; in fact, some of the scholars in the latter category have criticized the method as being merely an allegorical device developed by Origen for the purpose of obtaining for a particular Biblical passage a specific interpretation that would assist him in the development of some desired thesis. Today, Origen has limited prestige with some intellectuals because of his apparent tendency to denigrate the followers of Judaism and because of his often poorly conceived efforts to separate Christianity from its Judaic heritage.

Tertullian of Carthage, near the end of the second century, took the very important step of casting Christian polemic into Latin, which ultimately became the language approved by Roman Catholicism for use in the services of worship in all its churches irrespective of their location. It is only in very recent years that the universal use of Latin in services of worship by the Roman Catholic Church has been discontinued. Tertullian, like Origen, was a Christian philosopher. He seemed to reflect the ideas of Origen in his disliking for the Jews; in truth, it would appear that he made a deliberate attempt to portray the Jews as so unworthy of their own key traditions that of necessity such traditions became the property of the Christians. After the death of Tertullian a large number of his expositions on Christian practices and beliefs were destroyed because in some of them he had propounded ideas that some powerful Christian leaders regarded as heretical; unfortunately, such a tragic occurrence had become common. In one of his writings, for instance, Tertullian expressed his conviction that after the birth of Jesus, Mary married Joseph and then had other children; such an idea was anathema to many influential Christians.

As a consequence of the many and varied efforts of devoted Christian scholars, such as those whose work has just received brief treatment, the principles of Christian belief and the practices associated with Christian worship underwent the kind of analysis and study, often leading to new and revised formulations, that, it is clear in retrospect, had to precede any widespread acceptance of Christianity as a distinctive religion. Thus, by the time of the third century A.D., Christianity was being recognized widely as a new religious faith. Much of the substance of Christianity, however, remained deeply embedded in Judaism at the same time that the new faith was revealing in some important respects a pronounced tendency to deviate from its Judaic heritage.

While key persons in the Christian movement were perfecting both the theoretical and the practical foundations of their faith, the movement was also struggling for survival. Within a few decades after the death of Jesus, Roman officials had become alarmed by the steady growth in the number of Christians, whom they described as Nazarenes, in virtually all of the Roman Empire. At the start of the second century, the actual number of professing Christians was still very small, at least in comparison with the huge pagan population, but it was apparent to Roman officialdom that there was a continuing increase in that number, a remarkable fact since Christianity was essentially an underground movement. Although at that time new generations of missionaries were winning recruits for Christianity, still regarded generally by both Jews and non-Jews as a distinctive sect of Judaism, the efforts of the missionaries were receiving support, although not necessarily deliberate support, from merchant-travelers who throughout the Roman world were talking about the strange rabbi named Jesus who was reputed to be the son of God and who was crucified as a common criminal. The Roman world by that time comprised much more than the Mediterranean area; it included a substantial part of western Europe (Britain was conquered by the Romans in A.D. 43), and one historian has observed that the Black Sea had become a Roman Lake. Increasingly, Roman officials were bothered and mystified by the strange ideas that, according to rumor, the Christians were advocating. Moreover, the leading Romans were disturbed by the fact that the Christians seemed to disparage all Gods, even the powerful Gods of Rome, except their own one God. But Roman officials seemed to be most perturbed by the apparent political overtones of the new religious movement; influential political leaders in Rome regarded Christianity as a very dangerous subversive force within the Empire. Upon occasion, large groups of Christians, employing passive resistance, did indulge in acts of civil disobedience. And to complicate the political picture, it appears to have been a fact that some militant Jews were affiliating with Christianity because of their hope that the aggressive Christian movement, with such assistance as they could provide, would ultimately destroy the government that had been responsible for the cruel destruction and desecration of Holy Jerusalem and its great Temple. In connection with the charge made by many of the Roman leaders that

Christianity was a dangerous subversive force in the Roman Empire, it must be realized that Roman culture, including its political mores, was intimately related to the Empire's pagan system of religion which involved the deification of the Emperor.

The appalling ignorance of Roman rulers in regard to the nature of Christianity facilitated their ready acceptance of assorted rumors pertaining to political plots supposedly fostered by Christians, and it made it easy for them to believe strange reports about the indulgence of Christians in various kinds of outrageous behavior. The ignorance of Roman officialdom early in the second century is illustrated by the contents of some letters exchanged between Hadrian, who was Roman Emperor from A.D. 117 to 138, and the consul Servianus in Egypt. In the exchange of correspondence the statement was made that the Egyptian Christians appeared to be "lightweight gossipers." Moreover, one of the two men expressed the belief, after interviewing several Christians and listening to their talk about Jesus and the Kingdom of God, that the Christians, seemingly without realizing the meaning of their ideas and actions, were actually worshipping the Egyptian God Serapis. Serapis was usually portrayed by the Egyptians as an austere kingly character who always sat on a throne and wore a crown. Somewhat earlier the governor of Bithynia had written a letter to Trajan, who was the Roman Emperor during the period A.D. 98–117, in which he revealed his perplexity in regard to the seemingly innocent day-by-day behavior of the Christians in spite of the subversive activities in which, according to widespread reports, they were indulging. The Christians, the governor of Bithynia reported, sang hymns that did not appear to involve dangerous content, and often they ate together, eating quite ordinary food; moreover, he noted that his extensive analyses of Christian behavior had not been able to turn up any evidence that they indulged in "wicked deeds," and they never seemed to falsify their words or commit fraud, theft, or adultery. So he decided to try to ascertain the true facts in regard to Christianity by questioning two female slaves who were known as "deaconesses" in their church. To facilitate his examination of the two women, he tortured them. But, he asserted, apparently with great chagrin, "I could discover nothing more than depraved and excessive superstition."

As already noted, Paul was executed in Rome upon the order of Nero, who was Roman Emperor from A.D. 54 to 68. In fact, some of the earliest records of the systematic persecution of Christians pertain to episodes that occurred during Nero's rule. The historian Tacitus, writing in approximately A.D. 120, asserted that Nero, in attempting to place the blame for the great fire that swept Rome in A.D. 64, during which Nero is popularly believed to have fiddled, decided that the Christians were responsible. Tacitus states in his *Annals* that persons known as Christians belonged to a "detestable sect" which was suppressed for a while but then it "revived and spread not only in Judea but even in the city of Rome." He wrote further, "When some of these depraved and profligate wretches [the Christians] were induced to confess their guilt, Nero had some of them torn apart by dogs, some nailed to crosses, and others burned alive."

For many generations after the time of Nero, the persecution of Christians was a common phenomenon in the Roman Empire. Even Marcus Aurelius, Emperor from A.D. 161 to 180, who was a scholar and a stoic philosopher and who has been described by some historians of that period of history as the noblest of the Roman Emperors, permitted and actually seemed to encourage extensive persecution of Christians; numerous incidents involving the torture and death of Christians occurred during his otherwise notable administration. There is little doubt that Marcus Aurelius sincerely regarded the Christians as a superstitious and depraved lot, dedicated to the overthrow of the government; also he was concerned that his efforts to restore faith in traditional Roman culture, including its religion, as a bulwark against negative forces operating from within and without the Empire were continually being thwarted by the obstinate refusal of the Christians to cooperate.

But it was not until the short reign of Emperor Decius, 249–251, described as "an execrable animal," by one Christian writer of the time, that Roman officialdom decided, after many years of growing concern, that the Christian movement must be systematically crushed. Consequently, many thousands of Christians, men, women, and children, were subjected to various forms of horrible torture and death, often in connection with the popular Roman circus where as a featured event Christians were thrown into pits with hungry wild animals. In addition, large numbers of Christians were cast into slavery, inevitably leading to early death, to build vast public works, to do the work of drudgery in connection with military operations, and to work in Roman-owned mines, often in distant parts of the Mediterranean world. But even in advance of the officially sanctioned orgy of torture and death sponsored by Decius, a large number of acknowledged leaders of the Christian movement, Paul, Polycarp, Ignatius, Simeon, Justin, and many others had been tortured and slain upon the order of Roman officials. Moreover, for many years before the time of Decius a vast number of members of the Christian movement had suffered indignities and even death as a result of the intense hatred toward them by the vast majority of Roman citizens who remained staunch supporters of their pagan faith. Most of the people of the Roman Empire supported their officials in their acts of persecution against the Christians, for they found it impossible to tolerate the supposed attitudes and beliefs of the Christians on many subjects, sociological and political as well as religious. As a consequence, it had become common for Christian communities to seek refuge in out-of-the-way places; even caves provided sanctuary for a few of the groups; in much of the Roman world, Christianity was forced to remain an underground movement.

Decius was succeeded as Emperor by Gallienus, 253–268. Gallienus, apparently a wise man with an intuitive understanding of sound sociological and psychological principle, had become convinced that the program of persecution instituted by Decius was not the solution to the "Christian problem." Apparently he came to the conclusion, in spite of the fact that he believed that Christians held to religious beliefs which must be regarded as false, that the future of the Empire would be served best by offering clemency to Christians instead of persecuting them. Consequently, Gallienus, in A.D. 260, proclaimed an Edict of Toleration; the edict continued in effect after the termination of the administration of Gallienus. In fact, for forty years after the reign of Gallienus, Christians in most parts of the Empire were able to come out of hiding and lead a seminormal kind of existence.

After the time of Emperor Gallienus, there were five short-term Roman Emperors before Diocletian became Emperor in 285. Diocletian is universally regarded as one of the most capable of the Roman rulers. It is a curious fact, however, a fact which historians generally have been unable to explain, that he abolished the Edict of Toleration promulgated by Gallienus; in truth, an official policy of persecuting Christians was reinstated. It is the belief of some historians that in many parts of the Roman Empire the persecution of Christians by Roman officialdom, often involving the perpetration of unbelievable kinds of brutality upon large masses of people, actually reached its climax during the rule of Diocletian. But in political history Diocletian is best known for his many political reforms; among them was the creation of a so-called tetrarchy for ruling the Roman Empire, a scheme that represented a major reorganization of the government. The reorganization was conceived by

Diocletian as a device for introducing greater efficiency into the governance of the large and increasingly unruly Empire. In reality, however, the introduction of the new plan released new political forces in such a way that for a period of several years the political structure of the Empire was virtually demoralized by intrigue and by assassinations.

Probably the effects of the policies introduced by Diocletian upon the populace of the Roman Empire were felt most severely by the Christian segment of the populace in Egypt and in neighboring areas. Just before the time of Diocletian, Christianity in Egypt, due to a variety of causes, featured an extreme hatred of anything and everything pagan; in fact, a bitter feud had developed between Christians and pagans. Each one of the groups seemed to delight in engaging in injurious practices against the other. The Christians, in fact, destroyed Alexandria in A.D. 292, and simultaneously they murdered many of the distinguished scholars located there because of the fact that the cultural activities of Alexandria, in the sciences, in philosophy, and in the arts, featured pagan scholars. One writer has observed that the Christians of Egypt at that time, when dealing with pagans, had chosen to ignore the Christian concept of brotherly love.

So when Diocletian reinstated the official Roman policy of persecuting Christians, persons affiliated with Christianity in many parts of Egypt and in neighboring areas were treated by the Roman soldiers and by many members of the pagan population as if they were animals to be hunted down and slain. Eusebius, fourth-century historian, described in his *Ecclesiastical History* some of the horrible tortures to which Christians were subjected: Nude women were suspended by one foot until they died; the arms and legs of a person, man, woman or child, were lashed to the branches of trees that had been bent to the ground so that when the trees were released the body of the individual would be pulled apart; and many times, by using sharp shells, the flesh of the body of a professing Christian was scraped off the bones down to the skeleton. It is a part of the Coptic Christian tradition that during the reign of Diocletian, 140,000 Christians were slain and 70,000 were banished. The Coptic Church still pays tribute to the martyrs of that time, and the Coptic calendar dates from the year A.D. 284, the year in which Diocletian became Emperor, which is known among the Copts as the first year of the Era of the Martyrs.

Since Christians in Egypt during the time of Diocletian had only the choice of flight into the desert or horrible death, many, as one might expect, chose the former. Thus, suddenly, a tremendous stimulus was given to the expansion in the Egyptian desert of an already existing program of Christian community development that was unique within the Christian movement. In most of the communities of the Roman Empire where Christianity gained a foothold, its introduction, usually the result of the efforts of a missionary, was accomplished through the sponsorship of small closely knit communities of converts who usually practiced a semicommunal form of group living. But in Egypt and in most neighboring areas a different kind of Christian community, many of which had their origin during the time of Diocletian, became common; each such community usually represented the culmination of an interesting evolutionary process. The first step in the process involved the decision of an individual who was a devout Christian, and who may have been seeking safety and seclusion, to go into the desert and adopt a way of life that involved poverty and extreme austerity. Such a mode of living was regarded by a large number of early Christians as virtually necessary to satisfy the purported ideals of Jesus. Often the individual who had decided to adopt such a way of life became a hermit in some isolated location, possibly a cave. The solitary life of many of the hermits of Egypt frequently involved extensive fasting and many hours spent each day in prayer and meditation and even unbelievable self-torture. One hermit, Evagrius, is said to have lived on a diet that contained no meat, no vegetables, and no fruit; he never bathed; he frequently prayed one hundred times a day; and often he stood all night in a pit containing cold water. Upon occasion a hermit who gained attention and prestige because of his austere and supposedly holy ways would begin to attract pilgrims who sought to derive inspiration from his courage and from his demonstration of a style of life supposedly pleasing to Jesus; moreover, a well-known hermit frequently attracted disciples who might also choose to become hermits in close proximity to him. Thus, often, in the course of time, to serve the needs of pilgrims who may have been coming in large numbers from many communities in Egypt, and actually from almost any part of the Christian world, a chapel and accommodations for temporary living would be erected close to the abode of the original hermit. So frequently a Christian community, possibly with a monastery at its center, was the ultimate result of such an evolutionary process. The number of people attracted to the kind of Christian life thus conceived soon began to increase so rapidly in northeastern Africa that some members of the ruling hierarchy in Rome became fearful of the ultimate consequences of the movement on Roman society. The concern of the Roman authorities may have been especially great because the new Christian desert communities gave little recognition to Roman rule. Over a period of several decades, a vast congeries of virtually autonomous communities developed within the Egyptian part of the Roman Empire; the area which was involved extended from west of Alexandria into the Sinai to the east and then south for a considerable distance into the Nubian country.

In spite of the partial destruction of buildings and the massacre of many of their inhabitants through the centuries as several waves of conquering armies swept over Egypt and neighboring lands, several of the very early Christian monasteries in northeastern Africa still exist. Probably the best known is one of the four original monasteries at Wadi el Natrûn, only a short distance from one of the two main roads that connect Alexandria and Cairo. That monastery, its monks and its archives, as is true of several other similar monasteries, is a precious resource for students of the Christian tradition. According to legend, the monastery at Wadi el Natrûn was erected in A.D. 260. Jerome wrote in considerable detail of his visit to the monastery in A.D. 385.

During the early part of the period of intense political activity that resulted from the new organizational policies which Diocletian introduced to assist him in governing the Roman Empire, roles of considerable importance insofar as the present narrative is concerned, were played by Gaius Galerius, who was appointed a Caesar to serve under Diocletian in the East, by Maximin Daia, who had chief administrative responsibility for the Western part of the Empire out of Rome, and by Julius Constantius, who was made a Caesar to serve under Maximin Daia. All the key members of the new ruling hierarchy were confronted immediately with critical problems. Constantius, in particular, had to deal with major revolts in his part of the Empire, which included Britain and much of Middle Europe; he moved quickly, however, demonstrating great military efficiency, to crush all attempts at rebellion.

Constantius had a son named Constantine, who probably was born shortly after the year 280; his mother was a girl of very low social status. Shortly after the birth of Constantine, Constantius discarded the boy's mother in favor of a new wife who politically and socially was more acceptable. So Constantine, virtually an orphan, spent his youth in Diocletian's court in Nicomedia, a city in Asia that was only a short distance east of the Bosphorus; Nicomedia possessed a large Christian population. The son of Constantius was an extremely able and hand-some lad, and he used his unusual opportunities as a member of Diocletian's efficient court to become familiar with the problems of the Empire and with political and military strategy. Shortly after the year 305, when Diocletian suddenly abdicated because of ill health, Constantius decided that he could use the assistance of his brilliant son in connection with military operations then under way in Scotland. Galerius, who after the abdication of Diocletian assumed new powers in the ruling hierarchy, hesitated to permit Constantine to leave the court in Nicomedia, so the youngster, employing a brilliant bit of strategy, escaped and went to the aid of his father. Within a very short time, Constantius died. Since Constantine was on the scene, he moved quickly to take his father's place. It became apparent immediately that a new and powerful personage had moved into the Roman political picture, and the others in key positions of control within the Empire became duly concerned. Like his father, Constantine indulged in many tactics that pleased the troops in his legions and which won their respect. Consequently, the members of his armies, many of whom previously had been known as barbarians, accepted the rigorous discipline that he invoked; thus very soon Constantine had a very efficient military organization. In 312, after he had won several critical battles in areas of Europe north of Italy, he decided that the time had come to launch an invasion of Italy. The crucial battle of the campaign, one of the most meaningful in history, took place at Milvian Bridge where the badly outnumbered but well-disciplined army of Constantine crushed the forces sent out from Rome. The next day Constantine entered Rome, where he was given a great ovation and enthusiastic welcome.

The outcome of the Battle of Milvian Bridge must be regarded as tremendously significant as a factor in the evolution of Western civilization and in the development of the Christian movement, for Constantine, not previously known as a Christian, soon became strongly identified with the Christian faith. The victory of Constantine at Milvian Bridge took place during a time in Roman history that, from the point of view of historians of religion, was characterized by some curious developments in the field of religion. A new monotheism imported from the East, built around a Sun God, along with such monotheisms as Christianity and Judaism, was competing with traditional Roman paganism for acceptance by members of the populace. Moreover, a pronounced trend existed within the populace, especially among military leaders, to ascribe a success in some important endeavor to the approval of one of the Gods then being worshipped. Even before Constantine's victory at Milvian Bridge, he had decided that he had the goodwill of some God; his great victory at Milvian Bridge merely confirmed such a belief. But it seems likely, as indicated by a triumphal arch erected in 315 by the Roman Senate to commemorate that victory, that Constantine was convinced that his benefactor was the Sun God. Some Christians, however, believe that Constantine's victory was due to a miracle; they seem to have accepted as fact that a flaming cross appeared in the sky in front of Constantine before he led his troops into the crucial battle. Such a report, obviously legendary, originated, there is little doubt, with Eusebius, Christian historian already mentioned, who introduced the tale into his famous *Life of Constantine*, written after Constantine died. Although it is clear that Eusebius possessed great competence as a historian, probably his strong pro-Christian bias often became a factor in the functioning of his powers of imagination.

Although there is debate in regard to Constantine's religious beliefs prior to and immediately after Milvian Bridge, no historian doubts that he did become a confirmed Christian early in his political career. He was not baptized, however, until shortly before his death. Probably, his ultimate abandonment of religious beliefs built around ideas associated with the Sun God in favor of Christianity was a consequence of the fact that early in his political career he developed friendships with some outstanding persons whose religious inclinations were toward Christianity. Among such persons were Ossius of Cordova, of strong Christian background, Lactanius, a literary man who was very familiar with Christian doctrine, and, later, Eusebius, whose writings have added much to our knowledge of Constantine's life and to an understanding of the workings of his mind. Probably, after Milvian Bridge, one or more of Constantine's Christian friends succeeded in convincing him that his godly benefactor was really the God of the Christians, not the Sun God. There is little doubt that when Constantine first revealed his acceptance of the Christian faith he regarded it as something highly mystical; he seemed to believe that the cross was endowed with special mystical powers. In fact, probably Constantine never developed much understanding of his adopted religion, its doctrines and its practices, or even of Jesus and his message. It was many years after his apparent acceptance of Christianity before any mention of Jesus, or Christ, appears in any of his utterances. Ultimately, Constantine's military standard became the lab-arum, which was a long-handled staff with a chi-rho monogram (or christogram) on its banner, surmounted by a crown. Since the great majority of the members of the populace of Rome and of the Roman Empire, including most of the individuals of great influence in the affairs of the Empire, were still pagan, Constantine revealed his political acu-men by attempting in many of his political actions and pronouncements to bring about a reconciliation of Christian and pagan practices and ideas. In the year 313, for example, a medallion struck to conform to Constantine's orders portrayed the Emperor with a christogram on his helmet, the she-wolf of Roman paganism on his shield, and a cruciform scepter in his hand. When making appointments to office, he attempted not to discriminate between Christians and pagans.

The success of Constantine's campaign in Italy did not mean that he had obtained immediate control of the Roman Empire. Although he became the "senior Augustus," he still had to contend with several jealous and often powerful ruling officials, especially in parts of the Empire east of Rome. In about a year, however, as a result of deaths (some of which were planned) and military consolidations, his major opposition had been reduced to only two men: Maximin Daia, who had become ruler of Syria, Egypt, Illyricum, Thrace, and Asia Minor, and Licinius, who ruled the Balkan nations. Constantine was disturbed by the fact that both Daia and Licinius indulged in extensive persecu-tion of Christians. Consequently, exercising the authority associated with the superior position he now held in the ruling clique, Constantine demanded that Daia cease his harassment of Christians; then he ne-gotiated an understanding with Licinius, actually involving a strange and ambiguous document, that was used by Constantine in his in-sistence on freedom of worship in the part of the Empire which Licinius ruled. Shortly thereafter Constantine's opposition was reduced to one man, Licinius. This resulted from the fact that Daia had made the mistake of trying without proper preparation to conquer Byzantium, on the site of modern Istanbul, which was a part of the jurisdiction of Licinius. Licinius moved quickly and cleverly and soon routed the armies of Daia. Then, over a period of eleven years, Constantine, displaying his great genius as a politician, at times as an unscrupulous politician, as well as military strategist, slowly eased Licinius out of the picture; finally, Licinius capitulated, and in 324, upon order of Constantine, he was executed. So, in 324, Constantine, usually designated by historians as Constantine the Great, had become supreme ruler of the Roman Empire.

So, after the many dark days of the approximately first three centuries of the Christian era, when frequently the Christian faithful must have doubted whether the Christian movement could much longer survive, a powerful emperor, assisted in his decisions by a series of political and military successes, broke with tradition and produced a truly remarkable cultural revolution in the Roman Empire by accepting Christianity, not Roman paganism, as his personal religion. So, in effect, Christianity became the preferred religion of the state. As a consequence, history records the slow but steady demise of Roman paganism as the common religion of the vast population of people under the influence of Roman political and cultural forces. In truth, when Constantine succeeded to the title of Emperor, the future of Christianity, it can be seen in retrospect, became secure; soon, Christianity became an intimate part of the culture of a people who were destined to leave an indelible mark upon the development of Western civilization. A new era in history had been initiated.

Unfortunately, according to Egyptian historians, when suddenly Christianity became the religion in favor with Roman officialdom, vast numbers of Christians in Egypt took advantage of the unexpected happening by indulging in an orgy of destruction of existing pagan statuary and even of scholarly works. There was extensive destruction of many of the historically important edifices for which ancient Egypt was and still is famous; the destruction included the defacement of a vast number of the truly remarkable statues of pagan Gods that are a common part of the huge stone structures from antiquity that are now on the itinerary of modern tourists.

For a brief study of the career of Constantine the Great as Roman Emperor and as dynamic apostle of Christianity, we move to the next chapter.

Chapter Nine

CHRISTIANITY BECOMES AN IMPORTANT NEW FACTOR IN WORLD CULTURE

THE ERA OF CONSTANTINE

Even before Constantine gained his position of supreme authority in the political structure of the Roman Empire, he had become aware of the fact that the recognition he suddenly had received as the acknowledged Christian leader in the Roman world did not make it any easier for him to mediate disputes betwen squabbling Christians. Shortly after his conquest of Italy, Constantine found himself involved in a controversy pertaining to the appointment of a suitable person to be bishop of Carthage. Should it be Caecilianus or Donatus? The efforts at mediation which Constantine proposed, probably following the judgment of his friend Ossius, led to the designation of Caecilianus as the more desirable appointee. Consequently the followers of Donatus, known as Donatists, became angry, and they insisted that Constantine himself make the final determination. He agreed to review the case, but, after due consideration that probably involved the weighing of political factors as well as other aspects of the case, he upheld the previous finding and ordered strong action taken against the violently dissenting Donatists. Later, when he found himself confronted with critical civil disorders fostered by factions supporting the two candidates, Constantine rescinded the measures that he had instituted against the Donatists and announced that the controversy and those who were involved were being left "to the judgment of God." Thus a superficial analysis would seem to indicate that Constantine, the great military strategist, had suffered an early defeat on the religious front, but historians generally agree that he actually won a victory; members of the Christian community had revealed their acceptance of the principle that Constantine, technically a secular head of state, had become the proper person to make decisions pertaining to ecclesiastical appointments.

After Constantine had won complete control over the Roman Empire as a result of his victory over Licinius, he found that he had inherited a very difficult religious dispute, the so-called Arian controversy, that had been extremely troublesome for Licinius. Arius, an outspoken member of a dissident group of Christians headed by Bishop Melitius of Lycopolis, argued that Jesus the Son of God was not "of the same substance" as God but was of "similar substance." Such a point of view, vague though it is, seems to have been consistent with ideas advanced previously by several Christian scholars. By contrast, however, Bishop Alexander of Alexandria, as well as his immediate predecessor, promulgated the principle, which seemed to be accepted by a majority of influential Christians, that, simply stated, Jesus was of the same substance as God, who was his Father, and, in fact, with respect to their substance and the powers which they exercise, no distinction should be made among the Father, the Son, and the Holy Spirit, the three components of what was being described by Christians as the Holy Trinity. Much could be written and has been written about the strange, interesting, and difficult concept of the Holy Trinity, a concept that defies simple exposition; in brief, however, the Father, the Son, and the Holy Spirit, each one, represents, in a sense, a particular personality of the unique Godhead. An early and elaborate treatment of the subject was developed by Augustine, 354–430. Pope Leo XIII, 1878–1903, promulgated in his encyclical *Divinum Illud* an exposition of the concept that generally is regarded as acceptable by Roman Catholics. Some of the elements of the idea of the Holy Trinity undoubtedly had their origin in Judaic thought, but the primitive expression of the concept of the Holy Trinity as it was first introduced during the early centuries of the Christian movement smacks of Greek metaphysics—another illustration of the influence of Greek culture upon the early development of Christianity.

Arius, who was excommunicated from the diocese of Alexandria because of his beliefs, quickly embarked upon a one-man crusade in behalf of his theological position; he decided to pursue an aggressive campaign among Christians in areas to the east of Egypt, where he won much support from diocesan leaders. Amazing as it may seem in retrospect, the controversy that soon developed between those who supported Arius and those who held to a contrary point of view threatened to destroy any semblance of unity in the Christian movement just as a considerable reconciliation of views among diverse groups of Christians was beginning to take place, especially at the eastern end of the Mediterranean. The vitriolic writings and speeches of many Christians during that strange era in Christian history can hardly be reconciled with fundamental Christian ideology; passion rather than logic prevailed in the arguments that were advanced. It must be admitted, however, that probably logic was impossible in any analysis of the subject, which was so vague as to defy any attempt at definitive description. A modern scholar accustomed to processes of rigorous thought finds himself taxed to find any meaning in much that was said during the debates that took place. Apparently Constantine, the practical man who understood very little, if anything, about Christian theology, believed, as indicated in some of his letters, that the controversy was over trivia and at stake was nothing of real significance for the religious faith which he had accepted. Nevertheless, there is some reason to believe that Constantine at one time leaned toward the Arian position in spite of his ultimate denunciation of it, probably a consequence of his finally yielding to what seemed to be wise from a political standpoint.

After those who opposed Arius and who seemed to be well organized had strongly denounced him and his supporters at a meeting in Antioch and then had arranged for an even larger assembly to be held at Ancyra, Constantine decided that the situation had become critical and he must move to attempt to control the controversy. He ordered that the meeting at Ancyra be canceled and then hurriedly sent messengers in all directions to invite influential Christians from most of the Empire to attend a conference in Nicaea to consider the problem of heresy, especially the issues involved in the Arian conflict. Constantine promised that he would give the opening address at the meeting. Nicaea, like ancient Nicomedia, was located in Bithynia which, in modern geographic terminology, is an area in northern Turkey along the Black Sea. So on May 20, 325, more than three hundred church dignitaries, including the bishops at Alexandria, Antioch, Caesarea, Carthage, Nicomedia, and Rome, assembled in Nicaea. Some of those in attendance revealed physical disfigurement because of the persecution which they had endured in previous years. Constantine, when opening the meeting, exhorted the delegates to make a serious attempt to reconcile their differences and thereby restore unity to the Christian world. That, he emphasized, as would any good politician, was the prime purpose of the assembly.

Although many important actions were taken at the conference, including some pertaining to "heretical" writings, probably the best known was the formulation of the Nicaean, or Nicene, Creed, which, except for some relatively unimportant modifications made in it at the Council of Constantinople in 381, continues to the present day to be

217

accepted as basic to the creed of most Christian denominations. Traditionally it has been common for Christians to testify to their faith in the words that were introductory to the Creed: "We believe in one God, Father Almighty, maker of all things visible and invisible; and in one Lord Jesus Christ, the Son of God, begotten of His Father . . ."

The findings adopted at Nicaea essentially denied the ideas advocated by Arius but they affirmed common ideas that had evolved in regard to the Holy Trinity. The assembly confirmed the excommunication of Arius, an action that led to an order by the assembly to destroy his writings. The ideas of Arius were not dead, however; in fact, Arianism remained the chief cause of doctrinal disagreement within Christendom for most of the fourth century during and after the time of Constantine, and even in later years the Arian position was accepted by a variety of Christian populations, especially in the East. Even some of Constantine's successors accepted the Arian position, and for several centuries in regions on the fringe of the western part of the Roman Empire, where the religious control of the increasingly powerful Church at Rome was not very effective, the ideas of Arius prevailed. Many times, through all of Church history after the fourth century, in various parts of the world, strong spokesman for the Arian position have appeared.

The Nicaean Conference is known to many Christians because of the fact that among its actions was a specification that Easter, the day set aside by Christians to memorialize the Resurrection of Jesus, should be celebrated on the first Sunday after the first full moon following the spring equinox, which occurs on March 21; the formula thus stated is still followed in many parts of the Christian world. One can only speculate upon the nature of the reasoning that entered into the decision. In view of Gospel accounts of the Resurrection of Jesus, its celebration should take place each year at approximately the time that followers of Judaism celebrate the festival of Passover; such a circumstance is assured by the formula. (Before the development of the formula, some Christians had celebrated Easter at the time of the Judaic Passover.) A further motivation for those who designed the formula, according to a legend, was a desire to accommodate the many pilgrims who went to Jerusalem each year to celebrate Easter. As the pilgrims traveled down the eastern side of the Mediterranean, they were often harassed by brigands, especially at night. So the participants at Nicaea decided, the legend notes, that the journey of the pilgrims would be safer if they could travel under a full moon, which is assured by the formula that was adopted.

Possibly the most important part of the elaborate document drawn up at Nicaea was that which included the statement of twenty canons formulated to regulate church discipline and government. Thus, it is generally agreed, the Council at Nicaea, in 325, created the original charter for institutionalized Christianity.

At the conclusion of the Nicaean conference, Constantine expressed satisfaction in the fact that the assembly of churchmen, of whom he said he was merely one, had undertaken "the investigation of the truth." And, he assured the assembled members of the conclave, "all points which seemed in consequence of ambiguity to furnish any pretext for discussion have been discussed and accurately examined." Then, after asking the forgiveness of God for those who had previously indulged in blasphemies (obviously referring chiefly to Arius and his supporters), he urged all Christians to "embrace that doctrine which the Almighty has presented to us." Probably the profound influence of the Nicaean Creed on the early development of Christianity as an institutionalized religion is due almost entirely to the fact that Constantine, powerful and shrewd political leader and also recognized in his time as the responsible source of authority in Christendom, placed his tremendous prestige behind it.

In addition to the great impetus that Constantine gave to the development of the Christian movement, he made a decision that would have significant effects upon the future of the movement and, in fact, would have a pronounced influence upon historical processes that would be responsible for some of the later segmentation of organized Christianity. The important decision, made about the time that the great council was held at Nicaea, involved the removal of the seat of Constantine's government from Rome to ancient Byzantium, located on the Bosporus. Shortly after Constantine made the announcement of his decision, a decision that came as a tremendous surprise and shock to the Roman world, he initiated plans to rebuild Byzantium in the image of Rome but with a grandeur that Rome had not been able to attain. The re-created Byzantium, initially designated as New Rome, was soon renamed Constantinople, the City of Constantine; Constantinople became officially Istanbul in 1930 during the regime of Ataturk, great Turkish military genius, statesman, and national leader. Since Rome was to be continued as a subsidiary center of government, the net effect of Constantine's action was to split the Roman world into two segments, soon to be known as the Eastern and Western Empires. The reality of such a separation increased through the years, especially after Emperor Theodosius, approximately sixty years after the death of Constantine, placed each of his two sons in charge of a part of the divided Roman Empire.

Another consequence, a most important consequence, of Constantine's powerful attempt to elevate the city that bore his name to a position of eminence in world affairs was the fact that a tremendous stimulus was given to the development of a rejuvenated Greek civilization, generally described by historians of later years as Byzantine civilization. In fact, for about a millennium after the time of Constantine, Constantinople was the center of the magnificent Byzantine civilization that became a major factor in the cultural history of the world although during its time it was chiefly identified with an area that corresponded essentially with the Eastern Empire, often known as the Byzantine Empire. At its height the Byzantine Empire comprised all the Near East, from Libya and Egypt to the Caucasus and the Iranian frontiers, along with the Balkans, Greece, Sicily, and a small part of the Italian peninsula. Byzantine culture became the inspiration for some of man's finest achievements in art and architecture, in philosophy, in the development of ideas pertaining to the conduct of good government, and even in the creation of advanced notions in regard to proper human relationships, including medieval notions of chivalry. Byzantine culture had its foundation in earlier Greek principles and concepts, but its initial active ingredient was the new and dynamic Christianity of the East, nurtured in its formative days by Constantine.

One can only speculate upon the motives of Constantine when he moved the headquarters of his government from Rome to Constantinople, previously Byzantium. Just a short time before taking the action, he returned to Rome after an absence of many years; apparently he believed that he would receive an ovation similar to that of previous years. But much to Constantine's dismay, even the Roman Senate seemed to rebuff him; one cannot doubt that he was very unhappy with what he saw and heard. Undoubtedly there were other factors involved in Constantine's decision to move the headquarters of his government from Rome to Byzantium. For instance, since he had spent his youth at Nicomedia, only a few miles from the city that would bear his name, probably he had developed a strong affinity for the people of that area and for its culture. Moreover, the shores of the Bosporus, a narrow waterway separating Asia and Europe that carried and still carries heavy traffic between Mediterranean and Black Sea ports, provided a natural location for the establishment of a great commercial center. The specific site chosen for the central city of Constantinople was also easily defended; in fact, for approximately a thousand years after the time of Constantine the defenders of the city that bore his name were able to resist all would-be conquerors, thereby providing a kind of political stability to the Eastern Empire that the Western Empire did not have. Within a century after the death of Constantine, it may be noted, Rome was overrun by Germanic "barbarians," and, although Roman Christianity survived and actually continued to expand its influence, Rome did not recover its previous political stature for several centuries.

Probably an important factor in Constantine's choice of Constantinople for his chief seat of government involved his apparently sincere conviction that his government and Christianity were necessarily interrelated and that he, the political ruler, must accept great responsibility for the future of the Christian movement; certainly he would have been encouraged to develop such a point of view by the confidence displayed by the Christian world in his actions and decisions. Although many of Constantine's activities that pertained to the enunciation and elaboration of Christian principle undoubtedly bore the mark of political expediency, one cannot doubt that his dedication to the Christian faith continued to increase throughout his lifetime. During the latter part of his rule as Emperor he actually indicated a desire to be known as the thirteenth apostle, and he often revealed his belief that he had special status an an envoy of Christ on earth. Thus one must assume that the decision to make Constantinople the focal city of the Roman Empire revealed, at least in part, a preference by Constantine for the kind of Christian environment that seemed to be evolving in the East over that which was becoming associated with life in the West. There is little doubt that Christianity in the East, even before the time of Constantine, had scored a much more impressive victory over paganism than was true of Christianity in the West. Moreover, Greek culture with its strong mystical ingredient was giving Eastern Christianity characteristics that stimulated intellectual accomplishment. Although the new dynamic spirit in Eastern Christianity was making possible and actually encouraging some foolish controversy and even shysterism, religion and creative intellectualism in its many forms were becoming intensely compatible.

By contrast, a more passive brand of Christianity was developing in the West; great emphasis upon unquestioned acceptance of doctrinal pronouncements by those in authority in the Church hierarchy in Rome often was stifling individual initiative. This continued to be true for many years after the time of Constantine although the Byzantine culture of the East, with its powerful religious ingredient, exercised, especially during the first centuries after the era of Constantine, considerable influence upon Christian thought and practices in the West. As previewed in such early trends, which apparently did not escape the analytical mind of Constantine, Christianity in the East and Christianity in the West continued through several centuries to diverge with respect to some of their major characteristics. A superficial examination of the historical developments of the Church in Rome and that of the Church in Constantinople might reveal only growing hierarchial and administrative differences, but the widening divergence of the two bodies involved other elements that ultimately became very important. For instance, the fact of the intimate relationship in the East between the religious and the secular, which was continued into the new Church entities into which the Eastern Church ultimately was segmented, had very great political and religious significance through the years; in the West, by contrast, the Church remained independent of the secular and actually, upon occasion, dominated the political. In addition, as time progressed, differences in liturgy as employed in the Eastern and Western Churches became increasingly pronounced, and striking differences in fundamental doctrine and attitude on issues of Church policy became more and more apparent. The Eastern Churches have always given much more emphasis to the Resurrection than to the Virgin Birth, at least by comparison with the Western Church; in fact, the doctrine of the Virgin Birth of Jesus seems to receive little attention on the part of the clergy in many Eastern Churches. Some of the differences between the Eastern and Western Churches that had their origin in the early days after the time of their separation remain embedded in the accepted positions of the two Christian bodies. For instance, modern Eastern Churches, such as the Greek Orthodox Church and the Russian Orthodox Church, descendants of the original Eastern Church, permit priests to marry. The Roman Church, by contrast, has enjoined the priesthood to practice celibacy through most of its history although, admittedly, decrees in that regard were not rigidly enforced until Pope Gregory VII, in 1075, excluded married priests from all ecclesiastical functions.

When Constantine took his seat on his new throne in Constantinople, he did so as Emperor of the Roman Empire. In addition, he did so as reigning head of the Christian Church in the Eastern part of the Empire, a role to which apparently he believed he was entitled as a result of Divine designation. Constantine's arbitrary assumption of the position of ultimate control in the affairs of the Eastern Church was not challenged by prelates of the Church, including the Patriarch of Constantinople, in view of the powerful position within the Christian community that Constantine occupied. So, as already noted, an important tradition of vast consequences was inaugurated for much of later Christendom when for the first time in Christian history both the secular authority and the clerical authority within an important political entity were concentrated in one man. In 303, Armenia had become the first nation to adopt Christianity officially as the state religion when King Tiridates III became a Christian, but the role of Tiridates in the Armenian church was quite different from that of Constantine in the Eastern Church. Constantine fostered elaborate pageants as Emperor of the Empire; he also was the central figure, wearing royal purple and invested with scepter and diadem, in ceremonial events sponsored by the Eastern Church. At these latter events, which upon occasion must have been more elaborate than any other religious celebrations ever held at any time in Christian history, people prostrated themselves before Constantine. When making public appearances, Constantine expected to be greeted by shouts of "Holy! Holy! Holy!" His tremendous ornate palace and its grounds were regarded as sacred.

In keeping with his assumed position as the supreme officer of the Eastern Christian Church, Constantine sponsored a program of constructing grand houses of worship; the humble and often secret gathering places patronized by Christians only a few years earlier had become passé in the new regal atmosphere that Constantine had ordained for Christianity. Previously Constantine had been responsible for the initiation in Rome of plans for seven great churches, including the original St. Peter's; the present St. Peter's basilica is a Renaissance structure that was built during the sixteenth century While Constantine maintained his headquarters in Rome, the kind of pageantry associated at that time with the activities of a secular head of state were carried over to some extent into the religious realm, but when Constantine moved to Constantinople he instigated the staging of much more elaborate spectacles. The new church edifices in Constantinople for which Constantine was responsible, both in design and in construction, were more magnificent than anything previously conceived for religious worship. The great structures in Constantinople were designed to resemble imperial basilicas rather than the temples associated with the pagan culture of the Greeks; each structure consisted of a great hall with a very high ceiling supported by huge columns, with a portico in front and an apse in the back. Such churches themselves soon became known as basilicas. The Christian cathedrals of later years reveal the influence of Constantine's ideas. Constantine, clothed in his gorgeous robes, personally officiated upon a regular basis at religious services. When Constantine died in 337, he was buried, at his request, in the Church of the Holy Apostles. It has long been a tradition that Constantine also built many ornate structures on sites of significance for followers of Christianity, including a spectacular house of worship in Jerusalem at the location, venerated in his day, where it was believed that Jesus was crucified. Apparently such a tradition was confirmed in 1971 when archaeologists affiliated with the Greek Orthodox Church unearthed remains of a large structure that soon was identified by several scholars as the basilica of the Church of Constantine; its ruins provide part of the foundation of the present Church of the Holy Sepulchre in the Old City of Jerusalem. Other great churches within the tradition initiated by Constantine were constructed after his death. The most notable of the latter churches was the Hagia Sophia, the Church of Holy Wisdom, erected in Constantinople in 532–537; the Hagia Sophia, later used after the Muslim conquest of Constantinople as a Muslim mosque and currently as a museum, now is visited by many tourists and is still regarded as one of the wonders of the world. Because of the beauty, the size, and the structural characteristics of the Hagia Sophia, it is universally acknowledged to be one of the most remarkable edifices ever conceived and built by man.

Much of our information in regard to the rapid development of the Christian movement during the important era of Constantine is provided in the great mass of writings of Eusebius, whose *History of the Christian Church* was mentioned earlier. Eusebius, a contemporary of Constantine, was well-known in his day as the highly intellectual bishop of Caesarea. It is from the works of Eusebius that we obtain much of our information about people and events of his own time and of even earlier years; one can only hope that his obviously strong pro-Christian bias did not color his writings to any great extent. It is clear from the manner in which Eusebius documented his work that he had access to a tremendous library of manuscripts, many of which have since been lost. Eusebius must have been an intimate of Constantine, so he possessed a fine vantage point from which to observe history in the making; moreover, probably he deserves much credit for some of the important actions and decisions of Constantine and for some of the trends initiated at that time in Christian history. Eusebius wrote the first draft of the Nicaean Creed; apparently he, along with Ossius, exercised great influence in determining that the action taken at Nicaea in regard to Arianism should be negative. Moreover, Eusebius is designated by scholars as at least partially responsible for the great momentum that developed in the fourth century for the idea that Christianity was created by God as a unique religion for man. In so doing, Eusebius seemed to adopt some of Origen's views that the early traditions of the Jewish people had now become the property of professing Christians. Apparently such a point of view was also held by Constantine, probably the result of the influence of Eusebius. It may have been as a result of such a circumstance that in general the Eastern Church and its descendents became strongly anti-Semitic; this was especially noticeable in later years in the attitude and policies of the Russian Orthodox Church.

As a result of Constantine's actions in making Constantinople his official headquarters, and actually as the capital of the Eastern Empire, Rome became the nominal political capital of the so-called Western Empire. So the Patriarchs of the Western Church, who soon became known as Popes of the Roman Church, moved quickly to take advantage of the situation, even while Constantine lived, to make themselves the masters of the populace of the entire Western Empire. For many centuries thereafter the tremendous authority of the Roman Popes overshadowed that of the weak secular rulers of the Western segment of the Roman Empire; actually, until very recent years—and disagreements are still common—the Popes and the political leaders of Italy and the Holy Roman Empire engaged in an almost continuous struggle for dominance. The extent to which the Roman Popes became involved in civil affairs in their part of the world is a most interesting phenomenon in Christian Church history. The influence of the Popes upon the political as well as the religious life of the Western Empire was one of the factors that, in effect, separated the West from the East. And the early Emperors in Constantinople, although having some technical claim upon political control of the Western Empire as well as the Eastern Empire, provided little interference with the activities of the powerful Roman Popes.

The churchmen in Rome whose authoritative stance made them increasingly powerful in both the religious and political affairs of the Western Empire also enabled them to maintain their independence effectively from the religious and political authorities in the East. Nevertheless, the Roman Popes chose to adopt in church affairs the pomp and ceremony that were instituted by Constantine. The results of that decision can be observed today in the highly ritualized and often colorful procedures that are accepted as standard practice in the Roman Catholic Church and even in many Protestant churches which must acknowledge the ancestry of the Roman Church. Moreover, the Roman Popes could not completely ignore the intellectual ferment that was such a pronounced characteristic of the Eastern Church. But the members of the ruling hierarchy of the Roman Church, apparently motivated by the necessity of trying to satisfy the urgent needs of the demoralized society which they served, chose to give emphasis to social rather than to intellectual pursuits. In truth, church pronouncements and actions during that era of history actually reveal the existence on the part of Roman churchmen of a substantial amount of mistrust of the intellectual, probably a partial consequence of their growing belief that "Greek thought" was responsible for the fact that they had to contend with so much of what they regarded as heretical doctrine. For many centuries after the time of Constantine, the negative attitude of the Roman Church toward rational pursuits would prove to be a severe handicap to the development in the West of the highly rational intellectual disciplines, including the sciences.

The loose moral standards of the day in Roman life, a symptom of the obvious moral deterioration that was taking place in Rome and in many neighboring areas, became an early target of the Roman Church fathers. Prostitution was condemned, and a single moral standard was specified for husband and wife. The Roman clerics taught that the very institution of marriage comes from God, and the ends for which marriage was instituted as well as the laws that govern it were ordained by God. Thus the Roman Church could not recognize divorce. When a child was very young, at the insistence of Church authorities, he was inducted into Christian life under the auspices of the Church; he was taught how to worship and how to confess his sins. And at death, the burial and the rites associated with the burial became a responsibility of the Church. Throughout a person's life many elements of his conduct were the subject of Church directives, to which rigid adherence was expected; penalties for nonadherence, as those penalties were viewed by the faithful, could be severe. Such firm social policies cast in a religious format, as instituted by the Roman Church, seem to have had a salutary effect upon

Roman life; it is clear that the Church played an important and praise-worthy role in the society which it served. Such a statement continues to be true today.

Due to the very strong position in the West to which the Roman Church attained shortly after the era of Constantine, the time was opportune, and apparently it was so regarded by members of the Roman Church hierarchy, to advocate the idea of the primacy of the Roman Church and its headship in the overall structure of world Christendom. Thus the concept of the Papacy, which ultimately would be accorded great respect by much of the Christian world, was originated. In a complementary development, a high degree of episcopal organization of Christian Churches was instituted in the large territory over which the Popes of Rome claimed jurisdiction. In fact, during the latter part of the fourth century the foundation was created for the later worldwide organizational structure of the Papacy, with the Pope as bishop of Rome occupying the superior position and with its high offices generally filled by very competent men, that ultimately became what must be regarded as the most efficient and most effective nongovernmental organization the world has ever known. For more than a millennium and a half, the highly organized Roman Catholic Church, as expressed in the Papacy, has been able to surmount the vicissitudes of history. No nongovernmental organization has ever had more influence on the affairs of the world, political and sociological as well as religious, than the Vatican, located in Vatican City, an independent political entity since 1929 when the Lateran Pact was concluded between the Papacy and the Italian government. Even today, the chief Roman Catholic policy makers are at the apex of a vast and efficient enterprise that ministers to the religious needs of many millions of people in virtually all the nations of the world, and, in addition, they exercise tremendous worldwide influence on customs and attitudes and even on international political affairs, an influence that often is little understood by non-Catholics.

An argument strongly advanced by Roman churchmen in the fourth and later centuries to persuade Christians throughout Christendom to accept the Roman Church as the true Church of Christ was a strong emphasis upon the idea that the Church in Rome was founded by Peter. As already observed, great doubt exists on the part of probably most historians who are not Roman Catholics that Peter even went to Rome.

The significance for missionary purposes of the emphasis upon the role of Peter in founding the Church in Rome becomes clear when it is recalled, according to New Testament testimony, that upon one occasion when talking to Peter, Jesus asserted, "thou art Peter, and upon this rock I will build my church." Thus, at least since the fourth century, the Popes in Rome have been revered by persons affiliated with the Roman Catholic Church as members of a religious dynasty initiated by Peter, designated as the first Pope. With such a designation made for Peter, it became a task of the Church fathers in Rome to select from the Christian leadership in Rome after the supposed time of Peter those individuals who seemed to be worthy of being named in the succession of Popes immediately after Peter. This was not easy, for records pertaining to those who were involved in the affairs of the early Church were sketchy and untrustworthy. However, the Church fathers concerned with the problem received help from a reading of some of the writings of Irenaeus, for whom they had high regard. In about A.D. 180, Irenaeus in his treatise entitled *Against Heresies* mentioned twelve Christian bishops who lived after the supposed time of Peter and whose Christian works he regarded as notable. Consequently, the twelve men were chosen by the officialdom of the Roman Church to be designated as the Popes in the succession after Peter. At a later date, when a Papal history was prepared that was to be regarded and now is regarded as officially acceptable, some changes were made in the names and in the order in which they appear in the succession as given by Irenaeus.

Members of the Roman Catholic Church hold their Popes in very high esteem; a Pope's honorific is "Holy Father." An indication of the tremendous significance that most Roman Catholics now attach to the Pope's position in the Roman Church was revealed in 1870 when the first Vatican Council promulgated the so-called dogma of infallibility, which asserts that the Pope cannot err or teach error when he speaks ex cathedra—that is, on matters of faith and dogma. Such a doctrine had been widely assumed, however, before its promulgation.

So, by the latter part of the fourth century, Christianity had become the religion of a vast number of people of diverse cultural background. The Christian faith had become recognized as one of the major religions of the world, and it had developed sufficiently distinctive characteristics that it was no longer regarded as a special sect of Judaism. It is not surprising, however, that many students of the evolution of Christianity become concerned, possibly perturbed, when they realize that so early in the history of its organizational development it had become characterized by an extreme kind of institutionalization as revealed by its two diverging branches: the Eastern Church and the Western Church. It is inevitable that the thoughtful person must experience some wonderment that such grand religious enterprises, with their carefully conceived plans of organization, with their elaborate rituals and pageantry, with their plethora of doctrinal principles and proclamations pertaining to human conduct and belief, should bear the name "Christian," a title derived from the designation given by some of his early followers to a first-century evangelist from Galilee, regarded by many as the Son of God, who advocated a simple but powerful philosophy of brotherly love and human justice. That such enterprises so complex, called Christian, should be accepted as mere expansion and interpretation of endeavors so elementary, also called Christian, requires efforts at reconciliation that are not easy; such efforts must involve unusual historical, psychological, and sociological perspective.

The superficial student of history might be tempted to believe that because of the efforts of Constantine, Christianity had won its major battles; it is true that because of Constantine the future of Christianity became secure. Actually, however, the accomplishments of Constantine in behalf of Christianity merely made it possible for Christians to begin to grapple in a serious way with Christianity's most critical problems, those pertaining to substance. Christians could come out of their hiding places and openly debate and criticize. And that was necessary, for Christianity in the fourth century lacked most of the elements of maturity. Many ambiguities existed within the various doctrinal pronouncements and, in general, great confusion was to be found even among devout Christians in regard to proper and acceptable interpretations of Christian doctrine. The rudiments of a Christian theology as advanced by Paul were the conception of a Judaic-Christian mystic; in reality, a well-conceived Christian theology did not exist.

Chapter Ten

A CRITICAL PERIOD
IN THE HISTORY
AND PRACTICE
OF CHRISTIAN PRINCIPLE

IMMEDIATELY AFTER CONSTANTINE

During the era of Constantine, the early Christians in Egypt and adjacent areas regarded themselves generally as within the overall jurisdiction of the Eastern Church, administered from Constantinople. But, in reality, as noted earlier, special trends were developing and had been developing for many years in policies, in doctrinal matters, and in practices of worship that were giving adherents to Christianity in northeastern Africa a distinctive reputation in Christendom. Then, during the middle of the fifth century, a major controversy suddenly erupted in the Mediterranean world that seems to have had its origin in an argument between the Patriarch of Constantinople and a monk in a monastery near Constantinople; the argument pertained to the nature of Christ. The monk from the monastery had revealed his belief that the doctrine taught by some churchmen that Christ was both human and Divine was false; rather, he insisted that only the adjective "Divine" could properly be used to describe Christ. The monk's stated position is known in theological circles as an expression of the Monophysite Doctrine. Within a few months, controversy over the monk's position spread to a large part of the Christian world; many distinguished churchmen were involved. There was much denunciation of the opposition, even much name calling, and much politicking to line up forces. Finally, in 451, a council was called to be held at Chalcedon to consider several subjects but essentially for the purpose of coming to a conclusion in regard to the Monophysite Doctrine. During the discussions that took place, passions ran high, and it is now obvious that the issues became clouded by emotion and by semantic difficulties. Suffice it to say, most of the delegates to the Council were opposed to the views of the small group of dissident delegates from Northeastern Africa and the Near East who became known as Monophysites, persons who insist that Christ is made known to

230

man in only *one* nature, Divine. As a result of the disagreement, the dissident leaders and the Christians whom they represented decided to separate themselves from the rest of the Christian world. Through the centuries that followed, that separation has been complete; only in the last three decades have there been any significant attempts at reconciliation. At the present time there is in existence a collection of five significant church organizations, known as the Oriental Orthodox Christian Churches, that is the remnant of the collection of Christian organizations, after regroupings, that originally was composed of the dissenters at Chalcedon. The five major church organizations presently in the Oriental collection are the Coptic Church of Alexandria, the Ethiopian Orthodox Church, the Syrian Orthodox Church of Antioch, the Armenian Orthodox Church, and the Syrian Orthodox Church of Malabar (India).

Although few of the other disputes within the Christian movement shortly after the time of Constantine had the long-time consequences of the argument over the Monophysite Doctrine, the occurrence of that particular dispute reveals something of the primitive status at that time in history of even the doctrinal foundations upon which Christianity was based. The situation that existed provided a challenge to the creative endeavors of a number of very thoughtful and imaginative theologians and Christian interpreters, some of the greatest in the history of Christianity. In fact, the latter part of the fourth century and much of the fifth century constituted a truly remarkable period in the history of Christianity during which there was great acceleration in the refinement of the premises upon which Christianity was and still is based.

Theologians affiliated with the Western Church, more so than was true of those associated with the Eastern Church, had to work within a framework of strong doctrinal restraints enforced by dogmatic members of the Church hierarchy. But that fact did not seem to provide too much of a limitation upon those notable Western scholars of that period of history whom we still acknowledge as having made major contributions to the theological basis of Christianity; apparently they found that the existing restrictions were not too incompatible with ideas which they readily accepted. The names of Augustine and Jerome of the West are very familiar to most Western Christians, especially to Catholic Christians. Possibly it is one of the biases of our historical perspective on the accomplishments of the early churchmen that the contributions of the ecclesiastics of the West are better known than the contributions of those of the East, for Christianity in the United States and the rest of the Western world, whether Catholic or Protestant, has its historical foundation in the Western Church, centered in Rome.

Augustine, 354–430, was a product of North Africa, where a tremendous amount of genetic and cultural mixing had occurred among the people; for several centuries Romans had mingled freely and easily with native Africans as well as with immigrants from Asia Minor. Such a "melting pot" environment has often produced men of genius. As a youngster, Augustine, against the wishes of his Christian mother, indulged in the accepted pleasures of the day; in some of his later writings he admitted to extensive participation in sexual promiscuity. But he was an eager student of Latin, philosophy, mathematics, and music; his education in philosophy, since it was typical of that espoused by Roman scholars of that day, was essentially concerned with the work of the Greek philosophers. The influence of such an academic background upon his later writings as a Christian scholar obviously was very great. The latter part of Augustine's educational experience was at Carthage; there while still in his teens he was chosen to be an instructor. At Carthage he made the decision to give up his sexual promiscuity, for he had achieved satisfaction in a new way of life with a beautiful concubine, a social custom approved by Roman law. The concubine bore him a son for whom he developed great affection.

At the age of twenty-nine, Augustine decided to realize the ambition of many young men of his day in the Western world by going to Rome; there he continued his career as a teacher. But after only a year in Rome he moved to Milan. Augustine's mother, who was strongly protective of her son, pursued him to Milan where she tried to change his mode of life, which from her Christian point of view had to be regarded as intolerable; finally she was successful in persuading him to give up his beloved concubine in favor of a ten-year-old girl. The young girl was supposed to become Augustine's bride when she reached the age of twelve. Within a very short time, however, after asserting that he had become convinced of the merit of chastity but was not ready for it, Augustine took another concubine and forgot the girl.

Augustine's mother also succeeded in persuading her son to listen to some of the Christian teachers of the day, including the wise, articulate, and persuasive Ambrose, who was bishop of Milan and one of the most highly regarded Christian fathers in the Roman Church. Although Augustine soon decided that the simple faith of his mother had no meaning

232

for him, one cannot doubt that his introduction to Christianity at that time served to stimulate him to indulge in a great deal of speculative thought upon religious subjects. Such thought, however, became entangled in and often was in conflict with his philosophical interests which had their origin in his earlier academic studies. Finally in Augustine's thinking a reconciliation began to evolve between Neoplatonism and primitive Christian theology. Undoubtedly his interest in Christian theology was stimulated by his intensive study of Paul's writings. In fact, Augustine had become fascinated by what he had read about Paul and by the content of Paul's works, which rapidly became a source of much inspiration. The net result of the reconciliation in Augustine's mind between Neoplatonism and Paul's ideas was a dedication for the rest of his life to the perfection of Christian doctrine. Over a period of many years Augustine promulgated points of view on the fundamental tenets of Christianity that must be regarded as providing the next truly major step after the contributions of Paul to the development of Christian theology. The vast importance of Augustine's work is revealed by the fact that the principles of Christian theology advanced by him dominated Christian theological thought until the twelfth century. Even such later church reformers as Luther, 1483–1546, Calvin, 1509–1564, and Wycliff, 1320–1384, often justified some of the doctrinal changes which they advocated by arguing that they were merely trying to return to Augustinian principles from which they professed to believe the Roman Catholic Church had deviated during the centuries that immediately preceded their time.

Augustine was baptized into the Christian faith by his tutor, Ambrose, on Easter Sunday, 387. Then he went to North Africa with some associates to live the monastic life, involving poverty, celibacy, study, and prayer. The Augustinian religious order, the oldest monastic order in the Western world, traces its origin to Augustine's little community in North Africa. After only a few years as a recluse, however, Augustine was persuaded to become an assistant to the bishop of Hippo (near Bone in modern Algeria) on the coast of the Mediterranean. Shortly Augustine became the bishop, a position he held for thirty-four years, actually for the rest of his life.

From his very first days in Hippo, Augustine impressed members of his religious community with his ability as a thinker and with his eloquence as a preacher and teacher. Shortly after his arrival in Hippo, he found that he must contend with the aggressive Manicheans, whose basic doctrine was concerned with the supposed conflict between light and dark; material things were regarded as dark and evil. A debate was arranged between Augustine and the local Manichean bishop, a very strong religious leader in the community. Augustine's exposition and the force of his arguments overwhelmed his opponent, so much so that the Manichean leader left his post in disgrace. Augustine also challenged the pagans who still held a strong position in North Africa; moreover, he took issue with the Donatists, still an active Christian sect in the region. The Donatists, however, refused to accept Augustine's challenge to a debate; rather, they began to indulge in acrimony and actually in violence in their attempt to force the Augustinian Christians into a secondary position in the community; the government attempted to intervene in the bitter struggle that developed, but without success.

In spite of the heavy burdens of his office and the continuing opposition of the Donatists, Augustine was able to spend much time in meditation and in writing. Almost every day he wrote on some subject; much of the time he struggled with difficult topics of concern to the entire Christian world, but he did not ignore problems of local interest. He was dominated by the belief that by virtue of his position in the Roman Catholic Church he was a responsible representative of a unique agency on earth that was established by Christ. "The Church is spread throughout the whole world," he wrote, "all nations have the Church. Let no one deceive you, it is the Catholic Church." As he continued to study the writings of Paul, which he cited frequently in his works, and as he continued his consideration of the role of the Church in human society, his concept of the breadth of that role seemed to increase. Although purely theological analyses seemed to sustain his remarkable intellectual processes, it appears that he would have felt at home among the modernists of today who preach the "social gospel." In his active mind, undoubtedly because of the breadth of his knowledge and of his interests, many streams of intellectual endeavor, Christian and non-Christian, Biblical and non-Biblical, the philosophical, the social, and even the aesthetic seemed to come together. Among his extensive writings, filling many volumes, there were treatises on musicology, discourses pertaining to man's beliefs, attitudes, and practices, Biblical commentaries, tracts on human polity, many discussions of sacramental theology, and studies that must be described as concerned with human psychology.

Some of the premises upon which Augustine based his studies are revealed in the following words from his writings:

What the soul is to the body of man, that the Holy Spirit is in the body of Christ, which is the Church.

Between divinity alone and humanity alone there is as mediator the human Divinity and the Divine humanity of Christ.

In no way doth the benevolence of God's grace and the bounty of his omnipotence so plainly appear as in the Man who is the mediator of God and men, the Man Christ Jesus.

[The Lord Himself] helps us that we may shun evil and do good, which none can do without the Spirit of grace; and if this be wanting, the law comes in merely to make us guilty and to slay us.

There are two kinds of love: of these the one is holy, the other impure, the one is social, the other selfish; the one consults the common good for the sake of the supernal fellowship, the other reducing the affairs of the commonality to their own power for the sake of arrogant domination.

Some of Augustine's writings are notable for their attempt, always brilliantly conceived although usually lacking in logical nicety, to find a basis upon which Church doctrine, which he appeared to accept without much question, could be accepted by men whose mental processes feature the rational. Then, as now, the strange and difficult concept of the Trinity was a matter of deep concern for most people with an analytical mind and was the cause of many questions by prospective Christians and even by many persons who had accepted Christianity. So for fifteen years Augustine labored on his great work, *De Trinitate,* written for the purpose of justifying the notion of the Trinity. He also dealt with other debatable and difficult subjects; for instance, he tried to reconcile the concept of free will as an inherent characteristic of man with the idea of an all-knowing God, and he attempted to reconcile the fact that evil does exist in the world with the idea of God's benevolence. The sin of Adam, the Original Sin, was a subject that seemed to be very much in Augustine's thoughts; for him, the Original Sin was a basic factor in what he regarded as the natural tendency of each and every man toward evil, a condition that according to his belief can be changed only when an individual repents in a way that is acceptable to God. It was inevitable that Augustine's studies of controversial subjects would arose opposition; in fact, he and his expositions were often denounced by his contemporaries in very bitter terms, but such denunciations did not deter him from his studies and his writing.

Augustine was also the author of two long and truly remarkable works that are now generally regarded as classics in Christian literature. The first, *Confessions,* is his autobiography. He tells with sorrow and deep regret of his early life with its many sordid episodes that haunted him during his career as a representative of the Church, but then his auto- biographical treatment moves ahead to describe the contentment and happiness that had been his lot since he made the fundamental decision to devote his life to the work of Christ. The candid treatment, written in beautiful prose, is a truly moving document that had great influence in its time and is still a source of inspiration for many religious as well as others.

As already indicated, the Western Empire, a mere remnant of the once proud Roman Empire with its capital in Rome, would have only a few decades of independent political existence after the death of Constan- tine; afterward, in spite of the tremendous influence of the Church in the West, there would be many centuries of its political subservience to powerful conquerors. The fall of Rome was preceded by a pronounced de- terioration in Roman society with its consequent enfeebling effects upon Rome's political life and upon its military capability. Simultaneously many of the peoples on the fringes of the Empire, usually described by historians as barbarians, were showing unprecedented aggressiveness, stimulated in part by several instances of Roman mistreatment. In the year 410, the Goths under Alaric were able to conquer Rome, the first time in eight hundred years that the city had been taken by an enemy. The formerly prestigious capital of the Roman Empire was systematically pillaged, although the churches of St. Peter and St. Paul were spared, and vast numbers of citizens, especially the prominent and the wealthy, were massacred. When word of the terrible tragedy reached Augustine, he was shocked, and he began to give much thought to the nature of war, its origins, and its consequences. He himself would have a firsthand view of the terrible evils of war and the human miseries associated with it when in the last year of his life, the year 430, Hippo was overcome by Vandal armies which at that time were ravishing a large part of southern Europe and northern Africa and even parts of the Near East. During the inva- sion, Augustine, in spite of his age and attendant feebleness, attempted to maintain the faith of his followers.

Augustine's meditations upon the brutal conquest of Rome, its utter tragedy and irrationality, led him to the writing of his last great work, *City of God,* upon which he labored for thirteen years. Like the prophets of old, Augustine had to contend with the point of view held by many Christians to whom he ministered that a just God would not have permitted the conquest of Rome, the city of Peter and the Popes; also like the prophets of old, he chose to emphasize that the tragedy of Rome was God's way of punishing men for their sins. What was novel about the sacking of Rome, he stressed, was the lack of damage to the churches and the fact that mercy was accorded to Roman citizens who sought sanctuary in the churches. "Whoever does not see that this is to be attributed to the name of Christ, and to the Christian temper, is blind," he asserted. Moreover, he warned, "Whoever sees this, and gives no praise is ungrateful."

In very recent years some churchmen have been reviewing the traditional position of the Roman Catholic Church on the subject of war. Much of their attention has been focused upon the doctrine upheld by some churchmen, often adherents to Roman Catholicism, that "just wars" do occur; in fact, some students of the subject have regarded such a doctrine as a part of Roman Catholic teaching. One cannot doubt that upon occasion the Roman Catholic Church has adopted, at least by implication, a partisan position on a particular war, and has actually abetted some military operations that have been questioned by many neutral observers. The principle that there are just wars has often been ascribed to Augustine as its originator; subsequent refinements of the doctrine pertaining to conditions under which Christians may or should take up arms have been ascribed to Thomas Aquinas and to the later Scholastics. So a reading of some sections of Augustine's *City of God,* which reveals the torment of his mind as a result of his experiences with war, is revealing. In that dissertation, after providing a brief discussion of the "manifold disasters" known as wars, Augustine reveals in a few sentences the depth of his feeling about wars in general. "Let every one," he wrote, "who thinks with pain on all . . . [the] great evils [that are wars], so horrible, so ruthless, acknowledge that this is misery." And, he continues, "If any one either endures or thinks of them without mental pain, this is a more miserable plight still, for he thinks himself happy because he has lost human feeling."

It is a curious fact that Augustine, although exercising a powerful influence on Christian thought in the West, never received much recognition in the East. Many explanations have been offered to explain the phenomenon. Clearly, prejudice was involved, for there was some tendency for the Christian leadership in the East to denigrate the contributions being made to Christian thought in the West, and vice versa.

Probably of even greater importance, the work of Augustine was not within the spirit of the work receiving approval in the East; Augustine was obviously dominated in his writing by a desire to uphold orthodox doctrine and he had a pronounced tendency to subordinate the rational to the subjective.

Jerome, 340–420, is undoubtedly the best known of the churchmen in the West who were contemporaries of Augustine. Born near Aquileia, a town located at the northern end of the Adriatic Sea, and educated at Trier and Rome, Jerome inaugurated his career of passionate dedication to Christianity by establishing a monastic brotherhood in a location near his birthplace. Shortly, however, he entered a monastery near Antioch. In Antioch, after a short interlude spent in a desert hermitage, he was ordained a priest. In his early forties he returned to Rome where he became associated with Pope Damasus, who in Jerome's words "commanded" him to develop an improved Latin translation of the New Testament. So at the age of forty-five he left Rome and built a monastery for himself in Bethlehem; then, surrounded by great masses of reference materials, he devoted the remaining thirty-four years of his life to the writing of the Vulgate, the traditional Latin text of the Bible approved by Roman Catholicism. The writing of the Vulgate was an accomplishment that gave Jerome everlasting recognition in the world of the Roman Catholic Church.

Jerome left for posterity several commentaries on his grand project that provide an interesting insight into his methods and attitudes. Several earlier versions of the Scriptures, in Latin and in Greek, were available to him as he embarked upon his project of developing an improved Latin translation. His concern for his own fairness and accuracy as he necessarily had to pass judgment on previous versions is revealed in his comment, "In judging others I must be content to be judged by all." He made an early decision in the development of his own Latin text to return to the primary Greek version of the New Testament and not rely on translations. "Why not go back to the original Greek," he wrote, "and correct the mistakes introduced by inaccurate translators?" He noted that he soon discovered that he had the task of rectifying previous blunders committed by ignorant critics as well as by copyists "more asleep than awake." He exempted from his implied criticism of past efforts the versions of the Greek Old Testament that were available to him and which he accepted as a basic resource, for he expressed the judgment that, starting with the development of the Septuagint, competent scholars had given careful attention to the creation of authentic Greek translations from the Hebrew.

Jerome, so that he might have the necessary competency to achieve his goals, developed great proficiency in reading both Hebrew and Greek; his own language, of course, was Latin. Consequently he was able to utilize in his task, as he translated, checked, and compared, all the manuscript resources available to him, whether in Hebrew, in Greek, or in Latin. The distinguished Latin version which Jerome ultimately produced was revised with the approval of the Roman Catholic Church in 1592 and again in 1907.

Jerome, later designated by the Roman Church as a saint, was also concerned with many aspects of church doctrine and belief; he was such a crusader for the truth as he understood it that some of his utterances may seem to mark him as a very cantankerous person. As with many of the great scholars of history, he was extremely intolerant at times of the views and writings of others. His complaints in regard to some of his contemporaries in the Church often were bitter, and his sarcasm could be biting. In an age when some of the top Christians seemed to be watching for excuses to charge thoughtful Christian scholars with the crime of heresy, it is truly remarkable that Jerome did not hesitate to be objective and honest in his criticism. He was as critical of accepted principles and beliefs as he was of individuals. Upon occasion his comments did cause people who professed orthodox beliefs to be deeply agitated. He often expressed the judgment, based upon his exhaustive studies, that many of the teachings of the Christian Church were a mingling of fable with fact. Frequently, Jerome's assertions brought forth strong rebuttal, so feuding became a significant characteristic of his life. Possibly his caustic comments on the moral standards of his time have some modern relevance. For instance, he was highly critical of the revealing modes of dress that were featured by many women of his day, and he condemned in bitter terms the sexual promiscuity that was common; he also spoke out with righteous indignation against women who used drugs to prevent conception or to induce abortion. Jerome, in the judgment of some historians, observed more clearly than many of his contemporaries the existence of symptoms of moral decay in the society of his time, symptoms that were a harbinger of the fact that the Vandals would find it easy to crush the Western Empire while he was still alive.

During the approximately first century after the death of Constantine, many other churchmen could be mentioned as making significant contributions to Christianity in the West. However, it seems fair to say that Augustine and Jerome set a standard of accomplishment during the era that only one other, Ambrose, was able to attain. Already noted as the tutor and baptizer of Augustine, Ambrose left his mark on the Western Church in still other ways.

Born of distinguished parentage in Gaul in approximately 340, Ambrose had the background, intellect, and personality for outstanding political leadership. It appears, in fact, that it was his early expectation and plan to embark upon a political career. As a young man he became the provincial governor of northern Italy with his headquarters in Milan. But when he was in his middle thirties, rival Christian factions in his province became embroiled in bitter controversy in connection with the selection of a new bishop. Ambrose by his eloquence and through his powers of persuasion virtually forced the warring groups to listen as he admonished them to abandon their foolishness and to act as Christian statesmen. So impressed were the members of his audience with his appearance before them that they abandoned their candidates and insisted that Ambrose resign from his political position and become the bishop. Consequently, history reveals, Ambrose did make the hard decision to give up his promising political career; within a period of one week he was successively baptized, ordained to the priesthood, and then elevated to the post of bishop. He rapidly became known throughout the geographic area served by the Western Church as possibly its most influential and authoritative spokesman. Cassiodorus, writing a century and a half later, described Ambrose as an "utterer of eloquent speech, impassioned, but dignified, very agreeable in his calm persuasion." He also said of Ambrose, "Divine grace indicated its approval of him."

Ambrose, it appears, became the most powerful force in the Western Church during his time for obtaining adherence to accepted doctrine, including that incorporated in the Nicaean Creed; moreover, he successfully challenged Church and even political leaders who interfered in the orderly development of Church affairs. There is little doubt that Ambrose provided vitality to the still young Christian movement when even some of those in responsible positions in the Church had a tendency to waver in their support of some of its precepts. The prestige, ability, and integrity of Ambrose were such that his advice was sought by principal officers of both Church and state in the solution of complex problems, and many times he was entrusted with difficult assignments. And as an indication of his great versatility, he is reputed to have been the composer of some of the Church's earliest and finest hymns. Truly it can be said that Ambrose was a person of nobility; his influence on the early development of the Christian movement does not permit the specific type of documentation that is easily possible in the cases of Augustine and of Jerome, but it was real and it was of very great significance.

In the East, the segment of the Roman Empire favored by Constantine, shortly after the reign of the great emperor Athanasius (295–?), Basil (330–379), Gregory of Nazianzus (329–390), and John Chrysostom (344–407) seem to deserve special mention in the present exposition, for they displayed notable characteristics as creative thinkers and as leaders in the hurly-burly of Christian life that developed very soon after the death of Constantine. Without the rigid papal control of religious thought that existed in the West, and without the strong authoritarianism that Constantine had exercised in the Eastern Christian community, turmoil became a pronounced characteristic of Christian life in the East almost as soon as Constantine had been placed in his grave. There was bitter contention between strong and able advocates for a variety of conflicting ideologies and doctrines, and a variety of quacks found many opportunities to take advantage of existing uncertainties in Christian belief and practice. It was truly a painful period for Eastern Christians as they attempted to find their way through areas of religious thought that as yet had not been well charted. Although the names of many leaders of the Eastern community of Christians may have been comparatively well known during the century after Constantine, our knowledge of only a very few other than the four already named has survived the critical scrutiny of history.

Certainly few epochs in Christian history, possibly no other, can rival that of the latter part of the fourth century in the Eastern Empire with respect to the tremendous amount of religious ferment that existed. The many diverse manifestations of religion accepted at that time as Christian were a major factor in the life of the day. Even vendors on the street took positions on doctrinal questions and argued fervently and even violently in behalf of their ideas. The existing diversity of opinions on Christian justice and on accepted Christian practices actually became responsible for civil and sociological chaos in the nominally Christian society. In addition, the leading men in the Church hierarchy competed with each other for position and influence, and the organization of the Church was demoralized by the existence of a vast number of supposedly Christian monks who professed no real allegiance to any person or persons or to any set of religious principles. Actually the monks appeared to have little understanding of even the most simple aspects of Christianity; religion for them seemed to be a vehicle for the exercise of power and often served as a cloak to cover their pursuit of nefarious schemes. The total effect of the sudden removal of restraints exercised by the powerful Constantine was amazing. The turbulent religious situation that soon existed in the East after the era of Constantine was in marked contrast to the comparatively placid condition promoted by the orthodoxy of the West where the rule of the Popes was supreme.

Shortly after the time of Constantine, his official rejection of Arianism was soon forgotten, and there was a great resurgence in the East in the acceptance of the ideas of Arius. In fact, Arians took over several positions of power in the Eastern Church and soon were in control of the services at the great church, St. Sophia. Orthodox Christians, those who accepted the Nicaean Creed, rapidly became the "minority party" in Constantinople.

In 379, when religious controversy and turmoil were probably at their height in Constantinople, Gregory of Nazianzus, who had not attained any great distinction as an ecclesiastic and who was then living in the village of Seleucia in Isauria, was called by the small group of orthodox Christians in Constantinople to be their bishop. Since Arians had gained control of the pulpits in all the churches, Gregory held services in a home. But his eloquence, supported by his obvious devoutness, his great learning, and his apparent understanding of people and their needs, soon attracted tremendous crowds of people who came to hear him; it is generally acknowledged that his ministry in Constantinople stamped him as one of the greatest preachers of all time. Two centuries later it was written of him that he was the ideal pastor since he presented his expositions on the assumption that "one and the same exhortation does not suit all people, for they are not bound together by similarity of character." Apparently he was an early advocate of the principle, stressed by modern psychologists and of great significance for teachers, that when creating a learning situation, proper attention must be given to differences in individuals in their mental attributes and in their background of knowledge. The powerful sermons of Gregory of Nazianzus, directed as they were to the un-Christian attitudes and behavior of men of his day, are still a source of inspiration for many Christians, especially clergymen and prospective clergymen. Moreover, his emphasis on the values of religious drama, undoubtedly stimulated by his obvious appreciation of pagan classics and pagan religious practices, had a strong effect on the development of Christian religious observances. Gregory's pastoral triumphs created great animosity on the part of the Arians, but Emperor Theodosius, who was an orthodox Christian, was pleased; in due course of time, in fact, Theodosius decided to take advantage of Gregory's popularity by installing him on the throne of St. Sophia. But within a few months Gregory decided, in spite of his new exalted position in the Church hierarchy in Constantinople, that he could no longer tolerate the continual backbiting of a large number of bishops and other churchmen. So in sorrow he withdrew from his ministry to spend the rest of his life in obscurity.

After a short interval, the Emperor chose John Chrysostom, a priest from Antioch, to occupy the throne of St. Sophia. Whereas Gregory of Nazianzus, although displaying great confidence in the pulpit, was actually thin-skinned, John Chrysostom, virtually as eloquent as Gregory, possessed a tough hide; moreover, he possessed a sharp mind and he knew how to arouse his listeners to self-examination—a capability that, unfortunately, often caused anger. From his new position of authority John embarked upon a crusade to reform the clergy, whose newly attained affluent status in Eastern society had led them to indulge in much loose living. John also denounced the large number of professing Christians who seemed to have little or no appreciation of the ideals advocated by Jesus and who appeared to believe that their participation in the variety of immoralities that had become a characteristic of the age was not inconsistent with Christian precepts. Christians who worshiped the accumulation of wealth and the pleasures that wealth would buy became a special target of John; he asked repeatedly how they could profess to be Christians and ignore their responsibility, emphasized by Jesus, to assist the poor. He aroused the anger of such nominal Christians when he observed that if a piece of gold should be offered them as an award "for every man who was reformed," they would "use every exertion" and would spend "all day long—persuading and exhorting" a prospect in an effort to win the cash award. But, he noted, Jesus offers something that is greater than any sum of money, the kingdom of heaven and even more. John's attacks also were strongly focused on the gross immorality of the theater, the extensive prostitution that existed, and the common practice of concubinage. Even most members of the clergy had concubines. The large Christian population of Constantinople, including the clergy, squirmed under the lash of John's tongue. His verbal crusade was supplemented by a series of actions to eliminate Christian weaklings from position of influence in the Church; it is said that he dismissed thirteen bishops from their posts. The troublesome monks, some of whom were actually spreading terror in Constantinople, were cowed by John's threats and actions, and they became much more discreet in their behavior. As one would anticipate, John's courageous denunciations soon began to make enemies; among them was the Empress who claimed that the prelate had offended her; she demanded that her husband assemble a council of bishops to try Chrysostom. The Emperor, who had previously provided strong support for John, acquiesced to his wife's demand; so John was tried, deposed, and then recalled when the common people raised a tremendous clamor. In the end, however, as a result of sinner machinations in which jealous and antagonistic churchmen participated, John was ordered exiled. On his way into exile he died; he was utterly broken, mentally and physically. But John had made his mark on Christian thought; Christianity in Constantinople was beginning to change and was displaying definite signs that it was rising above its sordid state as it had existed just before the time of the ministries of Gregory of Nazianzus and John Chrysostom. John's popularity with the masses of people, who have always exercised strong but sometimes subtle influence on the nature of the evolving Christian movement, was reflected in the fact that after officials announced John's exile, tremendous riots broke out in Constantinople; even St. Sophia was burned.

Basil, bishop of Caesarea, successor to Eusebius in that position, must be named along with Gregory and Chrysostom as one who had tremendous influence on the development in the East of Christian thought and policy. Basil came from a family distinguished by the number of its members attaining distinction in Christian work; he studied in Constantinople and also in Athens when Gregory of Nazianzus was a student there. Apparently he was influenced strongly by his study of the writings of Origen. Basil was not a profound theologian or orator but he is regarded as one of the most powerful proponents in his day of orthodox Christianity; he was bitterly opposed to Arianism. In addition, he was a staunch defender of the Eastern Church against the constant claims made by the Popes of Rome that they had jurisdiction over all of institutionalized Christianity. Moreover, he took strong positions in behalf of his belief that the ascetic mode of life, then so popular and growing in popularity with many Christians in the East, was not in keeping with true Christian philosophy; he taught that the ideals of Jesus could only be realized by men working as active members of society. "The solitary life," he wrote, "has only one goal, the service of its own interests. That clearly is opposed to the law of love." In line with his beliefs, Basil taught his followers the values of physical work in a Christian society, and he initiated projects to assist the poor and the ill. Among the latter projects was the creation of hospitals and the organization of programs to educate medical personnel; often he is credited with the introduction of the principle that the maintenance of health-care facilities is a proper responsibility of the institutionalized Christian church.

Basil also worked on the ritual and the liturgy of the Church and was responsible for a new recognition of the importance of music in Christian worship. It is a curious fact, in spite of the continuing Judaic emphasis on music in the synagogues, that a trend away from the use of music in worship services had developed in several segments of the Christian movement. Basil realized the fallacies in such a trend. Moreover, it appears that he believed that the time had come to review the nature of Christian music as a recognized art form of Christendom. The result, for which Basil seems to have been essentially responsible, was a synthesis for purposes of Christian worship of contemporary models of Greek music with some other musical styles of the Near East. Christian music in the Eastern Church was strongly and permanently affected; the music in both the Greek Orthodox and Russian Orthodox Churches, for example, still reveals characteristics of the music introduced by Basil. Even in the West, Christian Church music took on some of the characteristics of the new music that resulted from Basil's efforts. Basil's versatility is reflected in the fact that he developed rules of governance for Christian monastic life that still are accepted as basic in present-day monasteries in Greece and in some of the Slavonic nations. The great variety of practical contributions of lasting duration that Basil made to the Christian movement mark him as unique in the history of Christianity; he was truly a genius.

Athanasius, bishop of Alexandria, sometimes known in the history of Christianity as Athanasius the Great, was probably the most militant theologian and possibly the most astute ecclesiastic of his age in the East. His influence upon the evolving nature of the Eastern Church and upon all Christian thought was very great. Probably Athanasius was born in Alexandria. Thus, like so many of the great churchmen whose background was Alexandrian, his mental processes were Greek. His aggressive pursuit of the truth, which for him was at the heart of orthodox Christianity, dominated his sayings and actions. He was one of the very few churchmen living during the time of Constantine who openly opposed the concept of secular control of the Church; after the death of Constantine he continued to battle with tremendous forcefulness for his notion of an independent Church. Athanasius was very sympathetic toward the monastic movement, which had become a strong factor in the Christianity of his region. His support of the movement was revealed in an emphatic manner in his writings about Anthony, who was a contemporary churchman and a renowned anchorite. Many people in both East and West became acquainted with monasticism through the works of Athanasius; they were translated into several languages. Of very great significance for Christianity as its advocates struggled to help it attain some semblance of maturity in its doctrinal foundation was the fact that Athanasius became embroiled in the major doctrinal controversies of his day; his positions were and still are strongly influential in theological thought. His strong logical mind, a product of his Greek background, was always apparent in the power of his arguments. He was especially bitter in his opposition to the Arians; he asserted that "infidelity is coming in through these men." In numerous tracts he insisted that the Arian position was intolerable and that it made a distinction between the Son and the Father that was completely contrary to Biblical teachings. Ultimately, because of his opposition to Arianism, Athanasius was removed by Constantine's successor from his position as bishop of Alexandria. Although Athanasius devoted much time to a rebuttal of Arianism, other important aspects of the young Christian theology received his thoughtful attention. It is true that his analyses did not possess the logical nicety of those of some later generations of theologians, but the standard of logical thought maintained by Athanasius represented a marked advance over that of most other theologians of his day; actually, the logical analyses of Augustine, regarded by many scholars as one of the truly outstanding theologians of Christian history, often seem labored when compared with those of Athanasius. The many present-day sects that are the result of the ultimate segmentation of the original Eastern Church owe much to the wisdom and persistence of Athanasius. Because of his contributions to the creation of the Ethiopian Orthodox Church, members of that Church still hold him in special veneration. In view of the latter statement, some brief comments pertaining to the origin and history of the Ethiopian Orthodox Church may be of interest.

During the fourth century, Frumentius, a Christian boy from Tyre, survived a massacre by native Ethiopians when the ship upon which he was traveling had to go into an Ethiopian port to take on provisions. Ultimately the boy became attached to the king's court—the Aksumite Kingdom in Ethiopia was then one of the most powerful in the Near East—and he became a court favorite. When the king died, Frumentius became an adviser to the new king, Ezana, who later conquered much territory on both sides of the Red Sea. While Ezana was receiving acclaim as a great conqueror, Frumentius converted him to Christianity. After that event occurred, many Christian Churches were established in the Aksumite Kingdom. Consequently, Athanasius, from whom Frumentius had sought help, accepted overall jurisdiction over the new churches, and then succeeded in having Frumentius appointed to be the first bishop of Ethiopia, then the Aksumite Kingdom. At about the same time, Ezana ordained that Christianity should be the official state religion, thereby originating the tradition, broken only in very recent years, that the Emperor of Ethiopia automatically becomes recognized as the nominal head of the Ethiopian Christian Church. Moreover, because of the fact that Athanasius of Alexandria was responsible for the appointment of the first bishop, a curious tradition was followed after that time until very recent years, which provided for the Coptic Patriarch of Alexandria to appoint the Patriarch as well as all bishops of the Ethiopian Church. In spite of the latter policy, the Ethiopian Church remained essentially separate from the Coptic Church, and it developed some distinctive characteristics. But it was not until 1929 that the Ethiopian clergy obtained control of the appointment of the bishops of their Church, and it was not until 1951 that the complete autonomy of the Ethiopian Church became established; upon the latter date Ethiopian clergy and laity gained the right to choose their own Patriarch. The Ethiopian Orthodox Church has an ancestry that served to cast it on the side of the dissenters at Chalcedon; thus, until very recent decades, it has been completely separated from the rest of Christendom. Such an unfortunate isolation has had great value for Christian historians, however, in view of the fact that the Ethiopian Church has retained many of the elements of belief and practice followed by fourth-century Christians of its area.

Again it may be observed that during Constantine's time, probably to a great extent because of the emphasis of Constantine, a political man, on the political aspects of Christianity, little systematic attention was given to the difficult issues inherent in Christian philosophy and theology that by that time in the evolution of the new religion were beginning to come to the forefront of Christian thought. But Christian history of the years

247

immediately after the death of Constantine, approximately a century, is distinguished by the fact that a few outstanding Christian scholars, such as those named in this chapter, identified and made penetrating analyses of the major issues and problems that confronted and would always confront students of Christianity. No problems were solved, nor would they ever by solved, in a manner that would satisfy all thinking men. But it is of notable importance that the Christian sages to whom reference has just been made succeeded in a significant way to clarify and to develop better definition of the issues and problems with which students of Christianity must contend, thereby making it possible for their successors to better indulge in intelligent discussion and debate.

It is conceivable, and actually probable, however, that some of the analyses of the early Christian scholars who served their church during the years shortly after the time of Constantine were basically responsible at a later date for stimulating within the Christian community a vast amount of discontent and argument. The sharpening of the issues that resulted from the work of scholars such as Augustine, Jerome, and Athanasius of the early post-Constantine period served to isolate factors in Christian principle and practice upon which it was virtually inevitable that thoughtful men would develop strong differences of opinion. Thus possibly it is not surprising that in later years, especially in recent centuries, partly because of the increased educational opportunities that have become available, doctrinal debates within the world Christian community have become more common and they seem to have increased in intensity. Consequently, there has been a significant amount of splintering of the Christian movement; a vast number of new Christian sects and cults have been created and continue to be created. So today, the religion that acknowledges Jesus as its nominal founder has become the most organizationally complex of the great religions. The many branches and cults of Christianity that now exist feature some interesting and often important differences in doctrine, but it is an interesting fact that, in general, the various branches and cults insist on retaining their status as members of the Christian community in the large. Perhaps a new definition of "Christian" is evolving that possibly, sometime in the future, will permit a merging with "Judaic."

Chapter Eleven

EPILOGUE

By the time of the sixth century, Christianity was widely accepted in the Roman world and was displaying some of the characteristics of a mature religion. Nevertheless, it can be seen in retrospect that a variety of signs were visible which warned that the new religion was facing a troubled maturity. In fact, until the sixteenth century, the constantly evolving Roman Church, the Christian Church of the West, would be required to contend in almost every century with a variety of challenges to its authority, to its doctrine, and to its practices, but the Church would survive and actually gain strength. The successes of the Roman Church were accomplished through the exercise of the power inherent in its political structure and by making carefully conceived modifications in its policies and, upon occasion, in its theoretical basis to accommodate changing mores and attitudes. Some of the great strength of the Roman Church throughout its existence has been due to its remarkable ability to maintain its stability while slowly making adaptations to new thinking and to new needs. The Roman Church even survived the serious lapse in its moral integrity that one must associate with the terrible Inquisition, which lasted from the latter part of the twelfth century through the early part of the nineteenth century. During the time of the Inquisition, the Roman Church, in view of its militant position on the necessity for stamping out heresy, seemed to give support to an unbelievable orgy of torture and execution in which many innocent people were victims.

In the sixteenth century, however, a series of major successful challenges to the authority of the Roman Church was initiated in Western Europe. In Germany, where the level of education had become exceptionally high, where a free spirit reigned, and where most of the secular princes had succeeded in becoming quite independent of the Roman Popes, a critical revolt against the Roman Church, led by an Augustinian friar named Martin Luther, took place in 1517. The immediate cause of Luther's action was his great disgust with the so-called indulgence system of the Church. Thus was initiated a titanic struggle between the powerful Roman Church and a large number of free-thinking Germans, many of whom possessed a long-standing resentment against many of the policies and actions of the Church. Germany was torn asunder by a violent civil war while men in other countries who were pro-Church and those who were anti-Church watched, and many of those who watched were following the action closely to obtain guidance before they took steps to instigate anti-Church movements. Although Luther, because of his leadership of the revolt, is usually designated as the first great Church reformer, the first man of the Reformation, some very influential clerics in all the nations of Western Europe had been arguing loudly over a time span of two centuries or more in behalf of reform in Church program, doctrines, and policies. For instance, John Wycliffe, 1320–1384, distinguished English philosopher located at Oxford, had attracted the bitter animosity of a large number of Church leaders by his denunciation of many of the Church's doctrinal positions; his arguments were hard to refute in view of his strong background in logic and philosophy. The crusade of Wycliffe received support from Jan Hus, 1309–1415, influential academician at the University of Prague, who contended that many of the teachings of the Church were false, that members of the clergy were dominated by greed, and that men should seek Jesus the Christ through his words instead of through the doctrines that were promulgated. Hus was executed because of his "heresies." After nearly four decades of the tremendous religious struggle in Germany that was initiated by the pronouncements of Luther, the bitter conflict was terminated at a conference of German princes at Augsburg. The date was 1555. As a result of the Augsburg conference, approximately half the population of Germany, now known generally as the first Protestants, became affiliated with Luther's protesting movement; the members of the movement, the first lasting "Protestant" movement of any consequence, became the original Lutherans, a descriptive designation now applied to members of the several versions of the Protestant Lutheran Church.

The success of the revolt against the Papacy by Luther and his followers in Germany gave encouragement to rebellious actions that soon erupted against the Roman Church in most of the nations of Western Europe. In fact, during the sixteenth century and into the seventeenth century, the spirit of the Reformation, as translated into specific kinds of action by many clergymen and their supporters in Germany, Switzerland, England, and other localities, was very strong in virtually all the countries of Western Europe, and new Protestant Christian denominations were formed. In England, King Henry VIII, as a result of a personal disagreement that he had with the Roman Popes Clement VII and Paul III, obtained the approval of the English Parliament in 1536 to break the bond that then existed between the English churches and the Papacy; the king had the assistance of dissident Roman Catholics in his country. Thus the Anglican Church, so influential in the political affairs of the United States in its early days, was created.

In view of such developments, a new era for Western Christianity was being inaugurated. The Roman Catholic Church, although still a militant advocate of its traditions, became involved in significant introspection, while the Protestant movement, displaying great strength and momentum, became splintered into many segments as a consequence of differing ideas, as expressed in doctrine and practice, pertaining to interpretations of the Christian ideal. During the years that followed, many Protestant sects, including some that now have large followings in the United States and in other parts of the world, would be created. But the widespread lack of agreement on even fundamental issues among the Protestant denominations, a condition that continues unabated to the present day, is regarded by many students of Christianity as an unhappy phenomenon within the Christian tradition. Disagreement still exists upon such subjects as an acceptable interpretation of the miracles, including the Resurrection and the Virgin Birth, that are described in the Bible, the actual significance of the Bible in the thought processes of Christians (Are nonliteral interpretations of the Bible to be encouraged? Should the Bible be regarded as an authoritative work in such fields as history and geography?), the nature of the inspiration of the writers who contributed to the Bible (Must the Bible be regarded as a unique literary work created by men inspired by God?), and the significance for Christians of the major rites and other practices that are widely accepted as a part of the Christian tradition.

In the East, as already noted, the Christian movement was subjected to tremendous stresses and strains within a very short time after the death of Constantine. Ultimately, however, as a result of unusual demonstrations of wise leadership by a few Christian scholars, such as those previously mentioned, and as a reaction against the turbulent religious situation that had developed after Constantine's death, the Eastern Church began to move in the direction of becoming deeply conservative. Such conservatism continues today and is implied in the rigid use of the modifier "orthodox" in the title of the individual Eastern Churches. In slightly more than a century after the time of Constantine, the Eastern

Church was beginning to adopt strong measures against the old and new "heresies" that always seemed to be present in spite of the adoption of repressive measures. But the Eastern Church, because of its uncertain and peculiar dependence on secular power, was revealing the fact that it did not have the internal strength of the Western Church when trying to cope with its problems.

Superficially, the two great Church organizations, the East and the West, in spite of their differences in several significant respects, maintained an association that was fairly cordial. But the Roman Popes and the Eastern Patriarchs always exercised caution when they dealt with problems of mutual concern; their political relationships often involved tricky gamemanship.

In 1095, Alexius Comnenus, Emperor of the Western Empire, wrote to Pope Urban II in Rome asking for the aid of Western Christians against the Turks, militant followers of Islam who then were in the process of conquering much of the Near East. The letter was a simple appeal for assistance by the person who was the nominal Christian leader of the East to the Christian leader of the West. But it served to signal the start of the Crusades, a nightmarish series of military campaigns, lasting over a period of two centuries, that were conducted by Western Christians against the Muslims. Historians of the Crusades usually identify eight major military expeditions, the first beginning in 1096 and the last ending in 1291, but passion-dominated mobs of Western Christians indulged in many other ventures in an attempt to dislodge the "infidel" Muhammadans from crucial positions which they held in the Holy Land. Militarism became accepted as a way of life by a vast number of Western Christians.

In 1204, a Crusade organized ostensibly to attack Egypt suddenly was diverted by its leaders to make an assault against Constantinople. It is likely that the decision to attack Constantinople was not made impulsively, for since the start of the Crusades there had been a steady deterioration in relations between the East and the West. Constantinople fell to the Western armies after a comparatively short siege. Thus, after more than nine centuries of independence, the great city founded by Constantine, which had provided the focus for Eastern Christianity and in earlier years had been at the heart of the magnificent Byzantine Culture, became secondary to Rome in the political world of Christianity. Although later half-hearted efforts were made to bring together the

Eastern and Western Churches, no meaningful union of the two bodies took place; they continued to maintain their particular traditions as well as their essential independence. In fact, the Eastern Church continued to refuse to recognize the primacy of the Papacy although the Papacy soon became known throughout Christendom as the most powerful jurisdiction within organized Christianity. The City of Constantine never regained its stature as a great center of Christianity, and it even began to lose ground as the focus of the Eastern Church. Then, in 1453, Constantinople was captured by a new generation of militant Turks, so Islam soon replaced Christianity as the dominant religion of the inhabitants of the city which for a thousand years had been a great showplace of Christianity. Consequently, some of the awe-inspiring Christian Churches of Constantinople became houses of worship for followers of Islam. And of very great importance, the Eastern Church, after the conquest of Constantinople by the Muslims, soon became splintered into a number of nationalized institutional churches, of which, the Russian Orthodox Church, the Greek Orthodox Church, and the Serbian Orthodox Church are typical. In the creation of each of the nationalized churches, the original Church in Constantinople was imitated in most of its policies and in its modes of operation, including the provision that the secular ruler of the nation, occasionally a despot, also received nominal designation as the chief religious officer of the state.

Consequently, today, two millennia after the death of Jesus, institutionalized Christianity has become a vast and complex enterprise. Overall, the Church that acknowledges Jesus as its nominal founder is regarded generally as being organizationally divided into three major branches: the Churches of the West (Roman Catholic and Protestant), the nationalized Churches of the East, and the distinctive collection of Churches usually known as the Oriental Orthodox Churches. But the world Christian enterprise has become increasingly complicated by the fact that we are witnessing the creation of new independent Christian sects, some of which have become militant crusaders for their ideologies. A new era of Christian thought and doctrine may be in the making.

At the present time, more than 580 million persons, over half of the Christians in the world, are served by the Roman Catholic Church, a very effective and mature religious institution that is the direct descendant of the original Western Church. The large collection of commonly recognized Protestant Churches, each of which must acknowledge the ancestry of the original Western Church centered in Rome, has a total worldwide constituency of approximately 220 million people. But not counted in this latter figure are the members of numerous churches, usually regarded as Protestant, that exist in the United States and in other nations of the world; a traveler to out-of-the-way places frequently discovers a house of worship of a rare Protestant sect, perhaps with a membership of only a few hundred or possibly a few thousand, that is unlisted in any directory and will never be listed.

Of the large number of nationalized Churches that had their parentage in the great Eastern Church originated by Constantine, probably the best known in the United States are the Albanian, Bulgarian, Ukrainian, Rumanian, Greek, Russian, and Serbian Orthodox Churches. It appears from several estimates that presently there is a world total of between 125 million and 145 million adherents to all the Eastern Orthodox denominations.

Only the roughest estimates are available in regard to the number of individuals who are now affiliated with the Oriental Orthodox Churches; the generally recognized Churches in the collection have already been named. There is little doubt, from a numerical point of view, that the strongest of the Oriental Orthodox Christian Churches is the Ethiopian Orthodox Church, which a few years ago had approximately 16 million adherents. Probably at the present time more than 4 million persons are affiliated with the Coptic Christian Church; most of the Coptic Christians live in upper Egypt and in Sudan.

So Christianity, based on a simple but powerful philosophy of brotherly love as espoused by Jesus of Nazareth, known to many Christians as the Judaic Messiah and as the Son of God, is acknowledged today to be a religion of tremendous influence upon a vast number of men and upon many nations. The very fact that Christianity has become such a powerful factor in world society provides impetus to an increasing number of studies of the evolutionary process that produced it. Within that long evolutionary process, the astute student finds a portrayal of man's weaknesses and his strengths, man's ability to hate and his capacity for love, and man's rationality and his irrationality. The person who indulges in a penetrating but sympathetic study of the evolutionary process, if he is able to overcome the feeling of disillusionment that upon occasion may intrude upon his thought, can see in it vivid demonstrations of man's tremendous and even miraculous creative powers of mind that enable him to enunciate for himself the characteristics of a purposeful life along with the principles necessary to assist him in attaining such a life, even as he struggles to find his way through the maze of hazards provided by a world that can never be fully charted.

INDEX

Abraham, 32–35
Academy of Hillel, 112
Academy of the House of Hillel, 113, 168, 171
Acts, Book of, 161,162–163, 169, 173, 190
Acts of Paul, Book of, 167
Adam and Eve, 60–61
The Admonitions of a Prophet (Ipuwer), 55
Against Heresies (Irenaeus), 228
Agrippa, 101–102
Aksumite Kingdom, 247
Alaric, 236
Albanian Orthodox Church, 254
Alexander, Bishop of Alexandria, 216
Alexander (the Great) of Macedon, 81–82
Alexandra, 92, 93–94
Alexandria, 82–84
Ambrose, 233, 240–241
Amenhotep IV, 21
Ammonites, 27
Amos, 64
Amos, Book of, 76
Anastasius, Pope, 135
Anglican Church, 251
Animals, and primitive Gods, 18
Annals (Tacitus), 206
Anti-Jewish attitudes, and death of Jesus, 154–155
Antioch, 164–165
Antiochus III, IV, 87
Antiochus Epiphanes, 80
Antipater, 91, 94, 95, 98
Antony, 97
Apocrypha, 84–85
The Apocryphal New Testament, 183
Aquila Bible, 123
Aquila Ponticus, 123
Aquinas, Thomas, 21, 237
Aramaeans, 27
Archelaus, 99

Arian controversy, 216–219
Arianism, 242
Arius, 216, 217, 242
Aristobulus, 92, 94
Ark of the Covenant, 47
Armenian Orthodox Church, 231
Art and religion, 19
Ataturk, 219
Aten, 21
Athanasius (the Great), 241, 245–246, 247
Atomic theory, 6–7
Augsburg conference, 250
Augustine, 61, 216, 231–238
Augustus, 97

Baalim, 52
Baal worship, 52, 58
Babylonian Captivity, 69–70
Babylonian Exile, 70
Babylonians, 27
    conquest of Jerusalem, 56
Baptism, 164
Barnabas, 173
Bartholomew, Book of, 182
Basil, 241, 244–245
Bethlehem, 134–135
Bible, Judaic, 32, 50, 75–81
Books of Wisdom, 78
Brain
    vs. computer, 2
    and creativity, 3–6
    and spirit of God, 7–8
British Museum, 131
Buddhism, 20
Bulgarian Orthodox Church, 254
Byzantine Empire, 220

Caecilianus, 215
Calendar, Jewish, 43
Calvin, John, 233
Canaan, 51, 52
Canaanites, 27, 51, 52